Lecture Notes in Computer Science

Lecture Notes in Computer Science

Edited by G. Goos and J. Hartmanis

109

Digital Image
Processing Systems

Edited by Leonard Bolc and Zenon Kulpa

Springer-Verlag
Berlin Heidelberg New York 1981

Editors

Leonard Bolc
Institute of Informatics, Warsaw University
PKiN, pok. 850, 00-901 Warszawa, Poland

Zenon Kulpa
Institute of Biocybernetics and Biomedical Engineering
00-818 Warszawa, Poland

AMS Subject Classifications (1979): 68-02
CR Subject Classifications (1981): 3.63

ISBN 3-540-10705-3 Springer-Verlag Berlin Heidelberg New York
ISBN 0-387-10705-3 Springer-Verlag New York Heidelberg Berlin

© by Springer-Verlag Berlin Heidelberg 1981
Printed in Germany

Printing and binding: Beltz Offsetdruck, Hemsbach/Bergstr.
2145/3140-543210

P R E F A C E

Pictorial information, in all its varieties, constitutes the most
important source of our sensory data as well as (apart from the
phonetic language) the most general means of communication between
people. Inevitably, use of this sort of information becomes steadily
the most important means of man-computer communication.

It has started to develop almost at the beginning of computer era:
in a sense, the tens of blinking lamps on the early computer panels
were a means of visual communication. Apart from this primitive "visual
communication", the use of true pictures to exchange information between computers and people can be divided into two main types:

    a) real-image processing and analysis
    b) computer graphics.

In <u>image processing</u>, the real images from the outside world (real
scenes photographs, microscopic images, satellite images, fingerprints,
and many others) are inputted to the computer (e.g. by TV means) and
processed by it. The results of processing can be of different types:
other pictures (e.g. enhanced, noisefiltered, etc.), quantitative
descriptions of the picture contents (e.g. number of objects, areas
of cells, positions of some features, etc.), recognition decisions (e.g.
name of an alphanumeric character, fingerprint classification code,
abnormal cell identification, etc.), interpretations (e.g. meaning of
a scene, description of a particle-collision event in nuclear physics,
etc.). The new use of image processing to store and retrieve pictures
in large pictorial data bases is also emerging presently.

In <u>computer graphics</u>, generally not the real images, but descriptions
of some, more or less "abstract" drawings are inputted by a human
operator to the computer. The input has the character of expressions
in some descriptive (artificial) language and/or manual "drawing"
(pointing out required positions) with a light-pen on the display
screen. The computer stores these picture descriptions in some internal
(usually non-pictorial) form and displays them in pictorial form on
the graphic display screen (or draws on the ploter) for the convenience
of the human operator. It can also introduce some "corrections" to
these pictures (e.g. straightening of crooked lines drawn by the
light-pen), manipulate them (e.g. zooming, rotation in space) and

calculate required parameters (e.g. transmittance of the electronic circuit from the scheme drawn, strain distribution along the beam, etc.). The computer animation of cartoons also uses these techniques. Generally, in image processing the input images are processed by computer (producing eventually some descriptions or "understanding" of their meaning), whereas in computer graphics the images are generated by a computer on the basis of their input descriptions. Both areas share, nevertheless, certain common features, which arise from manipulation of common type of data (pictures) and manifest themselves in the field of picture description and manipulation (for the display).

This book is dedicated to digital systems of image processing. Several European computer systems are described here in detail: GOP and CELLO from Sweden, BIHES ("Budapest Intelligent Hand-Eye-System") from Hungary, CPO-2/K-202 from Poland and S.A.M. (called previously MODSYS) from Federal Republic of Germany.

For various reasons, some other interesting European systems have not been included here. To compensate this, a fairly representative survey of European systems has been included. It reviews and compares systematically eleven systems, including all these listed above. The survey is a somewhat extended and reworked version of an invited paper presented at the EUSIPCO-80 Conference held in Lausanne in September 1980.

In order to show the readers possible practical usefulness of such systems and to introduce them into the methods and techniques of image processing, the book has been augmented finally by the paper by Milgram and Rosenfeld, the leading specialists in the field. This paper presents on a specific example of infrared images analysis a wide range of methods and techniques of image processing, analysis and recognition.

The editors sincerely acknowledge the collaboration of all the contributors to the book and wish to express their gratitude to the European Association for Signal Processing EURASIP for their kind permission to use the survey paper from EUSIPCO-80-Conference for this book.

The authors would like to express their thanks to Springer-Verlag for publishing this volume.

Warsaw, January 1981   Leonard B o l c
             Zenon K u l p a

TABLE OF CONTENTS

UNIVERSAL DIGITAL IMAGE PROCESSING SYSTEMS IN EUROPE –
A COMPARATIVE SURVEY

by

Zenon KULPA

Polish Academy of Sciences,
Institute of Biocybernetics and Biomedical Engineering
00-818 WARSAW, Poland

Abstract

In the paper, a selected group of eleven universal (computer based) image processing systems is surveyed and compared. They constitute a seemingly representative sample of the vast variety of such systems built in the last decade in European countries. The survey covers systems built for research purposes, either in image processing as such or for some other specific problem area, as well as more practically-oriented ones, including a commercially available routine picture analyzer. An overall classification of their general aims as well as basic parameters and features of their hardware structure, software support and application area is given.

1. Introduction

The purpose of this paper is to cast an overall glance at the vast European scene of universal image processing systems designs. In many different research institutions all over Europe there were designed or are being constructed various such systems, aimed either as tools facilitating basic research in digital picture processing or as practical devices for some more or less specific application. They are often constructed independently of the other analogical constructions existing or planned elsewhere. Their structure and parameters are frequently selected on ad hoc basis or result from specific limitations of chance elements (or building blocks) "just at hand" at the time of the system construction. As it is therefore understandable, they represent a great variety of structures, technical parameters as well as usage modes. Nevertheless, some general features can be found in this variety. The goal of this paper is to put some order in it, providing thus some guidelines for future designers, to help them in their own system development.

Because of rather great number of groups interested in picture processing and building their own systems, it was of course impossible to make this survey fully exhaustive. The main criterion of selection has been simply the familiarity of the author with the system, either personal or through generally accessible scientific literature and a sort of a questionnaire sent to the designers (see Acknowledgments section), or both. Several systems, less known to the author (lacking enough technical data to fill in the tables

below) have had to be therefore excluded. For example, it resulted
in omitting several seemingly interesting systems developed in FRG
(see [6]) about which I have got too fragmentaric informations and
too late to be able to collect them for this survey.

Furthermore, only <u>universal systems</u> have been considered, i.e.
that easily programmable for different tasks of sufficiently wide
problem area. In effect, all of them include such or another programmable digital processor used to process pictures: a general-
-purpose (mini-)computer or a special hardwired image processor.
Finally, all ERTS (Earth Resources Technology Satellite) image
processing systems have been deliberately excluded from this survey,
as they are a class by itself, having rather specific single source
of images and their own specific analysis techniques, emphasizing
classification of single pixels described by multispectral data,
rather than contextual processing of two-dimensional shapes in the
picture.

In spite of this non-exhaustiveness, the small set of only 11
systems surveyed here seems to be in several respects quite representative for the diversity of European image processing systems.
I apologize for all omissions of the systems whose features sub-
stantiate them to be included in any such survey pretending to be
representative. Any system designer confident that his system
should have been included here is encouraged to send the system
characteristics to the author - it will eventually help in prepara-
tion of the next version of the survey. The first version of this
paper was presented at the EUSIPCO-80 conference in Lausanne [34],
and was also included in the materials of the associated course on
Parallel Picture Processing [35]. The materials of this course contain also descriptions of several other image processing systems
(mostly of the d-type, see below), not surveyed here.

2. Image processing systems

All systems surveyed here are listed in Table 1. In the text
they will be referred to by names given in the first column. Those
having no name will be "called" by the first three letters of the
name of the laboratory head (see [6, 7]).

The systems can be classified according to their general goals.
The following classes are distinguishable:

Table 1. Some European image analysis systems.

Name	Country	Institution	References
CELLO	Sweden	Department of Clinical Cytology, University Hospital, Uppsala	[1 - 4]
(Nag)	FRG*)	Fachbereich Informatik, Universität Hamburg	[5, 6]
(Leb)	USSR	Institute of Information Transmission Problems, Moscow	[7 - 9]
BIHES**)	Hungary	Computer and Automation Institute, Budapest	[10 - 12]
MODSYS***)	FRG	Fraunhofer-Institut für Informations- und Daten-verarbeitung, Karlsruhe	[13 - 16]
CPO-2	Poland	Institute of Biocybernetics and Biomedical Engineering, Warsaw	[17 - 20]
VIP	Italy	Istituto di Cibernetica del CNR, Arco Felice (Napoli)	[21, 22]
PICAP	Sweden	Department of Electrical Engineering, Linköping University, Linköping	[23 - 26]
CLIP 4	England	Department of Physics and Astronomy, University College, London	[27, 28]
GOP	Sweden	Department of Electrical Engineering, Linköping University, Linköping	[32, 33]
Leitz T.A.S.	France & FRG	I.R.S.I.D. et École des Mines de Paris (license); Ernst Leitz Wetzlar GMBH, Wetzlar, and R. Bosch Fernseh-Anlagen GMBH, Darmstadt (production)	[29 - 31]

*) Federal Republic of Germany;   **) Budapest Intelligent Hand-Eye System;

***) Final version has been recently renamed S.A.M. (Sensorsystem for Automation and Measurement).

a) Systems created as tools to investigate some specific scientific problem with computational means: not intended to be multiplied in several copies; the principal goal is to solve the problem rather than to build a system (CELLO, (Nag), (Leb)).

b) Systems created as general purpose (although simple) image processing devices: intended for a wide range of processing tasks; rather research- than application-oriented; eventually with some perspective of building several copies for different users; the principal goal is to build a universal system for research in image processing itself rather than to solve some specific application problem (VIP, CPO-2).

c) Systems intermediate between the two above types: with some specific application in mind (e.g. "robot-eye") but universal enough and serving as a "research prototype" rather than a unique laboratory assembly or a finished production model; the principal goal is to build a fairly universal system, although good for some specific application (BIHES, MODSYS).

d) Systems experimenting with new computer architectures for two--dimensional data processing inherent for image processing: used to gain experience in effectiveness of the proposed set of hardware operations and memory organization; the principal goal is to build an effective and universal new processor rather than a simple and cheap "working" assembly of existing devices (PICAP, CLIP 4, GOP).

e) Commercially available systems for routine picture analysis: universal enough to be usable in sufficiently wide range of different practical tasks but simple enough to be feasible for production and marketing; the principal goal is to cover a wide range of rather simple routine applications, yet worth of automatization, due e.g. to massive amounts of analyses required (Leitz T.A.S.).

How these general systems goals influence specific construction features will be shown in the next three sections, discussing hardware, software and application aspects of the systems.

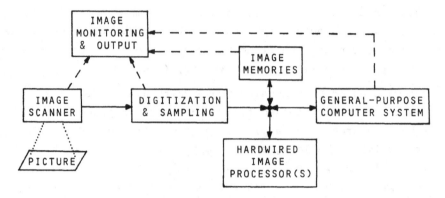

Fig. 1. General scheme of a universal image processing system

3. Hardware structures

The general configuration of a universal image processing system can be schematically drawn as in Fig. 1. Depending on the type
of the system as given in the previous section, different parts of
this scheme become more important. For the type (a), the central
part is the computer in which all processing is done, and the image
scanner and output are simply computer peripherals making it possible to input/output the necessary data. They are built (or bought)
to fit best the needs of the particular problem. Hardwired processors and image memories are usually absent - the latter are eventually used to extend the computer memory or as flexible display
buffers. In the systems of the type (b) and (c), the role of picture input/output and the computer is equalized, image memories are
used as input image buffers, hardwired processors are usually
absent due to cost considerations and not yet too advanced state of
the art. The type (d) systems are built around the proposed hardwired processor. The image memories are partially contained in the
processor and partially used as picture input/output buffers. The
computer serves as a supervisor facilitating programming and non-
-pictorial communication with an operator. In the systems of the
type (e), all parts are highly integrated, the hardwired processor
is an important part, although mainly capable of performing simple
counting of picture features on binary images (areas, components,
etc.) rather than full-scale of multivalued picture processing.

Table 2. Image input/output devices.

System	Input scanner Type	Scan time	Sampling: in pixels	Digitization Gray levels	Thresholds	Output devices
CELLO	OSIRIS: linear diode array mechan. scanned	30-60s	256 × 256	64 (256)	fixed, with software normalization	TV b/w & colour, Versatec
(Nag)	TV	~1s	574 × 512	256	?	COMTAL diplay, Facsimile writer
(Leb)	OPTRONICS P-1700 drum scanner	(large)	max: 1024 × 1024	256	fixed	TV b/w & colour, OPTRONICS P-1700 microfilm plotter
BIHES	TV (vidicon)	20ms	144 × 192	16	off-line control	Tektronix 613 (storage tube)
MODSYS	TV or diode array	20ms	380 × 256	2	fixed	(TV)
CPO-2	TV (vidicon)	40ms	512 × 512	16	hand & computer controlled	TV b/w & colour
VIP	TV (plumbicon)	20-320ms	256 × 256	2 - 16	single threshold computer contr.	Versatec
PICAP	TV	40ms	64 × 64	16	computer contr.	TV b/w & colour
CLIP 4	TV	(20 or 40ms ?)	96 × 96	64	?	TV b/w, Versatec, Tektronix 611, Microfilm plotter
GOP	TV, laser drum scanner	40ms, ?	512 × 512, 4096 × 4096	256	?	TV colour, laser drum plotter
Leitz T.A.S.	TV (plumbicon)	40ms	256 × 256 hexagonal	2: normal or "sliced"	settable to 100 levels	TV colour

The computer (frequently a microprocessor) is used mainly for further elaboration (e.g. statistical) of obtained counts.

In the Table 2 some technical parameters of the image
input/output part of the surveyed systems are given. The differences between various types of the systems can be seen quite markedly.
The (a)-type systems (CELLO, (Nag), (Leb)) are characterized by
usually large number of gray levels (256) and usually special input
scanners. For the (Leb) system, its application for image enhancement enforces an accurate and high-resolution image acquisition and
hardcopy output. In CELLO, to achieve densitometric accuracy in
medical specimens scanning, a special OSIRIS vibrating-prism
scanner was adopted (see references in [1, 3]) and the sophisticated light-sensitivity, shading and positioning correction software system run on a dedicated PDP 8/f computer was built [3], see
Table 3. In the (Nag) system, however, a standard TV input was
applied - it is justified by its use for off-line research in image
sequences analysis (e.g. road traffic monitoring), so that less
accuracy suffices. The scanning time is also not critical, due to
an off-line research-oriented mode of system's usage. It required
anyway the storage of sufficiently long image sequences. A large-
-capacity image memory was needed for this purpose. Here, an analog
TV-disk capable of recording 600 TV-frames (Table 3) was employed.
All the above systems are therefore characterized by rather slow
but usually accurate scanners (except partially (Nag)), great number of pixels scanned (except partially CELLO) and large number of
grey levels (usually 256).

All other systems use standard TV camera as an input scanner -
it is easily accessible, low-cost, easy in use and accurate enough
for general-purpose applications. It is interesting that none of the
systems surveyed use flying-spot scanners - they are expensive and
limit the form of input pictures, and are used rather in some
special-purpose systems (of the (a)-type, e.g. for particle tracks
images analysis in nuclear physics). The TV-camera input scanners
discussed here (other than (Nag)) sample and digitize the input in
real time, i.e. during a single TV-frame, or even half-frame in the
case of smaller resolution. The number of pixels is usually small
in the (d)-type systems (PICAP: 64×64, CLIP 4: 96×96). The small
number of pixels results from the dimensions of a special parallel
or semi-parallel processors array included in these systems -

larger dimensions would result in too big costs and less reliability of the hardware. This small picture "window" can be usually
moved over an entire TV-frame and used with different pixel spacing
(PICAP). In the CLIP 4, the window is unmovable - the aim of this
system is basic research in parallel image processing however, so
that an input flexibility has been of secondary importance and made
rather simple. The exceptionally high resolution of the GOP system
is due to different organization of the processor: the large (up to
512×512 pixels) image matrices held in the processor memories are
processed by four parallel "computation pipelines", reading the memory in a "rolling" fashion. There is, in fact, no parallel array
of processors: the parallelism exists in fetching pixels of the
neighbourhood (up to 64×64 pixels), but the image scan is performed serially (similar principle was actually applied also in PICAP
system).

Practically all systems employ sampling with a square raster.
The very interesting exception is the hexagonal raster of the Leitz
T.A.S. system. The hexagonal raster has advantages of uniform
structure of the local point neighbourhood (no connectivity para-
doxes), and smaller number of points in this neighbourhood (25%
gain in local operations specification). Its disadvantage, among
others, is nonuniform representation of the natural horizontal/ver-
tical coordinate lines [23].

The number of gray levels is usually 16 for most of the non-(a)
-type systems, except MODSYS, GOP, Leitz T.A.S., and partially VIP.
The latter operate usually on binary (2-level) images. It is much
simpler and faster than processing of many-valued images, and it is
quite sufficient in a wide range of applications, especially for
good quality, high-contrast pictures. Additionally, in many systems
the digitization levels can be shifted by the computer, making it
possible to discriminate potentially between great many shades of
gray (CPO-2, VIP, PICAP, Leitz T.A.S.). For example, in the VIP
system, which main aims were simplicity and low cost, a single, but
computer-controlled threshold allows an acquisition of images with
many (usually 16) gray levels in the course of several input cycles.
Similar solution was adopted in the Leitz T.A.S. system, where,
additionally, the threshold can be used in a "sliced" manner (setting to the value 1 all pixels between some narrow grey range
required).

All systems process basically black/white (uncoloured) pictures, although some experiments with colour input were done e.g. with (Leb) system and prospective processing of colour (or multispectral) images was assumed for GOP system [33]. The processing of coloured pictures is undertaken anyway by some other groups not reviewed here (see e.g. [6]). Nevertheless, most of the systems use coloured TV output devices to enhance legibility of pictorial results and facilitate interaction with the user with the technique of "artificial colours" (assigning any required colours to pixel values).

Most output devices used are TV monitors (black/white and/or colour), seemingly, like TV-cameras, because of easy availability, easy maintenance and low cost. Eventually TV-like graphic displays are used. For producing hard-copy output, an electrostatic plotters (usually Versatec) or similar facsimile writers are employed. High quality hard-copy output requires microfilm plotters anyway ((Leb), CLIP 4), or laser drum plotters (GOP).

Image processing devices are summarized in Table 3. Picture memories are of various types. Some are simply small buffers facilitating image data input into the computer memory (VIP), other larger TV-refresh memories (CPO-2, CELLO, (Leb)) or "true" image memories controlled by hardwired processors (MODSYS, PICAP, CLIP 4, GOP, Leitz T.A.S.). A somewhat uncommon solution was adopted in (Nag), where analog TV-disk was used - it is justified by the character of this system purpose (see above). TV-refresh memories should of course work with TV-speed, although sometimes, for slower memories (e.g. 1.5μs magnetic cores in CPO-2) it requires a little tricky read/write circuits organization. For small number of gray levels, pictures are usually stored as a stack of bit-planes (single-bit pixels packed into words; different bits of a pixel grey level representation placed in separate bit-planes: CPO-2, CLIP 4, GOP, MODSYS, Leitz T.A.S.). For larger number of gray levels, pixels fit well into bytes, so that the pictures can be stored as arrays of bytes (CELLO, GOP, probably (Leb)). A somewhat uncommon run-coding scheme has been also employed in MODSYS.

Hardwired processors are of course the heart of (d)-type systems (PICAP, CLIP 4, GOP). They implement parallel local (3 × 3 neighbourhood) logical and arithmetical operations on binary (CLIP 4) or 16-level (PICAP) images, or, in GOP, "general picture

Table 3. Image processing devices.

System	Picture memories			Hardwired proc.: operation types	Computer	
	Type	Pixel packing	Capacity		Type	Oper. memory
CELLO	semiconductor	array of pixels	512 × 512 × 8b.	planned: image segmentation units	PDP 8/f, PDP 11/55, LSI 11	128kwords 16b.
(Nag)	AMPEX MD 400 TV-disk	–	2 × 600 frames	–	4× MINCAL 621 (PDP 10)	784kBytes total
(Leb)	semiconductor	?	?	–	ALPHA 16 (US mini)	32kwords 16b.
BIHES	?	?	16kBytes	–	VIDEOTON R-10	20kwords 16b. (2μs)
MODSYS	?	pixel array or run-length contour coding	256 × 512b. + 4k × 16b.	propagation; counting	Z-80	potentially more than 8Mbytes (?)
CPO-2	magnetic cores	stack of 4 bit-planes	4 × 16kwords 16b.	–	K-202 (Polish)	44kwords 16b. (1.5μs)
VIP	shift register	16 one-bit pixels/word	4 × 16b.	–	HP 21MX (2108)	32kwords 16b. (0.8μs)
PICAP	shift register	–	3 × 64 × 64 × 4b. + 9 × 64 × 64 × 4b.	semi-parallel, local, logical & arithmetic	Datasaab D5/30 (Swedish)	128kBytes
CLIP 4	shift register	bit-plane stack	2 × 96 × 96 × 6b. + 96 × 96 × 35b.	parallel, local single-bit & propagation	PDP 11/10	?
GOP	?	array of pixels or bit-plane stack	16kwords 16b., 16kwords 20b., 8kwords 16b.	local semiparallel arithmetical convolution: "General Operator"	Eclipse	128kwords
Leitz T.A.S.	?	bit-planes	8 × 256 × 256b.	hexagonal, local & propag.; counting	LSI 11/2	64kBytes

processing operator" [32] local arithmetic convolution (with the neighbourhood size up to 64×64). They are realized either in a truly parallel fashion (CLIP 4: an integrated array of 9216 processors [28]) or semi-parallelly (PICAP: single many-instruction local processor shifted around the picture by means of the zigzag shift register [23]; GOP: four parallel pipelined processors scanning serially an image memory with a "rolling" fashion [33]). The propagation operations and also (in PICAP) sequential local operations can be performed. In GOP, the other part of the processor performs (serially) an analysis of the results of local processing and controls the local processing part (e.g., choosing an appropriate convolution mask). Anyway, in other systems, analogical (although simpler) picture processors can be found (MODSYS, Leitz T.A.S.), capable of performing local logical operations on binary images and "counting" operations. Their appearance in the commercial systems like Leitz T.A.S. signifies their coming into "mature age", as they acquire wider practical applicability, not only a laboratory, experimental status.

Computers used in the surveyed systems are usually single micro- or minicomputers of various types. It is interesting to notice two multiprocessor systems (not surprisingly, of the (a)-type: (Nag) and CELLO). Operating memories of these computers are as a rule not small (the minimum seems to be 40kBytes: BIHES), but rather large (up to the order of hundreds of kilobytes: CELLO, (Nag)). It is of course required for any nontrivial picture processing: real pictures carry rather large amounts of information.

4. Software support

The features of the software systems are listed in Table 4. The programming languages used for image processing are divided into three categories:
- basic language: in which all lowest-level picture handling is written,
- intermediate language: more problem-oriented, although not too high-level,
- high-level language: source language for easy application programming.

Usually the assembler of the system computer serves as a basic

Table 4. Image processing software.

System	Basic language	Intermediate language	High-level language	Picture representation
CELLO	FORTRAN IV-PLUS; MACRO-11 assembler	FORTRAN IV-PLUS	CELLO interactive	Array with 1 pixel per byte
(Nag)	Assembler	PASCAL (?)	SAIL	File of lines; line: packed array of bytes
(Leb)	ALPHA 16 assembler	–	FORTRAN	Array with 1 pixel per byte
BIHES	R-10 assembler	PLM macrogenerator	MODBUIL (in PLM) for 3-D objects manipulation	?
MODSYS	Z-80 assembler	PLZ/ASM (assembler-like)	PLZ/SYS (PASCAL-like)	See Table 3
CPO-2	ASSK-3 assembler	PICASSO-SHOW interactive	–	Bit-planes stack or packed (1, 2, 4 or 8 pixels per word)
VIP	HP assembler	–	FORTRAN IV	Packed array: 16 pixels per word or 4 pixels per word
PICAP	PICAP code; DAL 53 assembler	DEFPRO interactive macroassembler	FORTRAN; PPL interactive	Packed array; Run-length coding
CLIP 4	CAP-4 assembler	–	–	Bit-planes
GOP	Assembler	FORTRAN	INTRAC interactive	Array of pixels (?)
Leitz T.A.S.	(LSI 11 assembler ?)	TIP ("push-button" lang.)	TASIC (BASIC-like)	Bit-planes

language. For the (d)-type systems the machine language of the underlying image processor becomes basic: either only it (CLIP 4) or mixed with the computer language (PICAP, GOP). In other systems, sometimes FORTRAN becomes basic, eventually with some help of the assembler (CELLO). As intermediate languages we find various assembler-like languages (BIHES, MODSYS, PICAP), FORTRAN (CELLO, GOP), interactive picture processing language interpreter (CPO-2), "push--button" command language (Leitz T.A.S.), or even PASCAL (Nag). As highest-level languages often FORTRAN is reported (VIP, (Leb), PICAP) or other high-level languages standard for the given computer ((Nag), MODSYS). In other cases, various image processing languages designed specially for the given system or problem area (BIHES, CELLO, PICAP, CPO-2, GOP) or specialized versions of general-purpose languages (Leitz T.A.S.) are used. For several systems, a construction of new high-level image processing languages is planned (ILIAD for CELLO, PAL for CPO-2, PIXAL for VIP).

All systems, especially those having no image processing language, maintain growing libraries of subroutines for basic picture operations or picture processing algorithms. They are usually written in the basic language for run-time efficiency reasons, and sometimes constitute a base for the interactive image processing languages developed later on these systems (CELLO, CPO-2, Leitz T.A.S.). This way of development seems to give fairly good effects - it produces quickly something like simple high- (or medium-)level image processing language with widely applicable and effective (in run time) instruction set.

Representation of processed pictures in the computer memory is usually the same as in the image-memories (see Table 3). Sometimes it is adjusted to the features of the language used (Nag) or additional packing schemata are available (CPO-2, VIP, PICAP). The picture representation problem is quite important for efficiency of the processing (if it is done in the ordinary computer), especially for pictures having small number of grey levels (e.g. binary). In this case, appropriate packing of pixels saves memory space as well as allows for appplication of a so-called semi-parallel realization of picture operations on ordinary computers, which results in significant gains of the processing time for some classes of operations [17, 18, 20].

Finally, it should be noted that the task of surveying software

Table 5. Applications.

System	Mode of usage	Basic application areas	Main application example
CELLO	Algorithm development for biomedical applications	Automated cytology	Automated prescreening of pap--stained cervical smears [2].
(Nag)	Research in moving images analysis	Road traffic monitoring	Separating background from moving objects in image sequences [5].
(Leb)	Research and application of image enhancement and filtering	Space probing, Biomedicine, Digital holography	Noise cleaning in pictures from interplanetary MARS and VENUS stations [8].
BIHES	Research in 2-D and 3-D scene analysis	Industrial robot-eye, Workpiece handling	Recognition of bus-body sheets in a paint-spray workshop [12].
MODSYS	Practical visual sensor system for industry: research prototype	Industrial robot-eye, Automatic inspection, Workpiece handling	Recognition of noneverlapping workpieces on a conveyor belt [15].
CPO-2	Research in 2-D image analysis and applications	Biomedicine, Material engineering	Analysis of shape-changes of moving leukemia cells [19].
VIP	Research in 2-D image processing	Biomedicine	?
PICAP	Research in parallel image processing and applications	Biomedicine, Fingerprints, Automatic inspection	Malaria parasites detection [25], Fingerprint coding [26].
CLIP 4	Research in parallel image processing	Biomedicine, Automatic inspection	Basic research as yet.
GOP	Research in "general operator" processing and applications	Biomedicine, Material engineering, Fingerprints & other	?
Leitz T.A.S.	Commercial routine image analyzer	Biomedicine, Material engineering	Clustered cells separation (?) [31].

part of the picture processing systems is rather hard and tedious -
- available descriptions happen to be rather vague and tangled, the
software itself is often built in not very systematic way and is
hard to evaluate without going into actual writing of programs for
a given system.

5. Applications

General classification of systems according to their construction aims was outlined in Section 2. Here it should be repeated
that most of the systems were intended for research purposes,
either in image processing field itself (CPO-2, VIP, CLIP 4, PICAP,
GOP) or in some specific, more or less "pictorial" application
fields (CELLO, (Nag), (Leb), BIHES). Only two of them (MODSYS,
Leitz T.A.S.), although not without research aspect, are intended
to be more practical instruments, rather than research tools. However, also those of them intended for image-processing research are
frequently used to run practical application tasks (Table 5).

Almost all systems are being used for analysis of biomedical
pictures - it seems to be the richest source of interesting and
challenging as well as practically useful problems of 2-D image
processing. Also several systems are applied in the similar area
(with respect to the character of images), namely in analysis of
structure of materials.

The second numerously represented class of systems is devoted
for use as robot-eyes and in closely related problems of workpiece
handling and automatic inspection (BIHES, MODSYS, partially PICAP
and CLIP 4). Other application areas include space probing, road
traffic monitoring, fingerprints and digital holography [9].

Acknowledgments

The work reported here was supported by the Research Programme
No. 10.4. The author greatly acknowledges Dr. E. Bengtsson from
University Hospital in Uppsala, Dr. M.J.B. Duff from University
College London, Dr. J.P. Foith from Fraunhofer-Institut in Karls-
ruhe, Dr. G.H. Granlund and Dr. B. Kruse from Linköping University,
Prof. S. Levialdi from Istituto di Cibernetica in Arco Felice,
Prof. H.-H. Nagel from Hamburg University, Prof. J. Serra from
École des Mines de Paris, and Prof. T. Vámos from Computer and

Automation Institute in Budapest for providing detailed informations about their image processing systems which greatly facilitated the compilation of this survey.

References

1. Bengtsson E., On the design of systems for computer aided analysis of microscopic images, Ph.D. Thesis No. 428, Faculty of Science at Uppsala University, Uppsala 1977.

2. Bengtsson E., Eriksson O., Holmquist J., Nordin B., Stenkvist B., High resolution segmentation of cervical cells, J. Histochem. & Cytochem., 27, 1979, 621-628.

3. Bengtsson E., Eriksson O., Holmquist J., Stenkvist B., Implementation and evaluation of a diode array scanner for digitizing microscopic images, In: Pressman N.J., Wied G.L., eds., Automation of Cancer Cytology and Cell Image Analysis, 1979, 269-286.

4. Bengtsson E., Eriksson O., Jarkrans T., Nordin B., Stenkvist B., CELLO - an interactive system for image analysis, In: Bolc L., Kulpa Z., eds., Digital Image Processing Systems, Lecture Notes in Comp. Sci. 109, Springer-Verlag, Berlin 1981, 21-45.

5. Jain R., Nagel H.-H., On the analysis of accumulative difference pictures from image sequences of real world scenes, IEEE Trans. on Pat. Anal. & Mach. Intellig., vol. PAMI-1, No. 2, 1979, 206-214.

6. Aufstellung von digitalen Bildverarbeitungssystemen in der Bundesrepublik Deutschland (Ohne Anspruch aut Vollständigkeit), In: Triendl E., ed., Informatik Fachberichte, vol. 17, (Proc. 1st DAGM Symp., Obespfaffenkofen, 1978), Springer-Verlag, Berlin-Heidelberg-New York 1978, 379-385.

7. Lebedev D.S., personal communication.

8. Jaroslavski L.P., Digital picture processing (in Russian), Radiotekhnika, 32, No. 11, 1977.

9. Jaroslavski L.P., Merzlyakov N.S., Information display using the methods of digital holography, Computer Graphics and Image Processing, 10, No. 1, 1979, 1-29.

10. Vámos T., Industrial objects and machine parts recognition, In: Fu K.S., ed., Syntactic Pattern Recognition, Applications, Springer-Verlag, Berlin-Heidelberg-New York 1977, 244-267.

11. Vámos T., Báthor M., Mérő L., A knowledge-based interactive robot-vision system, Proc. 6th Intern. Joint Conf. on Artificial Intelligence, Tokyo 1979.

12. Mérő L., Csetverikov B.L., Báthor M., A system for recognizing metal sheets of a bus-body, Proc. MANUFACONT'80 Conference, Budapest, Oct. 1980.

13. Foith J.P., Geisselmann H., Lübbert U., Ringshauser H., A modular system for digital imaging sensors for industrial vision, Proc. 3rd CISM-IFToMM Symp. on Theory and Practice of Robots and Manipulators, Udine 1978.

14. Foith J.P., A TV-sensor for top-lighting and multiple part analysis, Proc. 2nd IFAC/IFIP Symp. on Inf. Control Problems in Manufacturing Techn., Rembold U., ed., Stuttgart, Pergamon Press 1979, 229-234.

15. Foith J.P., Eisenbarth C., Enderle E., Geisselmann H., Ringshauser H., Zimmermann G., Real-time processing of binary images for industrial applications, In: Bolc L., Kulpa Z., eds., Digital Image Processing Systems, Lecture Notes in Comp. Sci. 109, Springer-Verlag, Berlin 1981, 61-168.

16. Ringshauser H., Digitale Bildsensoren für industrielle Anwendungen in Sichtprüfung, Handhabung, Ablaufsteuerung und Prozess-Regelung, Microscopica Acta, 1980 (in press).

17. Kulpa Z., Nowicki H.T., Simple interactive picture processing system PICASSO-SHOW, Proc. 3rd Intern. Joint Conf. on Pattern Recognition, Coronado, Calif., Nov. 1976, 218-223.

18. Kulpa Z., Dernałowicz J., Raczkowska M., Piotrowicz M., Digital picture processing system CPO-2 and its biomedical applications, In: Selected Papers of the 1st Natl. Conf. on Biocybernetics and Biomed. Engng., PWN (Polish Sci. Publ.), Warsaw 1978.

19. Kulpa Z., Bielik A., Piotrowicz M., Rychwalska M., Measurements of shape characteristics of moving cells using computer image processing system CPO-2, Proc. Conf. BIOSIGMA'78, Paris 1978, 286-292.

20. Kulpa Z., Dernałowicz J., Nowicki H.T., Bielik A., CPO-2/K-202: a universal digital image analysis system, In: Bolc L., Kulpa Z., eds., Digital Image Processing Systems, Lecture Notes in Comp. Sci. 109, Springer-Verlag, Berlin 1981, 169-200.

21. Franchina V., Levialdi S., Pirri A., VIP: an image acquisition device for digital processing, Proc. Conf. on Computer Assisted Scanning, Padova 1976.

22. Levialdi S., Pirri A., Franchina V., An image acquisition device for minicomputers, Computer Graphics and Image Processing, 8, 1978, 113-120.

23. Kruse B., A parallel picture processing machine, IEEE Trans. on Computers, vol. C-22, 1973, 1075-1087.

24. Kruse B., The PICAP picture processing laboratory, Proc. 3rd Intern. Joint Conf. on Pattern Recognition, Coronado, Calif., Nov. 1976, 875-881.

25. Kruse B., System architecture for image analysis, In: Tarimoto S., Klinger A., eds., Structured Computer Vision, Acad. Press, New York 1980, 169-212.

26. Rao K., Balck K., Type classification of fingerprints - a syntactic approach, IEEE Trans. on Pat. Anal. & Mach. Intellig., vol. PAMI-2, No. 3, 1980.

27. Cordella L.P., Duff M.J.B., Levialdi S., An analysis of computational cost in image processing: a case study, IEEE Trans. on Computers, vol. C-27, No. 10, 1978, 904-910.

28. Duff M.J.B., Review of the CLIP image processing system, Proc. National Computing Conference, 1978, 1055-1060.

29. Leitz T.A.S.: System for automatic processing and evaluation of optical images, Ernst Leitz Wetzlar GMBH and R. Bosch Fernseh--Anlagen GMBH leaflet No. 121.521-073, Wetzlar 1980.

30. Nawrath R., Serra J., Quantitative image analysis: theory and instrumentation, Microscopica Acta, 82, No. 2, 1979, 101-111.

31. Nawrath R., Serra J., Quantitative image analysis: applications using sequential transformations, ibidem, 113-128.

32. Granlund G.H., In search of a general picture processing operator, Computer Graphics and Image Processing, 8, 1978, 155-178.

33. Granlund G.H., The GOP parallel image processor, In: Bolc L.,
    Kulpa Z., eds., <u>Digital Image Processing Systems</u>, Lecture
    Notes in Comp. Sci. 109, Springer-Verlag, Berlin 1981, 201-227.

34. Kulpa Z., Universal image processing and analysis systems - an
    overview of the European scene, In: Kunt M., de Coulon F., eds.,
    <u>Signal Processing: Theories and Applications</u>, (Proc. EUSIPCO-80
    Conference, Lausanne, Sept. 1980), North-Holland, Amsterdam
    1980, 7-14.

35. Granlund G.H., Kruse B., eds., <u>Parallel Picture Processing</u> -
    part II: <u>Hardware Structures</u>, a course material, EUSIPCO-80
    Conference, Lausanne, Sept. 1980 (issued by Linköping Univer-
    sity, Linköping, Sweden).

CELLO

An Interactive System for Image Analysis

Bengtsson E, Ph.D[1], Eriksson O, B.Sc[2], Jarkrans T, M.E[2],
Nordin B, B.Sc[2] and Stenkvist B, M.D[3]

(1) Dept. of Physics, Uppsala University, Sweden
(2) Dept. of Computer Science, Uppsala University
(3) Dept. of Clin. Cytology, Uppsala University Hospital

ABSTRACT

CELLO is an interactive, command oriented image analysis system. It has been developed for applications in automated cytology i.e. for the development of microscopic cell image analysis algorithms but is very flexible and can be used for a wide range of image analysis applications.

The system allows interactive as well as batch processing. In fact the degree of user interaction is easily adapted to the users needs. The image processing language is command oriented and is easy to expand by adding new commands. This is mainly due to the fact that CELLO has a high degree of modularity. Each command has its own independently loadable program module. The system monitor itself also consists of several relatively independent modules.

CELLO has been implemented on a large mini computer, a PDP 11/55 equipped with a custom-built image display system. The display interface of the software is general so that almost any type of display terminal can be used. A simpler CELLO version that runs on a PDP 8 computer has also been developed.

INTRODUCTION

The development of image processing algorithms is a highly experimental undertaking. Different tentative algorithms are applied to an image, the result is checked, the algorithm is modified and applied again until an acceptable result is obtained. To facilitate this kind of work a highly interactive system is needed.

On the other hand, when a promising algorithm has been found, it is desirable to apply it to a large number of different images in order to obtain reliable statistics about its performance. At that time it is only cumbersome if each step requires human interaction. Thus a system with a variable degree of interactivity is desirable.

Most image processing systems are heavily oriented towards image processing in a narrow sense i.e. transforming one image into other images. This certainly is a necessary facility in all image processing systems. To support this facility one needs a powerful way of specifying what operations should be performed. In order to keep the execution times reasonable a high performance computer is desirable. Such computers can very well take advantage of the parallell nature of most image processing operations.

However, many applications require a few scalar features, extracted from the images, as the end result of the algorithms. Thus for an application oriented system it is equally important to have good facilities for feature extraction and convenient handling of the extracted data in some kind of database. A system that is designed with both these aspects in mind can perhaps be called an image analysis system as opposed to a pure image processing system.

For a number of years research in the field of cytology automation has been carried out at the Department of Clinical Cytology, Uppsala University Hospital. Problems concerning automation of the uterine cancer cytology have been studied as well as more basic studies in computerized nuclear morphometry in relation to epidemiological and clinical aspects of breast cancer [1,2,3,4].

A number of interactive image analysis systems are continuously being developed in order to facilitate this research work. The first of these, SCANCANS [5], was a simple, easy to use, command driven software system implemented on a PDP-8 interfaced to a Leitz MPV II microphotometer, using a Tektronix 4010 storage tube terminal as the operator interface. This was a very limited system, although exciting enough to initiate the development of a new more powerful interactive software system on the PDP-8, basically using the same hardware. The new system, which was called CELLO-8, had a richer syntax and was highly modular in its structure [6]. It could be used in interactive as well as in batch mode, and could in fact be easily adapted to any level of interactivity. The success of this system was essentially the result of modern programming technology.

A PDP-8, however, is not an ideal computer for image processing, mainly due to the fact that it is a relatively old and slow computer and that the word length is 12 bits only. When a large modern mini-computer, a PDP-11/55, became available to us we therefore developed a third generation of our interactive image analysis system giving it the name CELLO-11. The basic system structure and command syntax is similar to that of the predecessor. However, the new system accepts several simultaneous users and also takes advantage of the greater flexibility of the larger computer system in several other ways. This paper discusses some of the design considerations that went into the system, outlines the structure of the system and gives some examples of its use. In a final section some of the experiences from using the system are reported and a new fourth generation system which presently is under implementation is outlined.

DESIGN CONSIDERATIONS

Although generally applicable in the field of image analysis, the CELLO system was developed for applications in automated cytology. The system was designed to fulfill two different needs:

1. A flexible interactive system for measuring and evaluating numerical parameters from cell nuclei and cytoplasms

2. A platform for algorithm and method development in automation of uterine cancer cytology

Both these applications require that not only image processing operations can be performed on the cells, but also that the results from such operations can be stored in data bases and that tools are available for evaluation of the data bases. They also require the possibility of varying the level of user interaction from a step by step control of each single operation to automatic batch runs that generate large sets of data which subsequently can be statistically analyzed.

These requirements were translated into the following design goals:

1. The user should be able to interact with the system by means of free format commands typed on the keyboard of a text terminal. This implies that the system has to scrutinize the input text string carefully for errors before any processing starts and write out suitable diagnostics if anything is wrong.

2. It should be possible to put commands together to sequences, to be used as procedures or new powerful commands (super commands). This feature enables the system manager to define commands suitable for use by unexperienced operators and non programmers, e.g. biologists and pathologists, in well defined studies of various kinds.

3. It should be possible to automatically repeat the same sequence of commands for a whole set of different images and save the result in a data base. This introduces a batch facility in the system.

4. The design had to be completely open-ended, i.e. it should be possible to add new functions to the system without having to modify anything in the old system. This was considered to be absolutely necessary, as the system was expected to grow more or less continuously during its lifetime in terms of new commands for new applications.

HARDWARE

Computer system

The CELLO-11 system was implemented on a PDP-11/55 computer running under the RSX-11/M multi-user operating system. The basic characteristics of the computer system are: 256 k bytes of core memory, an 8 lines multiplexed terminal interface, two 40 M bytes disk memories, an 800 bpi magnetic tape drive, a floating point processor and a Versatec electrostatic printer/plotter. The system also has a link to the old PDP-8 based image processing system (see Figure 1).

25

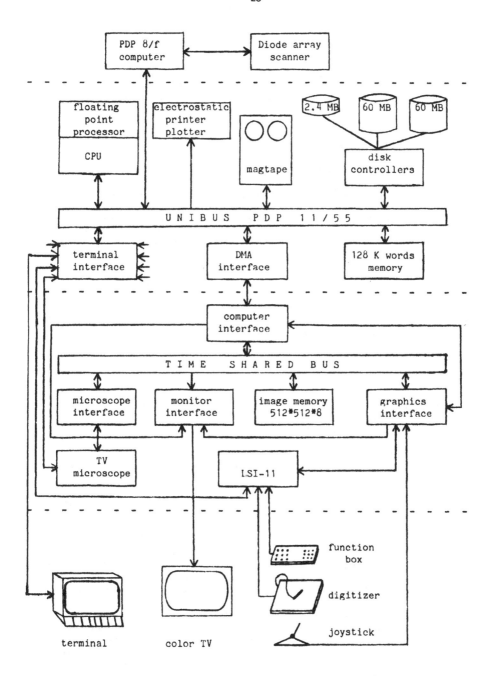

Figure 1. Block diagram of the hardware. The horisontal
dashed lines separate the different subsystems. These are
the image scanner, the host computer, the image display
system with the TV-microscope and the interactive workstation.

Terminals

Three alphanumerical terminals are connected to the system as well as three graphics terminals (Tektronix 4010, Tektronix 4006 and Hewlett-Packard 2648A). A custom-built image display system connected via a DMA channel is also available.

CELLO can be run from any terminal but a graphics terminal is needed for most image processing operations since the user otherwise will have very limited possibilities of interacting with the images. The simple graphics terminals are well suited for presenting graphical information such as histograms and object outlines but can also be used for grayscale images through the use of dithering techniques [7] i.e. each picture element is represented by a small matrix of black or white points. The grayscale obtainable in this manner is limited to a few gray levels but this is sufficient for many purposes. In fact, CELLO was originally developed for simple graphics terminals and is still frequently run from such terminals. However, an image display system capable of displaying a full 6 bit grayscale as well as graphics overlays in color is a more ideal tool for interactive image processing work. Such a system has also been built for us by the Department of Electrical Engineering at Linkoeping University and integrated with the CELLO software. It is briefly described in the next section. For a more complete description see [8,9]

Image display system

The image display system is built up around a high speed time shared data bus. The capacity of the bus is more than 40 M byte/sec. An image memory with a capacity of 512*512 picture points, each with 8 bits, and eight general I/O ports are connected to the bus. Three of these I/O ports are presently occupied, namely by a display processor, a microcomputer controlled graphics generator and an interface to the host computer.

The display processor is used for generating signals from the content of the image memory for a standard RGB monitor and a black and white monitor. The color tables in this processor can be loaded from the micro computer. This makes it possible to have full software control over the grayscale and pseudocoloring of the displayed images. Zooming and scrolling of the images is also possible. Finally the display processor has registers for controlling the position of a cursor symbol, allowing convenient operator interaction with the image display.

The microcomputer, a LSI-11 [10], is connected to an interface essentially intended for generating graphics using two of the bitplanes of the image memory. A function box and a digitizer pad are connected to the microcomputer via separate I/O interfaces.

The microcomputer software handles control functions and vector graphics to be overlaid on the gray level images. It accepts two different types of commands. The first type of commands are sent together with their data from the host to the microcomputer, where they are executed by a small interpreter. Some typical examples of such commands are

1. Draw/erase a sequence of vectors from the data that follows

2. Write/erase the text that follows

3. Set a subrectangle of the image to a given value

4. Enable the cursor and read back the cursor coordinates to the host

5. Enable the graphics tablet and track the stylus position until a termination signal is received

6. Load the color memory with the data that follows

The other type of commands are given via the buttons on the function box. These commands are typically used to control the video interface. Some examples are:

1. Turn the graphical overlay on/off

2. Zoom in/out

3. Move the display window up/down/left/right

4. Turn the cursor symbol on/off

The main communication line between the PDP-11 and the image display hardware is an asynchronous 16 bit parallel I/O interface working at a rate of about 0.5 M byte/sec. This interface can also be multiplexed to communicate with the graphics interface and thus with the microcomputer. Through this interface gray level images can be transferred directly from the host computer into the display memory and instructions can be sent to the microcomputer.

Image scanners

Image input to the system is presently through the link from the old CELLO-8 system. In that system a diode-array scanner [11] is used to provide high quality digitizations of microscopic images. This solution has some advantages in that image aquisition can either be done off-line using only the PDP-8 system or on line under direct control from CELLO-11. It is however a rather slow system and the added complexity of having to run two computers in order to obtain images is a disadvantage. We are therefore presently waiting for a new TV based automated microscope which will be connected to the high speed bus and thus input its images directly into the image memory of the display system. This microscope is being constructed by the group which constructed the display system.

COMMAND LANGUAGE

Syntax

The system is controlled by commands typed on the terminal keyboard. The syntax of the commands is defined by the grammar in figure 2, i.e. a command has the following general format:

$LABEL COMMAND QUALIFIERS (PARAMETERS) ->RESULT;

The only mandatory part of a command is the actual COMMAND verb. All other parts assume default values when absent. The qualifiers are used to request a special function of the command.

Two kinds of parameters, string parameters and numerical parameters, can be given to the command.

String parameters, which must preceed the numerical parameters, are made up from three different kinds of string data: string constants, string representation of numerical values and file references. Several substrings of different kinds can be concatenated to constitute a string parameter for a command.

Numerical parameters are arbitrary arithmetic expressions. Thus a numerical parameter can be a constant, a variable or a more complex expression. All arithmetic operations are performed in floating point representation.

```
Z ::= [<label>] <command> [<parameter>] [ -> <variable>] ;
<label> ::= $<identifier>
<command> ::=  <identifier>!<identifier><qualifierpart>
<qualifierpart> ::= <identifier> { &<identifier>}
<parameters> ::= ( {<strpar>,} {<numpar>,} )
<strpar> ::= '<char> {<char>}'
<numpar> ::= <expr>
<expr> ::= <term>|<term> + <expr>!<term> - <expr>
<term> ::= <factor>|<term> * <factor>!<term> / <factor>
<factor> ::= <const>|<variable>|(<expr>)
<const> ::= <unop><digit>{<digit>} [.{<digit>}] [E<unop><digit>]
<variable> ::= <identifier>
<identifier> ::= <letter>{<alphanum>}
<alphanum> ::= <digit>|<letter>
<digit> ::= 0 | 1 | 2 | 3 | 4 | 5 | 6 | 7 | 8 | 9
<letter> ::= A | B | ....... | Z
<char> ::= ASCII(40) ....... ASCII(176)
<unop> ::= + | -
```

Figure 2. Pseudo BNF-grammar describing the syntax of the CELLO command language. Entities enclosed within a bracket pair ([]) are optional, entities enclosed within curly brackets ({}) can occur from zero to any number of times in the definition.

Many commands can return a value or a set of values. These values can optionally be stored in a predefined data record by means of the assignment operator '->'. The values are stored in symbolic addresses, which implies that the same command can store its data in several positions of the data record. The names of these positions can be used as variables in arithmetic expressions. Originally this feature was intended for storing extracted numerical parameters from cell images and later for retrieving the information for e.g. statistical analyses , but it can also be used as a means of transferring information from one command to another.

Labels make it possible for one command to reference another one. In combination with the possibility of entering several commands in sequence before the execution starts, the labels can be used to impose a control structure on the language. In the CELLO system this has been achieved by introducing a set of conditional jump commands which transfer control to a referenced command when a certain condition is fulfilled. In this way conditional execution and loops become possible, although perhaps not always in a clean and structured way.

Below some examples of commands are shown:

```
DISPLAY;                    "display the image"
DISPLAY MASK;               "display the mask (binary image)"
AREA(0,40);                 "count all picture elements with gray
                             values in the range 0 - 40"
AREA(0,40)->NUCLEUSAREA;    "as above except that the computed
                             value is stored in a user defined
                             variable NUCLEUSAREA"
```

Command types

In an attempt to impose some structure on the wide variety of commands we try to classify them as belonging to one of eight different categories. These categories are:

1. System control commands.
    Controls the CELLO system providing the tools for writing and maintaining procedures, libraries, indirect files, data files etc.

    Examples:

    SET - turn various system options on or off.
         More than 25 different qualifiers.
    IF - conditional jump to specified label.
    GOTO - jump to specified label.
    RESET - open indirect file.
    RENEW - move pointer to next record in indirect file.
    DEFINE - insert a new command in the system tables
            making it immediately available for use.
    REQUEST - send instructions to the CELLO-8 system,
             mainly used to request the scanning of new images.
    VARIABLE - define new variables to the system and open
              a new data base where corresponding values
              can be saved

2. User interaction commands
    Display images, histograms etc on the terminal. Accept graph-
    ical input via joystick or cursor.

    Examples:

    DISPLAY - show an image on the terminal in one of many
              possible ways depending on qualifier.
    HISTOGRAM - generate and display the gray level frequency
                histogram
    HARDCOPY - make a paper copy of the display file.
    CROSS - show the density cross-section of the image along
            specified line

3. Image processing commands
    These are the traditional image to image operators accepting
    one or more images as input and generating one or more output
    images, either binary or grayscale.

    Examples:

    MASK - generate binary image through thresholding
           or some other procedure depending on qualifier
    ADD - add two images together with optional scaling
    GRADIENT - generate gradient image, either only magnitude
               or both direction and magnitude.
    SMOOTH - apply one of several selectable smoothing operators
             to the image
    ERODE - run the generalized erosion operator on the
            (usually binary) image

4. Feature extraction commands
    Extract numerical data from objects in the images. Usually
    the objects are defined through one of the binary masks.
    About a dozen such commands are available which together with
    their qualifiers and parameters makes it possible to extract
    hundreds of features.

    Examples:

    AREA - compute the object area.
    EXTINCTION - compute the integrated optical extinction value.
    DENSITY - compute various measures from the density
              distribution depending on the qualifier.
    SHAPE - compute various features based on a fourier analysis
            of the object contour.

5. Data base manipulation commands.
    Handle data that have been extracted from the images. Write
    out selected parts of the data base in numerical or graphical
    format. Create new populations by splitting or merging old
    ones etc.

    Examples:

SCATTER - show a scatter plot of two selected variables
MERGE - create a new data set from two old ones
FISHER - run Fisher linear discriminant analysis on
        selected features

6. Segmentation commands
Process images and other data in order to produce new representations of the information more useful for further processing. Both general purpose image processing algorithms and
specialized cell analysis procedures are available.

Examples:

KILL - delete all connected objects from a mask except
      specified ones e.g. largest, in certain size range,
      containing point x,y
OVERLAP - analyze contour of object and decide whether it is
      likely that it consists of more than one cell
      nucleus.

7. Miscellaneous commands
Various odd commands that do not fit any of the above categories.

Examples:

SIERPINSKI - Draw a Sierpinski curve on display.
TESTSEG - Compare an image segmentation to a reference one
      (see section 6.2)

8. Temporary commands
New or experimental commands that have not yet been accepted
as useful permanent additions to CELLO.

Command procedures

The power of the command language has been amplified through
the use of procedures. Procedures can be assembled from sequences
of commands and other procedures. When a procedure is called, the
call is replaced by its procedure definition. The syntax of the
procedure calls is a subset of the command syntax, implying that
the user can not see any actual difference between using a command
or a procedure. In this way a complex processing algorithm, which
can be expressed as a sequence of simple commands, can be defined
as a procedure and executed as a single command by the user. The
following is an example of a short procedure:

NUCLEUSVALUES('$1')

    MASK(0,$1);   "create a mask (binary image) of
                           all picture elements having gray
                           values in the range 0 - $1"
    EXTINCTION MASK->EXT; "compute the integrated light

                              extinction and store in the
                              variable EXT"
        DENSITY MEAN->AVLEVEL;   "compute the average gray level within
                              the mask and store in AVLEVEL"

This procedure is activated by giving its name and a formal parameter in replacement for its symbolic parameter in the description
above, i.e.

        NUCLEUSVALUES('35');

gives as a result integrated light extinction and average gray
level calculated from the gray level image, but only for the image
points with gray values in the range 0 - 35.

The help facility

        Presently we have about 150 different commands available in
CELLO. Of these about one third can be said to constitute the basic system. Another third are commands that have been developed
for various applications but found to be of general usefulness.
The rest are special purpose commands of little general interest.
The sheer size of the system makes it difficult for the casual
user to remember everything he needs to know. The fact that CELLO
is growing and changing with at least a few commands each week
makes it even more difficult to keep up with the present status of
the system.

        An aid in coping with these problems is the HELP command.
This is a command which gives various kinds of information about
the system. Used without any qualifiers or parameters it explains
its own use. With the qualifier SHORT it gives a compact listing
of the abbreviated names of all commands in the system. With a
command name as string parameter it explains the use of that command. This is done on two levels. Firstly the command syntax as
defined by the system tables is shown. Secondly approximately one
screen full of text is written about the use of the command. It
is the responsibility of the programmers to write such texts in a
standardized format as soon as a new command has been written and
permanently added to the system.

        Other qualifiers and parameters to the HELP command produces
other kinds of information about the system. Our general experience is that the help facility has been extremely useful in main-
taining an up to date documentation of the system available to all
users.

IMPLEMENTATION

        The main key to reaching the design goals within the limited
resources of the available hardware was modularity. Thus each
command corresponds to a single independently loadable program module (task). Adding a new command to the system requires writing
a program for it with a standardized beginning and end as well as
a standardized communication area. By means of prewritten subroutines in a library this is very simple. The new command has to be
identified for the system (a couple of system tables have to be

updated), which is done with a special command. The rest of the system is left completely unaltered. This procedure makes it quite easy to add new commands.

The monitor itself also consists of four tasks; a text editor, a macro processor, a translator and an interpreter. These tasks communicate with each other via a global common data area (one for each active user). The user enters and edits command strings with the text editor via the terminal keyboard. If any procedure calls are included they are replaced by their procedure bodies by the macro processor. Then these strings are checked for appropriate syntax and translated to internal form by the translator. Finally the internal form of the command strings is executed by the interpreter, which means one of two actions: either a command induces execution of a small piece of code in the interpreter itself, or, in most cases, an external task corresponding to the command is activated. Figure 3 shows the logical steps in the processing of a command or a sequence of commands. In the following paragraphs we briefly outline how these tasks operate. A more detailed description can be found in [12].

Text editor

The text editor has two different functions: firstly all input is entered and edited with it. Secondly, it is used to maintain a library of procedures as described above.

It works like any normal text editor: text can be entered and manipulated by means of simple commands. It has some similarities with the TECO editor [13]. Text can be entered either from the keyboard or can be read in from a file.

Macro processor

The procedure facility is implemented by using a macro processor. This processor is enabled when the LIBRARY command is used to specify which procedure library should be used. When the macro processor is activiated it processes the output from the text editor before it is used as input for the translator task. The macro processor replaces all procedure calls with the corresponding procedure definition. The macro processor is fully recursive allowing integer arithmetic, text string operations, conditional expansion, logical tests, etc. [14].

Command language translator

The input text string is checked syntactically and translated to interpretable code by the translator task. This task processes the input text in two passes. In the first pass all labels are entered into a special symbol table and assigned a relative value. The second pass performs the syntax checking, translates the input into an internal form and assigns an absolute value to the labels.

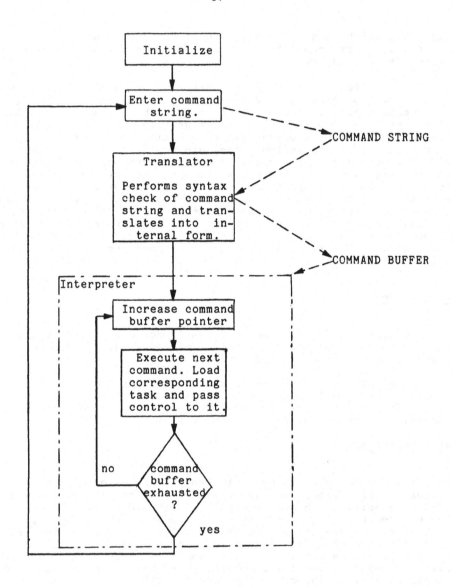

Figure 3. Flow chart showing the logical steps in the processing of a sequence of commands.

Internally the translator consists of a scanner which reduces the input into tokens (identifiers, operators ...) and a parser, which is a collection of procedures, one for each syntactic element. Each of these procedures performs the symbol table handling, the code generation and other tasks associated with its particular syntactic element. The input is checked syntactically and translated one command at a time.

The parser translates the commands into a useful form for the interpretation task, i.e. arithmetic expressions have to be stored in a form that is easy to evaluate at run time etc. If any errors are detected in the input text, an error message is written, the rest of that command is skipped and control is returned to the text editor rather than given to the interpreter when all commands have been processed.

The transition matrix technique [15] is used for syntax checking. This is a simple and fast method for parsing small grammars.

Interpreter and run time system

The input for the interpreter consists of the translated form of the input text together with the present state of the system. The system status is stored in a dedicated data area (the communication area).

Executing a command roughly consists of the following steps in order:

1. Read the internal form of the command with its parameter field and identify the command.

2. Evaluate the string parameters.

3. Evaluate the numerical parameters. The parser evaluates all numerical expressions which do not contain any variables. The remaining expressions are stored in a text pool and are evaluated by the interpreter at run time.

4. The final version of the internal form is stored in the communication area.

5. A check is made in order to see whether the command can be executed immediately, or if an external task execution is required. If the command is internal the code is executed and control returns to step 1. If the execution of an external task is required, that task is given control. The synchronization is accomplished using global event flags.

The external task also has access to the communication area, where it can leave calculated results, a modified image or mask etc. When completed the external task returns the control to the interpreter. Then the next command is executed or control is given to the text editor task if the input string is exhausted.

Graphics software

CELLO can be operated from any user terminal as was described in the hardware section above. The problem of incompatibility between different graphical devices has been solved by letting CELLO maintain a display file. The display file is a data area unique to each user containing primitive graphical operations, such as move to a coordinate, draw a vector from one coordinate to another. Text strings and image file identifiers are also stored in the display file. The display file is built up by different segments, where each segment corresponds to a particular subgraph to be shown on the display. Segments are deleted from and added to the display file by the various commands, each command having its own unique segment.

In order to be shown on a graphical device the display file has to be interpreted by an interpreter specific for the selected graphical device. Thus one interpreter exists for each device. Incorporating a new graphical device into the system requires a display file interpeter to be written for the device, which in general is very easy. This technique also gives a convenient hardcopy facility, as an interpreter has been written for the Versatec printer/plotter.

The graphics software in CELLO is a slightly modified version of a general purpose graphical package developed at our department [16].

Programming languages

The interpreter, translator, text editor and macro processor tasks are all written in the programming language PASCAL. PASCAL was chosen because of its possibilities for data structuring and clean control structure, making it a suitable high level implementation language. External tasks corresponding to commands are programmed in FORTRAN IV and compiled by using an optimizing compiler. FORTRAN is efficient for heavy calculations on relatively simple data structures, making it suitable for the commands, which perform the actual image processing operations.

EXAMPLES OF USE

The system internally handles two gray level images consisting of 128x128x6 bits each, and four masks (binary images) with 128x128x1 bits. The images and masks are referenced by commands by means of numerical parameters. Many commands in the system are designed for analysis of objects (particles) in the gray level images. An object in this context is a part of a gray level image defined by a connected region in a mask. Thus the gray level images and the masks are very closely connected to each other.

In this section two examples are given, illustrating how the system can be used. The first example is a purely interactive application, where only one command at a time is entered to the CELLO monitor. The second is a pure batch example comparing two methods for automatic segmentation of cytoplasms of cervical cells.

The selected examples represent two extremes - interactivity versus batch - , and it should be pointed out that it is possible to adapt the system to any level of interactivity between these limits. In a particular study procedures often are written for all well defined parts in the processing before the actual work begins, while the remaining parts are written as procedures when a couple of cells have been processed and experience has been gained.

Interactive application

This example discusses the processing of an image of cell nuclei from prostatic cancer. It is assumed that the images have been scanned earlier and reside on disk in special disk files. The command

    GET ('WEST1.PI',1);

loads image register 1 with the image file WEST1.PI,

    HISTOGRAM;

shows a histogram of the gray levels in the image on the display, and the command

    MASK (3,0,40);

generates a binary image of the picture elements with gray level 0-40 in mask register 3 and shows the mask on the display. Generally masks 0 and 1 are superimposed on image 1, mask 2 and 3 on image 2. Mask 3 was selected in this example in order not to overlay image 1 on the display. Figure 4 is a photograph of the TV monitor at this point of the processing. With the command

    KILL EXCLUSIVE(3);

the cursor is enabled, whereupon the operator is supposed to point at the object in the mask that he wants to keep. At this moment mask 3 contains the definition of one of the cell nuclei.

When an object is well defined and isolated, various numerical parameters can be extracted, e.g.

    AREA MASK(3) -> NUCAREA;

calculates the area of the mask and stores the value in the variable NUCAREA.

When an object has been processed and the numerical values have been stored in the data record, the data record must be saved before the next cell is processed. This is done with the command

    SAVE DATA ('WEST1DATA');

which saves the data record under the name WEST1DATA in a dedicated file that was allocated when the variables were defined. Later on commands are used for calculating statistics from the data file.

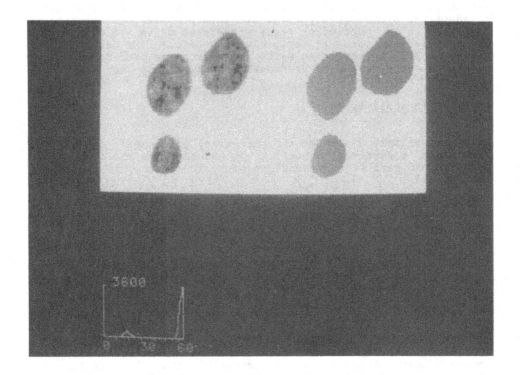

Figure 4. A photograph of the color TV monitor during the inter-active application example as described in the text.

Batch application

This example is somewhat more complicated than the former, but it shows how CELLO can be used as a more powerful tool in im-age analysis. It should be emphasized that we do not wish to dis-cuss the relevance of the selected image processing algorithms or experimental designs, but rather to illustrate the convenience and flexibility of the system.

Two methods for segmentation of cervical cells are compared. Both methods segment the images into background, cytoplasm and nu-cleus. In this study we are particularly interested in comparing the cytoplasm identifications. It is assumed that two gray level images of each cell are available from disk, one scanned at an il-lumination wavelength of 530 nm and the other at 570 nm [17]. Furthermore it is also assumed that three masks for each cell are also available from disk. The first one is an automatically pro-duced nuclear mask. The other two are a nucleus definition mask and a cytoplasm definition mask, both of which have been defined by user interaction in order to obtain a reference segmentation. The accuracy of this reference may be questionable but it is here treated as "the truth". In addition to these data a data file is required containing parameters extracted from the cell, e.g. the center of gravity of the automatically produced nuclear mask.

A fourth mask is produced during the processing in this example, an automatically calculated cytoplasm mask. This is done by means of a dynamic thresholding in the two dimensional gray level histogram obtained from the two original images. Thus an automated segmentation procedure is compared to a manual one.

As a criterion for comparing results from the different segmentations, the method proposed by Yasnoff et al [18] is used. A command, TESTSEG, was written and incorporated into CELLO for this purpose. Programming and testing of this command required only about two hours work which indicates how simple it is to add new facilities to the system. TESTSEG operates on the four mask registers and can return a value to be stored in a variable of the data record.

In addition to the new command a procedure, EVALSEG, was developed for processing a large number of cells without any operator interaction. The procedure is listed in Table 1. It has a file containing identifiers for all cells to be processed as a parameter. This file is called an indirect file. When a command references an indirect file (the file name is preceeded by '@'), the reference is replaced by the current record in the indirect file. Together with a command for moving the current record pointer this gives a convenient facility for obtaining different text parameters in commands each time a command in a loop is executed.

The first two commands in EVALSEG are outside the main loop. RESET sets the current record pointer to the beginning of the indirect file, while FATAL defines a label to which control is transferred when a fatal error occurs in the processing. The latter command together with

$NEXT RENEW ('$1');

at the bottom of the loop forces the procedure to continue with the next cell instead of stopping the whole run in case of an error.

The five GET commands at the beginning of the loop will load the two images, the two reference masks and the old data record of the cell.

HIST2D computes the two dimensional gray level histogram, stores it in a file (transparent to the user) which in turn is used by CYTMASK which does the two dimensional thresholding for defining the cytoplasm in mask 3. The next three commands will clean the cytoplasm mask by using an ERODE operation and by deleting all objects except the one containing the coordinates CENPOS[1], CENPOS[2], the center of gravity of the automatically produced nuclear mask. These coordinates are available via the data record.

The next three commands in turn load the automatically segmented nuclear mask, calculate the comparison measure between the
two segmentations, store that value in the data record and finally
save the data record.

The final processing consists in computing two difference
masks, i.e. masks showing the difference between the results from
the two methods. The first one shows the nuclear differences and
the other one the cytoplasmic differences. The cell image in image register 1 is loaded into image register 2 as well and the
masks 0 and 1 are cleared. At this point two identical gray level
images are shown on the display with the two difference masks superimposed on the right one. Figure 5 shows a photograph of the
TV-monitor at this time.

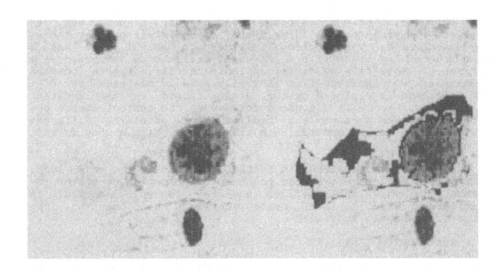

Figure 5. A photograph of the color TV monitor during the
batch application example as described in the text. The dark areas along the cytoplasmic- and nuclear borders which indicate the
difference between the two segmentation methods are shown in different colors on the TV.

The only thing that remains to do in the loop is to advance the current record pointer in the indirect file and jump to the beginning of the loop.

The next step in an evaluation of data in general is to plot frequency histograms and scatter diagrams over selected variables in a population of cells. As an illustration of this the result of the following command sequence is shown in figure 6:

```
WINDOW VIRTUAL (-1000.,11000.,-1000.,11000.);
SCATTER ('MALIGN','CMSRES','THRRES','X');
```

The first command defines a new coordinate system to be scaled down to the display screen coordinates. The second command draws a scatter diagram on the display of the population MALIGN (a data record file with the name "MALIGN") using the variables CMSRES and THRRES on the horizontal and vertical axes respectively. CMSRES is the variable which was stored in the data record by the procedure in the example above. THRRES is the same segmentation comparison measure but using a slightly modified method for producing the cytoplasm mask. Thus the scatter diagram illustrates the differences in performance of two different segmentation techniques tested on the same material. There are also commands available for more sophisticated statistical analyses such as linear discriminant analysis and cluster analysis.

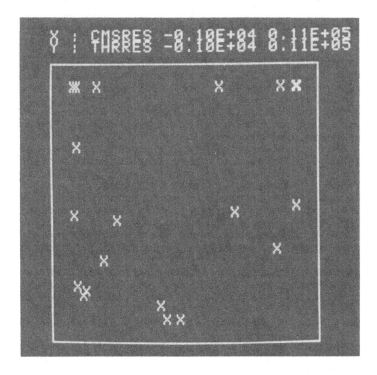

Figure 6. An example of a scatter diagram as produced on the TV-screen when the error measures from the two different segmentation experiments are compared (for details see text).

PERSPECTIVE

CELLO-11 has now been in routine use for about two years. The main application has been the development and testing of methods for automated screening of cervical smears. The general experience is that the system has been very useful. The reason for this is to a large extent the modularity and the fact that the system is programmable with procedures. Since the procedures can call other procedures it is easy to start with one part of a problem and write a procedure for it. When this part is solved, another part is attacked in the same way. Partial solutions can then be put together to new procedures and so on. This is known as the bottom up approach in computer science. In the procedure for segmentation of cervical cells [19] for instance there are several hundred commands. These commands are put together into subprocedures, each one solving a particular subproblem.

There are always possibilities to improve even an already successful system. Despite the fact that it is convenient to add new commands, a highly desirable feature would be the possibility to program all parts of an algorithm directly in the command language without having to write FORTRAN programs as external tasks for each command. The fact that CELLO has been used for programming in the command language to such a large extent further amplifies the need of improving this language. Thus what is needed is the development of a new interactive programming language with powerful general structuring facilities and with special data types for image processing.

Such a language has been designed and named ILIAD (Interactive Language for Image Analysis and Display). The general syntax is similar to that of PASCAL but the system is fully interactive. Thus new procedures and variables can be defined at any time. An image data type is available which makes the buffered access to images of any size and picture element type completely transparent to the user. The procedures can be of two types, internal or external. The internal procedures are procedures previously written in ILIAD and saved in libraries. The external procedures are similar to the CELLO command modules, i e independent programs linked to the system through certain global data areas. The syntax of the calls of both types of procedures is exactly the same. Thus the user will be able to develop his image processing algorithms entirely in the ILIAD language and, when he is satisfied with a certain procedure, reprogram the most time consuming parts in FORTRAN or assembler language to gain speed (if necessary).

The present status of our implementation of ILIAD is that we have the basic system working but that the handling of images, libraries and external tasks is still very primitive. We expect to complete the new system within the next year. Most of the CELLO commands will then be available in ILIAD as external procedures.

The custom-built image display system that is used by CELLO has an architecture that gives it the potential of doing much more than merely displaying images. Different kinds of image processors can be attached to the I/O ports of the high speed bus e g segmentation processors or linear filter processors. The modular structure of CELLO (and ILIAD) makes it very easy to adapt the system to control such hardware. One only needs to write simple programs that sends the appropriate control information to the hardware when certain commands are given.

The modular structure and device independent graphics also makes it easy to use CELLO with other display systems. All that needs to be modified is the display file interpreter for the image display and some commands that use special hardware features in the display system.

The modularity of the CELLO system has been mentioned several times in this paper as the key to the success of the system in several respects. But this modularity has a price. It does introduce a certain amount of overhead in the system monitor. This is in the order of one second per command. It also makes the total size of the system greater than it otherwise would need to be since significant parts of the code are used in several modules. Considering all the advantages of the modular structure we certainly think it is worth paying this price.

ACKNOWLEDGEMENT

This research was supported by the Swedish Board of Technical Development under grant no 77-3815 and the Bank of Sweden Tercentenary Foundation under grant no 77-112.

REFERENCES

1. Holmquist J.
   On analysis methods and software design for computer process-
   ing of digitized microscopic cell images.
   Ph. D. thesis from Department of Computer Science, Uppsala
   University, 1977.

2. Bengtsson E.
   On the design of systems for computer aided analysis of microscopic images.
   Ph. D. thesis from Department of Physics, Uppsala University, 1977.

3. Holmquist J, Bengtsson E, Eriksson O, Nordin B, Stenkvist B.
   Computer analysis of cervical cells. Automatic feature ex-
   traction and classification.
   J. Histochem. Cytochem, Vol 26, No 11, pp 1000-1017, 1978.

4. Stenkvist B, Westman-Naeser S, Holmquist J, Nordin B, Bengts-
   son E, Vegelius J, Eriksson O, Fox C.H.
   Computerized Nuclear Morphometry as an Objective Method for
   Characterizing Human Cancer Cell Populations.
   Cancer Research 38, 4688-4697, Dec 1978.

5. Bengtsson E, Holmquist J, Olsen B, Stenkvist B.
   SCANCANS - An interactive scanning cell analysis system.
   Computer Programs in Biomedicine 6, pp 39-49, 1976.

6. Holmquist J, Bengtsson E, Eriksson O, Stenkvist B.
   A program system for interactive measurements on digitized
   cell images.
   J. Histochem. Cytochem, Vol 25, No 7, pp 641-654, 1977.

7. Knowlton K, Harmon L.
   Computer-Produced Gray Scales.
   Computer Graphics and Image Processing, Vol 1, No 1, pp 1-20,
   1972.

8. Holmquist J, Antonsson D, Bengtsson E, Danielsson P-E, Eriks-
   son O, Hedblom T, Martensson A, Nordin B, Olsson T,
   Stenkvist B.
   TULIPS, The Uppsala-Linkoping Image Processing System
   Analytical and Quantitative Cytology. In press.

9. Antonsson D, Danielsson P-E, Malmberg B, Martensson A,
   Olsson T.
   A two Mbit random access memory with 512 Mbit/sec data rate.
   LiTH-ISY-I-0127. Dept of Electrical Eng., Linkoping Universi-
   ty 1977.

10. Microcomputer handbook.
    Digital Equipment Corporation, Maynard, Massachusetts 1978.

11. Bengtsson E, Eriksson O, Holmquist J, Stenkvist B.
    Implementation and evaluation of a diode array scanner for di-
    gitizing microscopic images.
    In the Automation of Cancer Cytology and Cell Image Analysis.
    Tutorials of Cytology, 1979.

12. Eriksson O, Holmquist J, Bengtsson E, Nordin B.
    CELLO - An interactive image analysis system.
    Proceedings of Digital Equipment Computer Users Society, Co-
    penhagen, Denmark Sep 1978.

13. OS/8 Handbook.
    Digital Equipment Corporation, Maynard, Massachusetts 1974.

14. Holmquist J.
    Mll - A general purpose macro processor.
    Report 77:7, Dept. of Clin. Cytology, Uppsala University
    1977.

15. Day A.C.
    The use of symbol state tables.
    Computer Journal 13, pp 4- , 1970.

16. Holmquist J, Johansson J, Bengtsson E, Eriksson O, Nordin B.
    MTGP - A device independent graphical package for RSX-11/M.
    Proceedings of Digital Equipment Computer Users Society, Co-
    penhagen, Denmark - Sep 1978.

17. Holmquist J, Imasato Y, Bengtsson E, Stenkvist B.
    A microspectrophotometric study of Papanicolaou-stained cervi-
    cal cells as an aid om computerized image processing.
    J. Histochem. Cytochem, Vol 24, No 12, pp 1218-1224, 1976.

18. Yasnoff W.A, Galbraith W, Bacus J.W.
    Error measures for objective assessment of scene segmentation
    algorithms.
    Analytical and Quantitative Cytology, Vol 1, No 2, pp 107-121,
    1979.

19. Bengtsson E, Eriksson O, Holmquist J, Nordin B, Stenkvist B.
    High resolution segmentation of cervical cells.
    J. Histochem. Cytochem, Vol 27, No 1, pp 621-628, 1979.

A KNOWLEDGE-BASED INTERACTIVE ROBOT-VISION
SYSTEM

by

T. Vámos - M. Báthor - L. Mérő - A. Siegler

Computer and Automation Institute, Hungarian
Academy of Sciences
Budapest, XI., Kende u. 13-17., 1111 Hungary

Abstract

A robot-vision project is reported which incorporates several
existing AI methods and some new results. The ambition of the project is a system which can economically complete various intelligent tasks within the scope of mini- and microcomputers. The tuned
composition of the applied methods provides a new and powerful
approach to R and D engineering and workshop-operation.

1. INTRODUCTION

This paper reports on a robot-vision system. A lot of its features
are similar to same existing systems, however, some of its characteristics are worthy of attention:
- a clear separation of four intelligence levels:
    system Research and Development /R and D/
    system Design and implementation
    task teaching and its adjustment
    production runs;
- a man-machine communication which controls the whole process and
  uses a real-time, simple graphic representation with special features for this kind of tasks;
- new real-time picture processing algorithms for contour following;
- a knowledge-based combination of picture processing and grammatical recognition methods;
- a 2D-3D inference mechanism;
- a well-performing system and application software.

2. GENERAL SYSTEM-PHILOSOPHY - HIERARCHY OF INTELLIGENCE

The goal of the project was a system which can complete various intelligent tasks economically, i. e. a system within the scope of
mini- and microcomputers. This creates an optimal trade-off between
the special task-oriented design and general problem solving. A
feasible solution is hierarchical: elaboration of a very general
methodology and a set of tools for a wide variety of problems combined by a shorthand design method for choosing the small subset of
methods for a specific task, all based on an interactive system.
Let us give details.

The highest level of hierarchy is the Research and Development in our special laboratory, containing all standardized system design tools, i. e. a special operations system, system design language, a sophisticated editor and the interactive graphics for displaying each step of the visual recognition, i. e. the result of each program segment, simulation of the robot manipulation and the teaching of the system. The graphic interaction is described in Section 4.

The system design languages are supported by a macroprocessor and Pascal-like special developments. The operating system and editor are display-oriented and especially designed for interactive operation.

The second level is that of the system design. The goal of the project consists of creating an industrial workplace, the elaboration of the hardware configuration, selection and improvement of software, system simulation, debugging. This is a CAD activity mostly started in the R and D lab using all of its facilities.

The third level is the adjustment and teaching of a single special task for a given site, including the selection of an even smaller subset of the software, parametrization and experimentation. This is a typical workshop-engineering problem.

The fourth level is the operational level. On the fourth or the operational level the user has similar responsibilities to that of a computer operator, for example, supervising the actual job stream, e.g. an assembly operation, the selection of a specific part etc.

The hierarchy of the levels is such that no level can modify any of the levels above it. However each level can communicate with the system by adding its own heuristics to the problem-solver.

The system is aimed at serving primarily assembly and material handling tasks. Later the system should also be extended to carry out inspections /texture, dimensions, contours/. The main limitations are:
- the objects should have well defined contours and/or surfaces;
- the number of objects used in the recognition process should be

limited /not exceeding 10-15/;

- human interaction is always necessary.

The limitations refer to the economy of intelligence as mentioned above: the low 4 decimal dollar range, which is set by the robot-hardware prices /$ 25-35.000/ and the economy of human replacement. This is a rather uncommon approach of AI, but more common in many other engineering problems: e.g. a systematic optimization of services within a certain price limit. This limit is rapidly changing with technological progress, although this change is much less rapid for a complete system /including sensors, I/O, software etc./ than for single components, but the time complexity of the problems increases at a much steeper rate. That means that a rationale for limitation the complexity and the most economical man-machine division of labor is a useful design criterion. By applying the philosophy of the intelligence and task-levels this optimization problem can be approximated gradually as each level requires different resources, so that a very general operating framework is given for a wide variety of problems and the final result can be simple, comprehensive and very restricted.

3. PICTURE PROCESSING

After several experiments with special optical inputs such as laserscan /23/, at present the system uses a standard closed loop TV camera which yields a 192 by 144 matrix of pixels. This device was the result of a recent economic trade-off between input and processing hardware. 16 grey levels are used, the level-scaling is adjustable, each level can be turned on or off separately. The full picture can be windowed, zoomed and stored in memory. These functions are realized by a special hardware-unit. The preprocessing algorithm covers the picture by overlapping windows. The Mérő-Vassy operator /11/, which is a simplified and faster version of the Hueckel operator, fits an optimal line or a stroke in each window. The local operator uses only two linear templates instead of the 8 used by Hueckel; if the pictures are not too noisy, the fit serves as an adequate basis for a future procedure /Fig. 3/. The goodness of the fit is measured by a statistical estimator and this value is later used as a weight of the stroke. At this point the algorithm can branch depending on the special application. The

strokes themselves can be used as input data of the common brute-
force qualitative comparison methods /momenta, area/perimeter etc./.
This first approximation can accelerate the succeeding steps.

The rather hairy picture of the strokes is elaborated by looking
for optimal paths between hypothetical branching points where 3 or
more homogeneous regions meet. A branching point is supposed in a
region where the variance of the slopes of the strokes attains a
local maximum.

Some arrays of strokes are assembled, each beginning and ending at
hypothetical branching points. These arrays of strokes are called
streaks. Some mathematical criteria are stated on the streaks
expressing that the streaks are to follow the contour lines in an
optimal way and that each contour line should be followed by just
one streak /Fig. 4/. The streak assembling algorithm can be proved
to satisfy these mathematical criteria. The erroneous hypothetical
branching points can be corrected or neglected by this algorithm.

The algorithm extracts lines from the streaks by uniting the approximately identically directed consecutive strokes by comparing
the slope-differences. This interpretation is generally weak, due
to the uncertainty of the whole process, thus a probability value
is assigned to each possible interpretation - while each streak
may have various interpretations /Fig. 5/ - and this serves as an
ordering of hypotheses in the linguistic recognition /Section 5/.

4. MODELLING OBJECTS - GRAPHIC INTERACTION

Recognition of objects, location, orientation and their manipulation - all need a representation of geometrical knowledge which
should be optimal from the point of view of
- human interaction /simulation, programming aid, debugging, visual
  control/;
- display-manipulation, computation, memory requirements;
- 2D-3D conversion;
- access to the numerically expressed features realized by different programs /similar or easily convertible data structures/.
Considering these, a 3D-model data base was chosen for the recogni-

tion. Comparisons of the input pictures are made with computed 2D views. This approach avoids the 2D-3D restoration and makes use of the rotational and fast hidden-line computational abilities of the system.

According to the recognition procedure only linear and circular line sections are defined, the surfaces are planar, spheroidal, conical and cylindrical, although other second order surfaces are not excluded. The surface boundaries are real or imaginary edges, the latter separating "smooth" connections, visible and invisible parts as well as contours. The surfaces are directed, this is an important aid to the hidden-line algorithm /Fig. 7-10/. The data structure of the model contains not only the numerical geometric components but also additional information used for manipulation /grasping surface, orientation, grasping force etc./.

Teaching of the system is accomplished by interactive graphical programming. Although a direct input from the camera is available even in this phase, a human model building looks more straightforward. The available procedure is the following:
- menu-driven display of the numbered standard line and surface elements and stored complex or parametrized representations;
- human line-drawing and automatic correction in terms of the standard elements;
- pointing at picture elements.

An effective device for the robot recognition and manipulation is a development of the homogeneous coordinates concept /14/, a 4D augmented representation of the 3D objects, which helps in easy calculation of different views, rotation, linear transformations applying simple matrix multiplication. This method also serves for model building on the screen and at the same time in the data base.

Complex objects are formed by unification - the intersections are not calculated, because of the high computational requirements. For everyday problems of robotics this generally can be omitted, and if not, an easy manual intervention helps.

The hidden-line problem is essential in producing the 2D views for comparison with the TV pictures. This algorithm is very fast, it always rotates the wire-frame model in the positive direction with respect to the z /vertical/ axis, calculates the contour edges of curved surfaces and by taking the orientations into account selects the "forward" and "back" surfaces and ignores the latter in cases where permitted, for example closed polyhedra bounded by convex polygons. The intersections of the edges are systematically ordered by the measure of hiding and checked logically for visibility. The algorithm is a modification of Loutrel's /8/.

5. RECOGNITION

The recognition process finds the highest probability fit between the 2D picture received from the interpretations of the strokes and those which can be derived by different views of the available 3D models. The chosen method is a kind of grammatical search.

An available a priori knowledge consists of a set of faces /"countries"/ which appear in at least one of the 2D views of the 3D models and, in addition, all possible arrangements of these faces which can compose a meaningful picture in the scenary of the knowledge-base.

Thus at first all possible kinds of faces are assembled from the interpretations of the streaks. A streak in each face can be represented by only one of its interpretations. A reliability value of each face is computed from the probabilities of the interpretations of the streaks used in assembling that particular face.

All those combinations of the lines and arcs from the interpretations of the streaks which constitute meaningful faces, are assembled into possible faces. These planar configurations /e.g. parallelograms, triangles, loops etc./ are guessed by allowing some tolerance-thresholds and the reliability-value of the guess is computed. /Fig. 6/

Finally the possible faces are assembled into complete pictures /line drawings/. The a priori knowledge of the model data-base concerning the connections and relations of the faces is utilized again, each meaningful 2D line drawing is tried to be assembled from the possible faces. The assembled variants are also provided with reliability-values derived from the reliability values of the constituting faces. The highest probability yields the supposed recognition, an identification of the 3D model and the TV picture /Fig. 11/. Symmetry can cause some ambiguities but this may be irrelevant or easily eliminated. Coarse evaluators or parameters can also be included in these final procedures as search accelerators.

The search procedures have been implemented by using V. Galló's /6/ parsing program.

The final result of the recognition process is a matrix which describes the transformation of the object from the model's coordinate system to its actual position. The size of the models are the same as the real size of the objects and the projection matrix of the input camera is also supposed to be known. Thus a best fitting matrix that transforms the 2D projection of the model into the input picture, can be computed from the one-to-one correspondences between the vertices of the two pictures. If there are several one-to-one correspondences, the matrix of realized least-square error will be accepted.

6. HARDWARE AND MANIPULATOR CONTROL

The visual input was shortly described under Section 3. The computer is a 16 bit, 40 KB mini /VIDEOTON R-10 - a licence of the French CII-Mitra 15/ equipped with a minidisc, magtape unit, graphic display. The manipulator has two versions: an orthogonal and a polar one /Fig. 12/, both 6 degrees of freedom plus the grasp movement, force and torque feedback, similar to the Draper Lab solution /12/. The computer controls the robot via a 3D CNC equipment /17/ simultaneously in all degrees of freedom. Important features of the robot-control:

- it can be simulated and controlled on graphic display;
- it can be taught by manual operation or by graphic simulation;
- it uses the same spatial transformation algorithms as the model building and recognition, i. e. the relative positions due to
  - object location

x arm movement

    x visual recognition errors etc.

can be calculated quickly and effectively.

7. TIME REQUIREMENTS

The whole recognition procedure takes about 30-50 seconds for an object shown e.g. on Fig. 2. The times of the particular algorithms are as follows:
The hidden line algorithm is extremely fast, e.g. it produced Figs. 10, 11 within 2 seconds each. The edge detection operator takes approx. 4 seconds for a TV input picture. The algorithm which assembles the strokes into streaks requires 10-15 seconds. The grammatical searching procedure to find the possible faces and the possible object drawings from the streaks takes 5-8 seconds. The other on-line algorithms take less than 1 or 2 seconds altogether.

All the times listed are experimental results on the R-10 minicomputer with a 2,5 μus add-time. These time data enable this system to meet on-line requirements on a faster computer and possibly make use of some parallel processing.

8. APPLICATIONS

The system is primarily assembly-oriented. This task seemed to be a good paradigm of the problem and in fact, till now it has been handled in this way. It means that only laboratory environment tasks have been solved and a system as a mass-produced workshop-robot will not be available for the next two years. Less ambitious applications of the operating results are being realized recently: a recognition system in a bus-body factory identifies the metal sheets for controlling a painter robot, and an application in neuro-biological research. The latter is an interactive system which should detect neuronal nets in microscope-sections.

9. FUTURE TRENDS

Our goal of paramount importance is how to collect enough experience with the complete laboratory system to enable research and the in-

dustry to make a real-life environment design. We are well aware of
the many problems that naturally arise in similar projects. E.g.
illumination - how to use different light sources in solving the
trouble-making shadow and shine effects by applying the knowledge-
base in a highly intelligent way. Robot control and pattern recognition are centralized in one computer. Our future plans include
considerations, whether to use distributed systems. Some important
components realized in the new CNC-system and graphic display are
already available thanks to the achievements of other groups of the
Institute.

Especially in Section 5 we described our approach to the problem of
similarity and distances. Distance is a very common notion in statistical pattern recognition. The metrics - which is the decisive
part of the problem - lies in the very statistical nature of the
approach; a good metrics is such that it can discriminate the
clusters with the greatest reliability. By this way a good statistics provides an optimal metrics. In our case the metrics is more
logical than statistical, being bound to the individual object
which should be identified for the individual task. What to consider similar, which details to suppose identical /e.g. three
straight lines or one arc/ are task dependent. Some approaches for
a general quantification of similarity or distance in this logical
sense are known /5, 15, 18/ but these methods are applicable only
in a priori evaluable situations. In the knowledge-based interactive system most measures of distance should be taught and experi-
mented. The crucial features can be very diverse /one dimension,
one certain detail, a complex interrelation of characteristics/,
their selection is within the scope of human experience. We think
that the best solution is to provide the human operator with interactive linguistic and graphic tools so that he can find these distances /if they are not well-known before/ and communicate them to
the system.

The above ideas should be outlined and elaborated much better
during the next experimental period.

CONCLUSIONS

A knowledge-based man-machine intelligent robot system is reported having special features in fast real-time pattern recognition, teaching, modelling and control, which makes use of graphic inter- action. A very general industrial problem solver is outlined with a hierarchy from R and D level to the operational level. The limita- tion of intelligence is a practical, economical trade-off which provides a variable optimum for the man-machine distribution of tasks.

References

/1/ A.P.Ambler, H.G.Barrow, R.M.Burstall, R.J.Poppelstone: A Versatile Computer-Controlled Assembly System. Proc. 3rd IJCAI /Stanford/, 1973, pp. 298-307

/2/ M.Báthor: Interactive Picture Manipulation. 2nd Hungarian Computer Science Conference /Budapest/,1977, pp. 168-177

/3/ M.Báthor: Hidden-Line Algorithm for a Robot Experiment. Ph.D. Thesis /Budapest/,1977 /in Hungarian/

/4/ B.G.Baumgart: Geometric Modelling for Computer Vision. Stanford Memo AIM-249, 1974

/5/ K.S.Fu: Stochastic Tree Languages and Their Applications to Picture Processing. International Symposium on Multivariable Analysis /Pittsburgh/,1978

/6/ V.Galló: A Program for Grammatical Pattern Recognition. 4th IJCAI /Tbilisi/, 1975, pp. 628-634

/7/ V.Galló: Sistema dlya obrobotki spiskov dlya intelligentnovo robota. 2nd Hungarian Computer Science Conference /Budapest/, 1977, pp. 400-411 /in Russian/

/8/ P.P.Loutrel: A Solution to the Hidden-Line Problem for Computer-Drawn Polyhedra. IEEE Trans. Comp., C-19, 1970, pp. 205-213

/9/ L.Mérő: A Quasi-Parallel Contour Following Algorithm. Proc. AISBIGI Conf. on AI /Hamburg/, 1978

/10/ L.Mérő, T.Vámos: Real-Time Edge Detection Using Local Operators. 3rd IJCPR /Coronado/, 1976, pp. 31-36

/11/ L.Mérő, Z.Vassy: A Simplified and Fast Version of the Hueckel Operator. 4th IJCAI /Tbilisi/, 1975, pp. 650-655

/12/ J.L.Nevins et al.: Exploratory Research in Industrial Modular Assembly /Cambridge, Mass./, 1977

/13/ M.Potmesil: An Implementation of the Loutrel Hidden-Line Algorithm. Rensselaer Polytechn. Inst., TR CRL-49 /Troy, N.Y./, 1976

/14/ L.G.Roberts: Machine Perception of 3D Solids. MIT Press /Cambridge, Mass./, 1965, pp. 159-197

/15/ A.Rosenfeld, R.A.Hummel, S.W.Zucker: Scene Labelling by Relaxation Operations. IEEE Trans. SMC-6, 1976, pp. 420-433

/16/ Y.Shirai: Analyzing Intensity Arrays Using Knowledge about Scenes, in the Psychology of Computer Vision /ed.P.H.Winston/ /New York/,1975

/17/ A. Siegler: Computer Controlled Object Manipulation. 2nd Hungarian Computer Science Conference /Budapest/, 1977, pp. 724-738

/18/ E.Tanaka, K.S.Fu: Error-Correcting Parsers for Formal Languages.
IEEE Trans. Comp. C-27, 1978, pp. 605-616

/19/ T.Vámos: Industrial Objects and Machine Parts Recognition, in
Applications of Syntactic Pattern Recognition /ed. K.S.Fu/,
/Heidelberg/, 1977, pp. 243-267

/20/ T.Vámos: CAD-Marriage with AI Methods, Views Based on Dual
Experiments. Prepr. of IFIP WG 5.2 Conf. on AI and PR in CAD
/Grenoble/, 1978, Session 5

/21/ T.Vámos: Automatic Control and Artificial Intelligence /in-
vited survey/. Prepr. of 7th IFAC World Congress /Helsinki/,
1978, 4, pp. 2355-2369

/22/ T.Vámos, Z.Vassy: Industrial Pattern Recognition Experiment -
A Syntax Aided Approach. Proc. 1st IJCPR /Washington/, 1973,
pp. 445-452

/23/ T.Vámos, Z.Vassy: The Budapest Robot - Pragmatic Intelligence.
Proc. of 6th IFAC World Congress /Boston/, 1975, Part IV/D,
63.1

Fig. 1: An object in the scene

Fig. 2: Digitized input

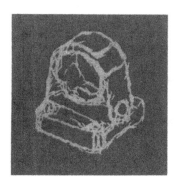

Fig. 3: The strokes found in
the picture

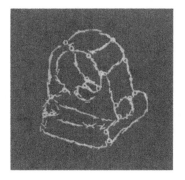

Fig. 4: The streaks of strokes with
the branching points found

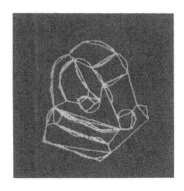

Fig. 5: All possible interpretations of the
streaks

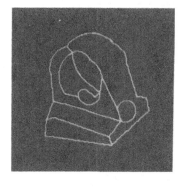

Fig. 6: The lines from the streaks
used in the recognition

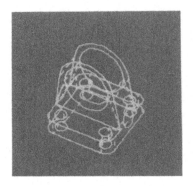

Fig. 7: 3D wire-frame model
of the object

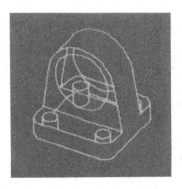

Fig. 8: The model being built
(hidden line version)

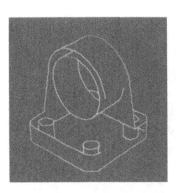

Fig. 9: The model, some surfaces
are not defined yet

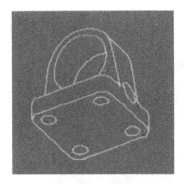

Fig. 10: A projection of the
perfect model

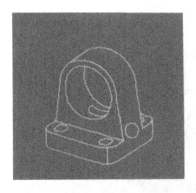

Fig. 11: Another projection to
be matched to Fig. 6

Fig. 12: The robot arm

REAL-TIME PROCESSING OF BINARY IMAGES FOR INDUSTRIAL APPLICATIONS

Foith, J.P., Eisenbarth, C., Enderle, E., Geisselmann, H.,
Ringshauser, H., Zimmermann, G.

Fraunhofer-Institut für Informations- und Datenverarbeitung
Karlsruhe, W-Germany

Summary

This paper deals with problems and solutions in applications of Image Analysis
Systems. Important applications are visual inspection, sensor-controlled
handling and assembly, and the control of tools, machines, or processes. When
designing Image Analysis Systems one must not only solve image analysis
problems: the whole workplace must be engineered in order to reach practical
solutions.

One particular requirement for Image Analysis Systems is the capability of
real-time processing. Selected methods of image processing and analysis are
discussed under this aspect. It is pointed out why practical systems perform
binary image processing, and it is argued that this suffices for many
practical tasks. A brief survey of existing systems shows the state-of-the-art
and a discussion of applications illustrates the power of these systems.

In the third part is presented a system -- 'S.A.M.' (for: Sensorsystem for
Automation and Measurement) -- that the authors have developed. S.A.M. is a
kit whose modules can be combined into configurations that are adapted to
particular tasks. S.A.M. hardware consists of three groups of modules that
perform: 1) video input processing, 2) image processing and analysis
(including image storage), and 3) data processing. The purpose of the second
group of processors is the reduction of data (TV on-line feature extraction).
Extracted features are: component labels, area, perimeter, number of holes,
and centroid coordinates for up to 255 blobs in a binary image. These data
are collected and highly organized by the Data Processing Modules. S.A.M.
software is implemented in three layers: 1) basic software, 2) problem
oriented software, and 3) operator oriented software. With the aid of S.A.M.
hardware and software the analysis of complex binary images can be performed
in less than 500 ms -- despite the use of a micro-processor. In concluding,
the authors give an example where a S.A.M. configuration was coupled with
an industrial robot for grasping parts from a running conveyor belt.

1. DIGITAL IMAGE ANALYSIS SYSTEMS FOR INDUSTRIAL APPLICATIONS

The present economic times are marked by high costs for labor and material, lack of trained workers, avoidance of inhumane work, demands of reliability, safety, and quality, as well as aspects of environmental protection. In the last years, industrial nations have put a lot of effort into the development of more efficient productivity technologies in order to cope with that situation. Improvements in this area appeal for social, economic, and techno-logical reasons.

Manufacturing operations are generally classified as either mass production, batch production, or job shop /ABRAHAM et al. '77/. While mass production is automated since long,this did not hold for batch manufacturing until a decade ago. With the advent of industrial robot technologies,we are about to ex-perience improvements in batch production that will continue to increase within the next two decades /COLDING et al. '79/. In the early days of research and development in robotics technology emphasis was on manipulator arms and control algorithms. In the meantime it has become obvious that these manipulator systems must be equipped with sensors in order to be applicable in a wide variety of tasks. Sensor systems can be based on many different physical signals. In robotics mostly visual and/or tactile sensor systems are put to use. In this paper we will only deal with visual sensor systems.

Microprocessors and other integrated circuits facilitate the construction of special digital systems for practical image analysis. Various aspects of Digital Image Analysis systems (DIA-Systems) will be discussed in this paper. After a general discussion, a particular system will be presented that the authors have developed.

1.1 TASKS

Tasks for practical DIA-systems can be classified from different view points. We choose 3 categories into which these tasks fall: inspection, handling, and control.

1) Visual Inspection

Quality control is an important task in automated production processes. In many   operations the human worker performs an "implicit visual inspection" while handling parts (i.e. he just glances at the part in order to check it superficially). In other instances he makes an "explicit inspection" in order to check the quality of parts more scrutiniously. Boths kinds of inspection

are open to automation and it is in this area that we expect widespread use
of DIA-systems.

2) Part Handling

Historically seen, interest in DIA-systems stems from the development of robotics technology: while the first generation of industrial robots was "blind",
it was soon felt that a sensor-equipped generation was needed. Obvious tasks
for DIA-systems are in the control of industrial robots in handling workpieces. This handling occurs during part transfer, loading and emptying of
machines, assembly or sorting. Despite many efforts to introduce industrial
robots in a wide range, progress has been slow so far in Europe. This is due
to a number of reasons that are outside the scope of this paper. However,
this implies that the application of DIA-systems in this area will be even
slower.

3) Control of Tools, Machines, and Processes

This category of applications is of somewhat younger origin, yet there is a
high potential of applications to be expected. Here, emphasis is on "in-
process"-control. Examples are the control of tools (e.g. screwdrivers in
assembly tasks), the control of machines (e.g. cutting machines), or the control of processes (e.g. welding). This category may be the most challenging,
but with progress in efficiency of DIA-systems a wide range of applications
can be expected.

Let us briefly resume these 3 categories with the aid of a few examples
(cf. Fig. 1.1 - 1). In row A we list examples for inspection tasks such as:
check the presence of parts or presence and completeness of labels on bottles
(A1); check the shape of the screw or the completeness of a part coming out of
a press (A2); check the surface of running metal sheets or check liquids for
particles (A3).

Row B shows examples for control tasks: determine the identity of parts on a
conveyor belt including their position-class, location (x-y-coordinates) and
orientation (rotation ϕ in the image plane) (B1); determine the position of
goal sites for assembly tasks (B2); determine the position of the weld head
along a seam (B3); in this last example we may also observe the weld pool in
order to control welding process parameters. For a systematic view of tasks
see /ROSEN '79/.

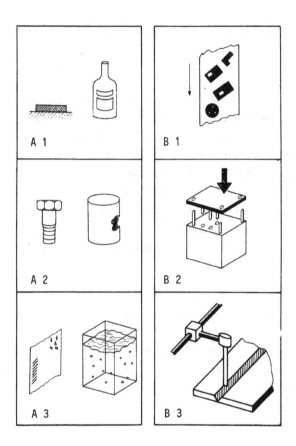

Fig. 1.1. - 1: Examples for Industrial Applications
(see text for explanation)

1.2 CONSTRAINTS

A number of constraints determine how effectively a workstation can be automated. In particular one must consider (cf. Fig. 1.2. - 1):

- geometry of the set-up
- degree of order of workpieces
- illumination
- imaging system
- architecture of the DIA-system

- output processing
- transport & handling of objects.

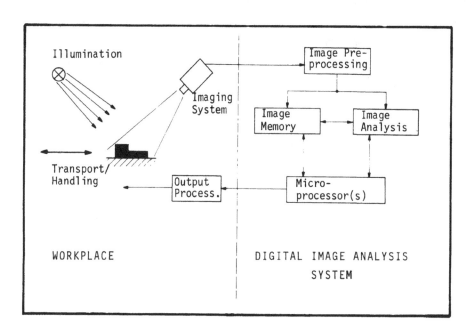

Fig. 1.2. - 1: Components of a workplace

All these components are related with each other and must be considered as a whole in order to obtain cost-effective solutions. For example, if the illumination is chosen poorly then one will need a much more powerful DIA-system in order to cope with the inferior quality of images that must be processed.

The geometry of the set-up is determined mainly by the angle and the distance between camera, workpiece and illumination. This geometry can either be fixed or variable. In the latter case the camera is mounted directly onto the manipulator arm and is moved together with the arm. Then both, distance and angle from camera to the workpiece will change permanently and must be considered accordingly. Since that may require a lot of computations (or table look-ups) it is advisable to use fixed geometry whenever possible. If there is a working plane (e.g. conveyor belt) and if the optical axis coincides with the normal of this plane there will be fewer aspects of the objects. It is therefore recommendable to mount the camera directly above the working plane at a fixed distance.

The <u>degree of order</u> of the workpieces is an important factor and a lot of attention must be paid to this part of the problem: the higher the degree of order, the easier the task that the DIA-system must solve (cf. Fig. 1.2. - 2).

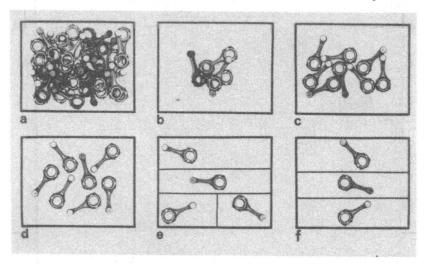

Fig. 1.2. - 2: Complexity of scenes
    a - parts in a bin (multiple overlap)
    b - few overlapping parts
    c - touching parts
    d - isolated parts at random
    e - isolated parts in semi-order
    f - isolated parts in linear order

The complexity of the scene may range from completely loose positions of the parts to completely fixed positions. In the first case parts will overlap and occlude each other (parts in a bin). At the time of writing no DIA-system is known that could analyze such scenes. In the other extreme, when the positions of parts are completely fixed, then there is no need for a DIA-system. Practical tasks for DIA-systems are found in the mid-range. It is obvious that the complexity of the scene determines the required competence of the DIA-system and thus the costs of the solution.

In general, it can be said, that order is expensive to introduce and maintain. Quite sophisticated mechanical periphery is necessary in order to separate parts. If one wishes to maintain order it is often necessary to use special magazines. One must therefore find a balance between the costs for mechanical periphery and the costs of the DIA-system.

Illumination can be used in a number of ways to facilitate image analysis. One has the following options (cf. Fig. 1.2. - 3):

- back lighting
- top lighting
  · diffuse
  · directed
- light sectioning.

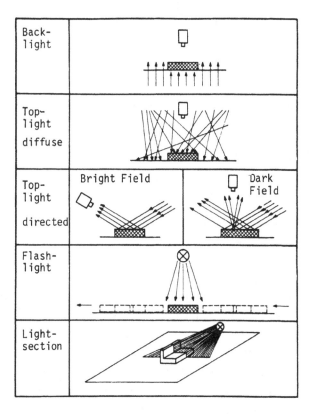

Fig. 1.2. - 3: Illumination techniques

These different illumination techniques can be applied either in steady or in strobe mode. Strobe mode is particularly suitable when motion blur must be suppressed. Back light leads directly to binary images since one only ob-

serves the silhouettes of parts. Top lighting can be used in different ways:
a diffuse light source will in general provide homogenous reflections and
thus facilitate the image segmentation process. For inspection tasks (such as
measurement of surface smoothness) directed light will often prove to be useful. Here one may observe either directly the reflected light (bright field
observation) or the stray light that stems from surface flaws (dark field
observation).

Light section techniques provide different informations about the scene than
the other illumination techniques. While these deliver surface reflection
functions, light sectioning informs about the 3-D structure of a scene. These
techniques will not be discussed in this paper. Yet in general, they can be
powerful methods for many practical purposes (cf. /HOLLAND et al. '79/).

There are basically two types of imaging systems: 1) CRT-cameras and
2) solid state cameras. In the latter case one can either work with linear
cameras or with diode arrays. CRT-cameras have been around for a long time
and are readily available. Yet it is assumed that solid state cameras will
prevail in the near future.

The architecture of the DIA-system depends on many constraints: required processing speed, image resolution, type of image to be processed (binary vs.
gray level), complexity of the images, to name the important ones.

All practical DIA-systems must work in real-time: quite often this notion is
meant as image processing at TV-speed. Here we understand by "real-time image
analysis" a process which follows the cycle of the production process. Typical cycle times range from several hundred milliseconds to several seconds.
There are of course shorter as well as longer cycle times that can occur in
practice. If short cycle times are required, then much of the image processing and analysis must be done by hardware; if long cycle times are allowed
one may easily store the image and perform the task by software. The issue of
system-architecture will be discussed in greater depth in a later section of
this paper. Typically, the output that a DIA-system provides, is some kind of
quantified description of the observed scene: what objects are there?;which
way do they lie?; what is their exact location?; which way are they rotated?;
and so on. Before this information is handed over to the handling system, NC-
machine, etc. there is often the need for output processing. Two examples may
clarify this point. In the first example, one encounters problems with coordinate spaces when dealing with a sensor-driven industrial robot: DIA-systems

work in cartesian coordinate spaces (x, y, z) while robots have their own
coordinate space which is given by the structure of the robot (polar or
cylindrical systems constitute the easy cases; sometimes one has to deal with
quite complicated systems). It is therefore necessary to perform coordinate
transformations which may be computationally demanding.

A second example may be taken from visual quality control. Once the DIA-
system has determined the quality of a part, it must output commands for
further treatment of the part. Assume that there are different classes of
flaws: those that can be repaired by further processing and those that cannot.
That means that the system must decide which step to initialize next.

This brings us to the first/last step in the systém: parts must be transported
and handled. This issue is related with some of the other components of the
system. Parts must be brought to the workplace and also transported from it.
While being brought, the parts may be separated and a certain degree of order
may be installed. Thus the complexity of the scene is determined in this step.
If the parts are moved at constant speed across the sensor field then one
might well apply a one-dimensional imaging system (diode line) since the
second dimension is provided by the transport system. Transport of parts to
the next workplace may also be a crucial step since here input to the next
processing system is prepared. If in this step, one is able to maintain the
order of pieces then the efforts that have to be made at the next station
can be   reduced.

Let us briefly summarize the issues of this section. If one wants to automate
a workplace it does not suffice to substitute a worker by a handling system/
robot and a sensor-system. Rather, one must consider all components in order
to reach an optimal solution. Since most of the components are related with
each other, one may reduce the costs of one component by making another component more efficient. This will certainly require a much better cooperation
between the mechanical engineer and computer scientist than exists today.

1.3 EVALUATION OF PRACTICAL SYSTEMS

From the previous section it has become clear that the performance of a DIA-
system cannot be evaluated per se. Rather, it has to be seen in the context
of the complete system. Though one cannot specify a-priori what a good DIA-
system should look like, one can at least list the features that determine
the quality of a DIA-system.

COST

Here one must differentiate between costs for the installation and costs for operation and maintenance. The costs for the DIA-system must be related to the complete system whose costs quite often range from 100.000 $ to 300.000 $. It would therefore seem appropriate to allow 10.000 - 35.000 $ for the costs of the DIA-system. The costs of operation are rather low and can practically be ignored.

RELIABILITY

This is an important feature since malfunction of the DIA-system could lead to bad damages in the workplace. It is therefore necessary to build fail-safe systems that monitor their own out-put. As an example: prior to data-transfer of object coordinates from a DIA-system to a robot controller it must be checked that the coordinates are within allowed ranges.

PROCESSING SPEED

The required speed is mostly determined by the cycle of the production process. Typical cycle times range from 100 ms to up to 10 s although exceptions in both directions occur.
Thus DIA-systems should be able to operate at processing speeds between a few hundred milliseconds and a few seconds. If one wants to process TV images on-line, i.e. without storing them, then one must operate in the 20 ms range.

FLEXIBILITY

Flexibility is required whenever there are frequent changes of workpieces that must be inspected, recognized or located. This is typical in inspection tasks or robot handling. In these cases it is imperative that the DIA-system can be easily adapted to the new task. This requirement is strongly related with the operability of the system.

OPERABILITY

Since the DIA-system must be operated at the worksite it should not require familiarity with programming languages in order to operate the system. Rather, the operator ought to be supported through dialogue-systems, menuing techniques, and problem oriented programming languages that are easy to use.

MAINTAINABILITY

Ease of maintainability is a requirement that applies to all kind of equipment
and is not a special feature of DIA-systems. Since some of these systems can
be rather complex, it may be advisible to install diagnosis routines that help
find the source of trouble fast. Modular hardware design for easy replace-
ments is state-of-the-art.

ACCURACY

The required accuracy that the DIA-system must obtain may vary considerably.
Thus one can only specify a typical range: from our experience it can be
stated that an accuracy in coordinate measurement around 1 % of the visual
field and angle resolution around 1^O are quite typical.

COMPETENCE

There is a wide variety of tasks that determine what a DIA-system must be capable of. This begins with simple measurements (width, length, area, ...) and
stretches out to complex scene analysis tasks. A very crucial point is the
following: whatever analysis the system performs, it must be absolutely
reliable. There is no use to implement algorithms that "work most the time"
since these will not be suitable for practical applications in the industry.

2. SELECTED METHODS OF IMAGE AND SCENE ANALYSIS FOR PRACTICAL SYSTEMS

It is outside the scope of this paper to give a detailed survey on image
processing and scene analysis. Rather, a few methods will be selected that
seem appropriate for implementation in practical DIA systems. Emphasis is
here on practicability, i.e. methods that are feasible for industrial
applications in an economic way, now.

Let us briefly define the terms 'Image Processing' and 'Scene Analysis'. In
Image Processing one transforms an image into some other image; in Scene
Analysis one starts with an image and ends with a description of the underlying scene. Figure 2.-1 illustrates this process: we begin with a gray-
level image; the task is to decompose this image into meaningful elements
from which a description can be built. In the computer an image is represented as a discrete picture function. In the three-dimensional plot of
Fig. 2.-1 we see how the objects in the gray-level image correspond to
certain structures in the 3-D plot. By going through a number of processing
steps, higher and higher levels of abstraction are obtained until one has
eventually reached the desired description.

It is clear that the nature of the description depends on the task the DIA-
system must fulfill. In industrial applications such descriptions could be:
number and type of objects in a scene, their positional class, position
parameters - in fact all the information that a robot needs in order to
grasp objects; statements about the completeness of an object or the quality
of a surface (for visual inspection); and so on.

A digital image is a matrix of N x N pixels whose values correspond to gray
tones. While the human observer sees lines and regions with meanings rather
than pixel matrices, the machine initially "perceives" N x N pixels with
no apparent interrelations. It is the task of the processing step to group
together spatially neighboured pixels into ensembles that "belong together".
This first step is called 'segmentation'. It partitions the image into
regions.

There are two basic approaches to segmentation: either by outlining contours
or by specifying all pixels inside a region. In the first approach one makes
use of differences between the gray values of neighbouring regions; in the
second approach one utilizes gray value similarities between pixels within

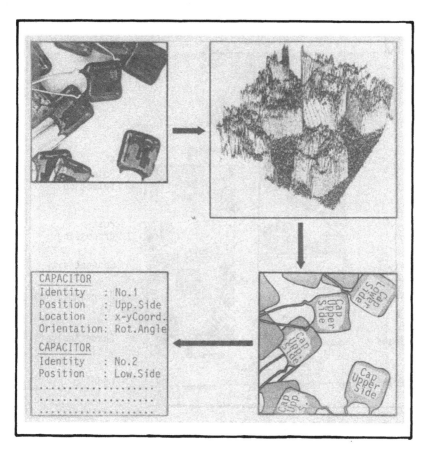

Fig. 2.-1.: Scene Analysis: From Gray-Level Images To Descriptions
(the 3-D plot is inverted, i.e. black pixels are high
and vice versa)

a region. Sometimes combinations of these two approaches are used - but that
will not be considered here (for examples cf. /MILGRAM '77 A,B/ or
/SCHÄRF '77/). Despite the differences between the two approaches both are
based on four discrete steps with the same underlying idea: selection/
detection of appropriate points, postprocessing, connectivity analysis, and
representation of the resulting structures (cf. Figure 2.-2).

74

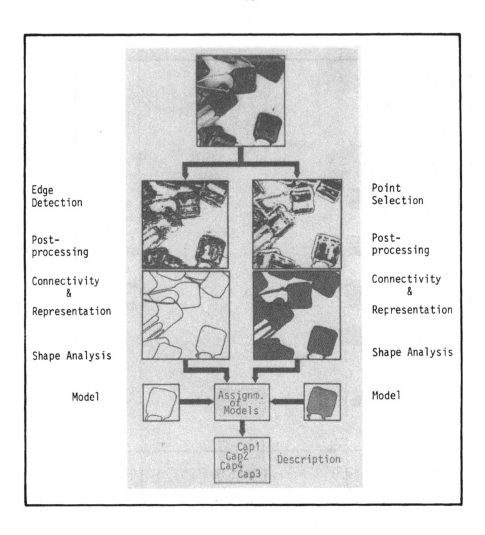

Fig. 2.-2.: Processing Steps During Scene Analysis

With this in mind we can now specify the steps that transform an image into
a description:

1) Pixel Selection: in the contour approach this step is the application
   of edge detection techniques; in the region approach this step can be
   determined as feature value determination;

2) Postprocessing: Pixel Selection usually leads to noisy results that
   must be cleaned before further processing is feasible; in the contour
   approach this could be thinning and gap filling; in the region approach

this could be the removal of isolated points;

3)   Connectivity Analysis: this is an important (and as will turn out, also crucial) step; here one must determine which of the selected pixels "belong together"; in the contour approach this step is performed by line finding; in the region approach this step is usually done by label propagation (or 'component labeling');

4)   Representation of Connected Components: once connected components are determined, they must be represented by appropriate means; in the contour approach this can be done by using straight line and curve segments; in the region approach this is somewhat more difficult. Here techniques such as representation by overlapping convex sets can be brought to bear;

5)   Shape Recognition: each of the (sub-)structures that are a result of the segmentation process must now be recognized. For this the shape of the element can be used. Shape analysis may be used to assign symbols to each of the elements. These symbols may be compared to some kind of vocabulary with which to describe the visual appearance of objects;

6)   Assignment of Models: by using the afore mentioned vocabulary we can express through appropriate data structures what objects 'do look like'. With the aid of this a-priori information we can now compare extracted elements and structures with stored models and assign matching models to groups of image elements. The record of these assignments is then the desired description (this implies that the models contain all the information that one seeks).

This scheme is a rather generalized one which completely ignores control structures among the various steps. There are many ways how to introduce feedback loops between all processing steps; quite seldom will the analysis proceed as straightforwardly as has been presented here. Ideally, all steps should be provided with as much a-priori as well as a-posteriori information as possible. Yet, it is outside the scope of this paper to discuss any issues of control structures.

In the following we will briefly discuss various techniques for segmentation, shape analysis, and assignment of models. We will emphasize here which techniques are ready for real-time applications and which are not.

2.1 SEGMENTATION

As has already been mentioned the goal of segmentation is the partitioning of an image into meaningful entities. In Scene Analysis there are of course many semantic levels. It must therefore be determined at which level the image is to be described. Low levels describe the image in terms of local features such as boundary elements or homogenous reflections and provide only general information. Intermediate levels describe the image in terms of regions and lines and provide knowledge about object surfaces. Higher levels describe the image via object parts or objects and provide specific knowledge. In workpiece recognition it seems appropriate to segment the image into regions that correspond to visible surfaces. Due to variations in illumination, reflectance, and surface orientation it will often be impossible to establish exactly that correspondance. The process of segmentation will therefore result in an incomplete partitioning.

There are two basic approaches to segmentation: via contours or via regions. Both approaches will be discussed in this section. It has been pointed out that both approaches are based on 4 steps. Of these, 2 steps are most important: pixel selection and connectivity analysis. It is important to understand that these two processes are principally different: the process of pixel selection is based upon properties of the intensity array, connectivity analysis is based on spatial continuity.

2.1.1 SEGMENTATION VIA CONTOURS

The basic idea of this approach is to delineate the regions into which the image is to be segmented. This implies that neighbouring regions must differ sufficiently in gray level from each other. We exclude here the problem of texture discrimination. The state-of-the-art is still a long way from segmentation through texture discrimination. We therefore assume for the remainder of this section that all regions in the image are homogenous to some degree or at least not heavily textured. This is often true in industrial environments. If not, other techniques must be brought to bear for the segmentation process.

Boundaries of homogenous regions are in general edges, i.e. step-like structures in the intensity array. As can be seen from Figure 2.1.1.-1 real edges are not clear cut steps but vary considerably in shape. The first step in segmentation is the process of edge detection. Here one determines which pixels are possible edge points and which are not.

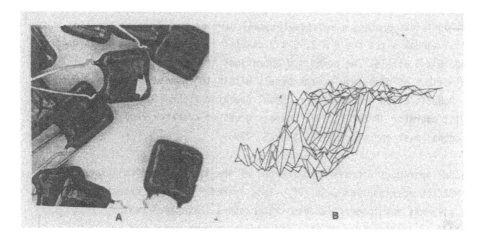

Fig. 2.1.1.-1.: The Three-dimensional Structure of A Real Edge
                A - Gray Level Image (see arrow!)
                B - 3-D Plot

Basically, the following kind of information can be extracted during edge detection:

- local orientation ef edge elements;

- strength of edge elements, i.e. the contrast in brightness between neighboured regions;

- width of edge elements (since edges are not ideal steps they can vary in width considerably);

- placement of edge representant; since edges may be more than 1 pixel wide, it is necessary to determine where to place the edge point;

- polarity of the edge element (which of the regions is the brighter one?);

- gray value of the edge element;

- gray value of the neighbouring regions.

There is a huge number of operators available for edge detection. Since there exist excellent surveys /DAVIS '75/, /LEVIALDI '80/ we will not give any details. Typically, most operators fall in one of the following three classes: local, regional or global operators.

Local operators process a relatively small part of the image at one time. Typical window sizes are 2 x 2, 3 x 3 pixels; in general window sizes don't exceed 5 x 5 pixels. The performed operations are linear or non-linear combinations of gray-levels from pixels within the window. A few examples are: Roberts cross /ROBERTS '65/, Sobel operator /TENENBAUM et al. '69/, Prewitt operator /PREWITT '70/, compass gradient operator /ROBINSON '77/, or orthogonal mask operators /FREI & CHEN '77/.

Regional operators process larger areas of the image. A typical example is the HUECKEL operator /HUECKEL '71/. This operator does not detect point-like edge elements but longer elements that cross a (circular) region. Simplified modifications of this operator have been developed by /MERO & VASSY '75/, /O'GORMAN '78/, /BUROW & WAHL '79/ and a number of other authors.

Global operators are those that process the complete image. Typical examples are filtering approaches such as high pass filtering /ROSENFELD & KAK '76/ or Wiener filtering /FRIES & MODESTINO '77/.

Fig. 2.1.1.-2.: Local Edge Detection
        A - Gray Level Image
        B - Gradient Image (Sobel Operator)
        C - Thresholded Image (B), THRSH = 40
        D - A Reminder: We still have a matrix of points, and no lines!

Figure 2.1.1.-2 shows an example for a local edge detector - the Sobel operator. There are at least 4 problems that one has to cope with at this stage:

- noise (even background pixels yield some edge value);
- smear (parts of the contours are rather thick);
- fragmentation (some parts of the contours are missing);
- misplacement.

These problems make it necessary to apply some postprocessing which provides
line thinning, gap filling, as well as noise suppression. The most obvious
technique is of course thresholding, i.e. the suppression of all points
whose edge value is below a given threshold. Clearly thresholding removes
noise to a certain degree, yet it is neither suited for gap filling nor line
thinning. Better postprocessing techniques make use of local context and
yield far better results. The most commonly used techniques are:

- non-maximum suppression
- local connectivity analysis
- relaxation.

All three techniques are based upon much the same idea: if a pixel shares
similar edge directions with its neighbouring pixels then it is likely to
be an edge point and will be enhanced; otherwise it will be suppressed. In
non-maximum suppression the considered neighbourhood consists of the left
and right neighbour across the edge. If either of these has a higher edge
value, the considered pixel is suppressed. For discussions of these techniques see /ROSENFELD & THURSTON '71/, RISEMAN & ARBIB '77/ or /PRAGER '80/.
In local connectivity analysis one looks at a 3 x 3 window around the actual
pixel. Here, continuation along the edge point is checked: if there are
preceeding and succeeding pixels with similar edge directions, then the
actual pixel is considered an edge point. In the approach of /ROBINSON '77/,
/ROBINSON & REIS '77/ similar edge values are also required; if these exceed
an adaptive threshold value and edge continuity is given, then the pixel is
entered into a binary edge map.

The techniques of non-maximum suppression and connectivity analysis work in
one single step and throw away all the information that is contained in those
pixels that are suppressed. The third technique, relaxation, makes use of
these informations as well and constitutes a generalization of the other
techniques. The basic idea of relaxation is to set up a 'cooperation and

competition' between neighbouring pixels with respect to their local interpretation. Let us rather briefly clarify this point: contrary to non-maximum
suppression the edge values of weaker elements are not thrown away but are
'collected' by the stronger elements. In other words, strong edge points
that are consistent within their local context are enhanced further and
further while weak and/or inconsistent elements are gradually diminished
in importance. Relaxation schemes work basically in parallel and iteratively;
strength or weakness of elements is expressed by probabilities of labels and
the process of 'value collection' is performed by changing these probabilities
in dependence of local context. We are not going to discuss these techniques
any further but refer the reader to /ROSENFELD, HUMMEL & ZUCKER '76/,
/ZUCKER, HUMMEL & ROSENFELD '77/, /ROSENFELD '77/, /RISEMAN & HANSON '78/,
/RISEMAN & ARBIB '77/, /PRAGER '80/ or/PERKINS '80/.

As a result of these postprocessing techniques one obtains edge images with
thin lines and filled gaps. Yet, while the human eye sees clear lines, in the
computer we still have a matrix of single edge points that must be linked in
order to form lines. The process of line finding is certainly one of the
most difficult steps in image analysis. In comparison with the huge variety
of edge detection techniques there are only few line finding techniques
available today. We want to classify these into 3 basic approaches (although
other classification schemes might well be more suitable):

- local methods
- global methods
- iterative methods.

Typical local methods link edge points by starting at an appropriate point
and looking for good continuations in the next line /ROSENFELD & KAK ' 76/,
/KORN '78/. If some criterion doesn't hold any longer that line is abandoned
and another line is started. Yet another local linking scheme consists in
binding edge points pairwise into 'streaks' /SLANSKY '78/, /NEVATIA &
BABU '79/. Among the global approaches we see two different types of methods:
1.) tree search techniques that evaluate a 'goodness' function while they
    go along and
2.) transform or template matching techniques that determine what prevails
    in the image.
Among the tree search approaches we find techniques such as heuristic search
/MARTELLI '72/, dynamic programming /MONTANARI '71/, /EHRICH '77/, minimum

cost tree search /ASHKAR & MODESTINO '78/, and locus search /YACHIDA, IKEDA, & TSUJI '79/. Among the important transform techniques for line finding there is the Hough transform which transforms an edge image into a 2-dimensional parameter space where collinear points cluster /IANNINO & SHAPIRO '78/. It can be shown that this transform corresponds to template matching /STOCKMAN & AGRAWALA '76/. All these techniques only make use of information that is available in the image.

The last (iterative) approach makes use of a-priori information as well: here one first extracts major contours that indicate what object is present; finer contours are then found by model-driven programs /SHIRAI '78/.

Let us evaluate how well line finding approaches work. Very generally speaking, it can be said that line finding methods deliver results that are far from what the human observer perceives. Figure 2.1.1.-3 shows a typical example of the problems that one encounters in line finding: lines are missing, lines are too short, lines are too long, lines have the wrong direction, lines are fragmented into small pieces, there are duplicate lines.

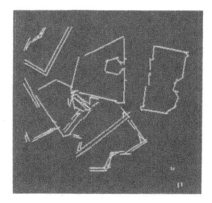

Fig. 2.1.1.-3 : Line Finding

A - Gray Level Image

B - Lines Extracted By Line Finder From /KORN '78/

The final step in contour finding is yet another postprocessing with the aim of cleaning up resulting lines. Here, short line elements are removed or linked into longer segments, if possible. Thus one finally obtains a list of contour lines that are the result of the segmentation process.

How well suited is this segmentation approach for real-time processing and for practical applications in the industry? Recall from the introduction that there are three important issues which are related with the practicability of DIA-systems. These are: real-time processing capability, cost effectiveness, and reliability.

Let us briefly discuss real-time processing via contour segmentation. Given the processing speed of today's micro-electronics one must rely upon local computations where relatively few data have to be handled. It would therefore seem most appropriate to develop dedicated hardware for local edge detectors. This is indeed happening in a number of various efforts. Examples are: the Sobel chip in CCD technology /NUDD et al. '77/; a multifunction chip which includes a 5 x 5 programmable transform, a 3 x 3 Laplacian operator, a 7 x 7 mask programmable kernel, a 5 x 5 cross shaped median and a bipolar convolutional filter for 26 x 26 pixels /NUDD et al. '79/; discrete circuitry for the on-line computation of the gradient /ZURCHER '79/; or a development of JPL which performs computation of gradient, construction of an 'Edge Map' and postprocessing within an 8-pixel-neighbourhood /ESKENAZI & WILF '79/; one even investigates VLSI technologies for image processing algorithms /EVERSOLE et al. '79/. All these processors are specified to work with TV speed, i.e. they are capable of real-time processing. There are also developments that support real-time postprocessing: connectivity analysis is performed by a 'real-time edge processing unit' from Northrop /ROBINSON & REIS '77/; the development of cellular structures would support the application of relaxation algorithms /WILLETT et al. '79/; the development of a local gradient direction histogrammer /BIRK, KELLEY et al. '80/ prepares the extraction of straight lines. The really hard problem is the line finding stage. Since this is a search process backtracking may be necessary. Today, we are not aware of hardware projects that would support search processes. A step in the right direction seems to be the development of 'SPARC'/ALLEN & JUETTEN '78/. Although postprocessing facilitates the line finding process it is only possible to extract major contours in a reliable way. In general it can be said that contour segmentation requires high computational time (or much specialized hardware), large memories, and a fine tuning of

many parameters and thresholds. Despite the developments for real-time edge
detection it does not seem feasible to base practical DIA-systems upon
contour segmentation. With few exceptions it will take some time before
these techniques can be applied for industrial purposes.

2.1.2. SEGMENTATION VIA REGIONS

The alternative approach to segmentation is to specify which pixels belong
to a certain region. Again, segmentation is based upon 4 discrete steps,viz.:
point selection, postprocessing, connectivity analysis, and representation.
We will advocate the use of thresholding techniques and completely ignore
methods of region growing since these do not seem appropriate for industrial
applications.

When using thresholding one should state the assumptions that one makes
about the nature of the images:

- at least some of the object surfaces must reflect homogenously;
- there should be no heavy textures in the image;
- illumination should be homogenous.

In industrial applications these assumptions are often true. Most workpieces
(metal, plastic, ceramic, and so on) tend to have smooth surfaces. Most often
parts are presented to the DIA-system during the process of manufacturing;
they are therefore 'brandnew' and rust or other soiling are scarce.Since
the illumination can be adapted to the task one can make sure that it will
be homogenous. Even if not, one could still apply local adaption techniques
which can be applied as real-time preprocessing systems /WEDLICH '77/.

Let us briefly discuss the various steps of region segmentation. Fig.2.1.2.-1
shows a simple gray value image that fulfills our basic assumptions. The
3-D-plot of Fig. 2.1.2.-1.C reveals that there are basically two different
populations of gray levels, viz. gray and bright ones. These appear in the
gray level histogram as one large mode (for gray values) and a small
plateau to its right (for the bright pixels). Of course gray pixels correspond to the background, bright pixels belong to object surfaces. If we now
select a threshold such that it lies between the right flank of the mode
and the beginning of the plateau we obtain a binary image as in
Fig. 2.1.2.-1.D (above-threshold pixels are colored black as 'figure',

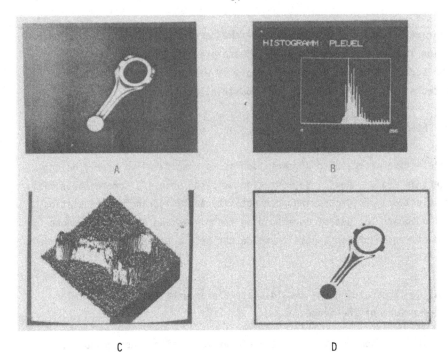

Fig. 2.1.2.-1 : Image Segmentation Trough Thresholding

               A - gray level image
               B - gray level histogram
               C - 3-D plot
               D - binary image

below-threshold pixels are colored white). Obviously much depends on the choice of the right value for the treshold.

The selection of thresholds has found quite some interest in the literature and there are various approaches. One can work with

- fixed thresholds
- adaptive thresholds
- image dependent thresholds
- result dependent thresholds.

Fixed thresholds are determined interactively by a human operator; usually the same threshold value is used all over the image. This works well when one has complete control over the illumination and observation conditions.

Adaptive thresholds are determined from local information (either by computing an average gray level /TOKUMITSU et al. '78/ or a histogram in a local
neighbourhood /NAKAGAWA & ROSENFELD '78/). Adaptive thresholds can cope with
local changes in the illumination. Image dependent thresholds are selected

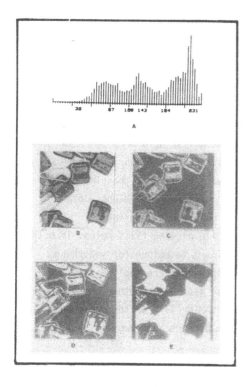

Fig. 2.1.2.-2 : Threshold
Selection From Histogram Analysis
A - gray level histogram
B - gray level image (0   - 255)
C - gray level slice (32 - 120)
D - gray level slice (121 - 183)
E - gray level slice (184 - 255)

from global histograms. Fig. 2.1.2.-2 shows the basic idea of this approach:
often, modes in the gray level histogram correspond to pixels that belong
to the same region in the image. Thus by selecting threshold values at
valleys that separate modes in the histogram one is able to extract exactly
those regions. The classic example for this approach is /OHLANDER et al. '78/
(although they used color images). Instead of using gray values one may also
analyze edge value histograms. Here one determines the right shoulder of the
histogram where the second derivative is maximum /BAIRD '77/. Yet another
and more powerful technique is the analysis of 2-dimensional histograms;
here gray value is plotted against edge value /PANDA & ROSENFELD '78/,
/MILGRAM & HERMAN '79/. As a result one obtains varying thresholds that
depend on the location of pixels: pixels within a region are thresholded
differently than those on a boundary. This technique is reported to lead to
good results. Finally, result dependent techniques start with some threshold

that was randomly selected and use the result to derive a new threshold
/RIDLER & CALVARD '78/. Even after selection of a good threshold there can
still be noise in the resulting image. Typically this noise occurs as:

- small blobs or isolated points
- small holes within blobs
- fringed border lines of blobs.

We therefore need postprocessing techniques that can perform suppression of
small blobs, hole filling, as well as border smoothing. There exist indeed
operators that are well suited. These have long been known in the literature
as 'shrink' and 'blow' /ROSENFELD & KAK '76/ and are realized in several
systems such as the T.A.S. /KAMIN '74/, /NAWRATH '79/ or others /LÖFFLER
& JÄGER '79/. Shrinking erases all pixels that have a neighbour in the
background and thus 'erodes' the blobs; blowing works just the other way
and adds another layer of border points thus 'dilating' the blobs. Both
techniques can be applied iteratively. It is obvious that shrinking
eliminates small blobs and isolated points while blowing fills holes. If both
techniques are applied sequentially one obtains a technique for smoothing
border lines. Here the order in which these operators are applied plays an
important role: 'blow - shrink' tends to close gaps and smoothes border
lines; it is therefore called 'Fermeture' /KAMIN '74/. On the other hand,
'shrink - blow' tends to deepen cracks in the borders and removes small
noise; it is therefore called 'Ouverture'.

After postprocessing the connectivity analysis must take place. Since at this
step all connected components in the binary image are marked with an
identifying label, this process is often called 'component labeling'. There
are many algorithms that perform component labeling. A few examples are
/ROSENFELD & KAK '76/, /KRUSE '73/, /MORI et al. '78/, /DUFF '76/, /VEILLON
'79/, /AGRAWALA & KULKARNI '77/. Instead of discussing any of these algorithms
let us briefly give the basic idea of those algorithms that are based on a
top-down, left-to-right image scan (such as the TV scan); cf. Fig. 2.1.2.-3:
when we scan the image in this fashion we store linewise the intersections
of the scan with connected components (determination of linewise connectivity
is obvious); each time we cross a component that was not previously
encountered, a new label is assigned to that section; while scanning the next
line one checks for overlap of sections in the two lines; if an overlap
occurs then the actual section gets assigned the same label as the section

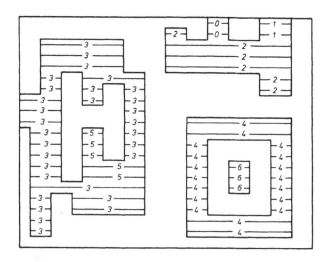

Fig. 2.1.2.-3 :   Component Labelinq   In The Order Of Appearance
                  During A TV-scan

from the previous line. As can bee seen from Fig. 2.1.2.-3 care must be
taken when two different labels converge; here one stores this event in
an 'equivalence table' which can later be used for relabelinq.

After component labeling each blob in the image can now be identified
through its set of labels. If the labels are assigned to each pixel of the
blob then this constitutes a representation of that blob already (though not
a very efficient one!). Another way of representation maybe the decomposition
of each blob into regular subfigures such as convex sets, cf. for instance
/ZAMPERONI '78/. More decomposition techniques can be found in /PAVLIDIS '77/,
/HARALICK & SHAPIRO '77/, /FENG & PAVLIDIS '75/, or /PAVLIDIS '72/. All these
techniques represent blobs explicitly in terms of substructures or primitives.
Such techniques are seldom used for industrial applications. Far more often
one derives directly some shape feature from the labeled blobs (see the next
section) and stores those features together with the labels.

Let us briefly evaluate how well suited the region segmentation approach is
for real-time processing. It is clear that thresholding can be easily
performed with TV speed; the same holds for operators such as shrink and
blow: these are local operations that can be easily performed with high speed
(and this has been done a long time). Thus the only critical step could be

the component labeling but here experience tells us that it can indeed be
done with TV speed (cf. chapter 3.). One example for a hardware realization
in CCD technology is /WILLETT & BLUZER '77/. Thus we may conclude that this
approach is well suited for industrial applications and real-time processing.
Therefore it does not come as a surprise that almost all practical DIA-
systems that are available today for industrial purposes are based on the
analysis of binary images that are obtained through thresholding.

2.2 SHAPE, MODELS, AND MATCHING

After the process of segmentation (and postprocessing) the image is decomposed into a set of discrete structures. An ideal segmentation would yield
exactly the silhouettes of all workpieces that are present in the image; we
understand here by 'silhouette' the set of all pixels that the image of a
workpiece covers. In reality perfect silhouettes are only obtained when back-
lighting is used (since this leads directly to binary images). Otherwise one
must expect segmentation results that are quite imperfect and where only
parts of the silhouettes are extracted. In the contour approach we may obtain
only some of the major contours (cf. Fig. 2.1.1.-3); in the thresholding
approach silhouettes will fall apart into a set of blobs as in Fig. 2.1.2-1.

In order to analyze the complete image we must therefore:

- assign some meaning to the extracted structures;
- group these structures such that they correspond
  to the images of workpieces that one is looking for.

In order to assign some semantic label to the extracted structures one must recognize them. This is done by shape analysis of contours or regions (although other information such as contrast, polarity, or gray level could also be used).Approaches for shape analysis for both kinds of structures will be discussed in this section. After recognition of structures one must determine in which way they "belong together". The search for meaningful ensembles cannot be performed efficiently in a blind way. Rather, it must be guided by models that specify what to look for. Therefore, the system must contain a set of models that describe all aspects of workpieces that are to be recognized; the process of recognition then consists in matching the extracted data with those of the models. Model structures and matching techniques will also be discussed in this section.

Shape analysis is a difficult problem (cf. Fig. 2.2.-1). There is no "Theory of Shape" but there are many - sometimes singular - approaches to shape analysis. Let us look at two principles according to which the manifold of approaches can be cast into some kind of scheme (cf.Fig.2.2.-2):

1) what spatial property is used for the analysis?

2) Is the result of the analysis a number (or a vector) or is it a structure (such as strings, trees, graphs,..)?

Matching	Direct	Indirect
Templates		

Features	Scalar	Structural
Contours		
Regions		

Fig. 2.2.-1 :   Methods Of Shape Analysis

We can either take the complete figure and compare it with some reference
(template matching) or we can derive features from contour or regional
properties. If we obtain numerical features we talk about 'scalar' methods;
if the result of feature extraction leads to structures we call these
methods 'structural'. It should be noted that there are no clear boundaries
between these categories.

Template matching can be performed either directly by using iconic
references or indirectly by applying an artifical template (such as circles
around the centroid of the figure). The resulting intersections between the
template and the figure deliver features that can be used for classification as well as for the determination of orientation in the image plane.
Direct feature extraction can be based on contour or region analysis. In the
first case "one walks around the figure", in the second case "one walks

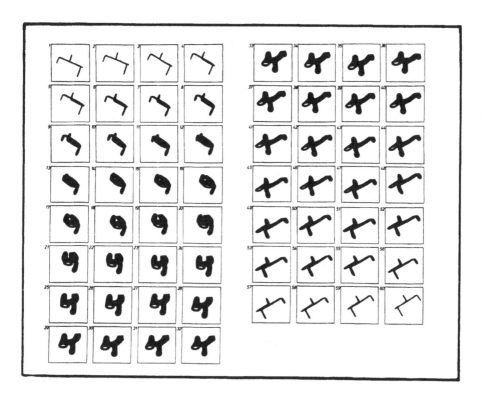

Fig. 2.2.-2 : Shapes Of Workpiece Silhouttes /FOITH '78/

inside it" /PAVLIDIS '78/.

Examples for scalar features that can be extracted from contours are:
perimeter; minimal, maximal or average curvature; minimal, maximal or
average polar distance (= the distance of contour points from the centroid).
Scalar features that can be extracted from regions are: area, moments of
inertia, number of holes, ... If one works with scalar features then usually
numerical classifiers are used for the assignment of semantic labels.
Typically, nearest neigbour classifiers prevail /DUDA & HART '73/. These can
be modified to improve their performance by adding tests in each feature
dimension /FOITH '78/. Another powerful classification technique is the
decision tree approach where features are tested sequentially in order to
determine an optimal path through a search tree /ROSEN et al. '76/,
/GIRALT et al. '79/.

Examples for structural features that can be extracted from contours are:
straight line elements or elements with constant curvature. Structural
features that can be extracted from regions are: convex subsets or other
regular substructures. Structural features require different analysis methods;
here either syntactic or heuristic approaches are used. In the syntactic
approach structural elements are considered as primitives of a vocabulary;
shape analysis is then performed through parsing. It is outside the scope
of this paper to discuss the merits and drawbacks of the syntactic approach.
Generally, it can be said that the basic weakness is the sensitivity of this
method to disturbed data (although work is going on to make this approach
more flexible). Heuristic approaches are far more flexible in this respect,
yet they sometimes lack generality.

In practice, all kinds of approaches have been used for industrial applications. Let us give a few examples. /BAIRD '76A/ uses local and global templates
to determine the corners of IC chips (see also /BAIRD '78/). Indirect template
matching techniques are used by: /BRETSCHI '76/ who uses TV-lines to intersect object silhouettes or by /HEGINBOTHAM '73/ and /GEISSELMANN '80/ who use
circles around the centroid. Examples for scalar methods of contour analysis
can be found in: /AGIN '75/, /PAVLIDIS '77/, /DE COULON & KAMMENOS '77/,
/DESSIMOZ '78/, /NAKAGAWA & ROSENFELD '79/ or /ARMBRUSTER et al. '79/. One
particular advantage of working with contour features is the fact that
these can be used when parts are overlapping each other.Here, contour features
provide local cues that can be used for recognition of partial views
/McKEE & AGGARWAL '77/, /PERKINS '77/, /KELLY, BIRK & WILSON '77/, /DESSIMOZ
et al. '79/, /TROPF '80/.
Regional features such as area and moments have been used by /BIRK, KELLEY
et al. '76/, /BAIRD '76/, /HASEGAWA & MASUDA '77/ or /FOITH '78/.
The syntactic approach, finally, has been applied by /MUNDY & JOYNSON '77/ and
/BJORKLUND '77/, among others. Structural, regional features seem to have
found only little interest - probably because decomposition into regular
substructures involves high computational costs. With the support of
dedicated hardware most methodes discussed here are well suited for real-time
processing and industrial applications.

As can be seen from these examples the boundary between shape analysis and
model matching is rather fuzzy. The simplest models that can be constructed
for workpieces are just lists containing shape features; model matching then
turns into classification of the feature vector. More complex and more power-

ful are 'relational models' that contain substructures and their interrelations such as distance and relative orientations. These informations
are usually stored in graph-structures -- an approach that goes back to the
early seventies /BARROW & POPPLESTONE '71/ /BARROW et al. '71/.

The matching of relational structures is known to be an NP-complete problem
/SHAPIRO '79/. One must therefore keep in mind to use only graphs with few
nodes or to partition the graph into subgraphs such as suggested in /BOLLES
'79A/. Relational models can be constructed for binary images /HOLLAND '76/ as
well as for gray level images·/PERKINS '77/. In the first case, blobs are
used as substructures, in the second case one typically chooses contour
segments. In both cases one is well advised to include as much information
as possible in the description of each substructure in order to facilitate
the search through the model. For example, if local orientations of model
elements are stored in the model, then the search for neighbouring elements
can be confined to restricted areas in the image. Encouraging results have
been obtained in the area of model driven analysis, yet there are many open
questions and a lot of research will be necessary to make this approach
applicable in a general and powerful way.

2.3 EXAMPLES FOR PRACTICAL DIA-SYSTEMS

In conclusion of the discussion of approaches from the literature we want
to point to some specific examples that clarify the state-of-the-art. Early
approaches for industrial applications have started in the seventies; as
off the mid-seventies such applications are finding an ever increasing interest. The first approaches were typically simulations which did not perform
in real-time, i.e. most often processes had to be slowed down or simulated
completely. Also, these approaches were oriented towards very particular
problems; only few approaches tried to tackle more general problems. Yet,
with the development of this area, there is a strong tendency for more
generality and we are seeing the first examples of systems that are commercially available.

In this section we will first give a survey on some approaches that seem
rather typical. Due to the vast amount of literature a complete survey would
be outside the scope of this paper, so we will more or less point to some

articles. We will conclude this section with examples of DIA-systems that can be used in general ways with emphasis on those systems that are commercially available. As was pointed out in the introduction, important tasks for practical DIA-systems fall into the categories of visual inspection, handling, and control. In the literature, especially the first two categories have found a lot of interest.

Visual inspection and handling are two tasks that often go together for 2 reasons: parts that are to be inspected must be presented to the DIA-system (often in a determined way); 2) if parts are presented to a DIA-system for handling tasks one might as well inspect their quality (provided that the DIA-system is powerful enough).

Most inspection tasks are performed with binary images. These are not always obtained by thresholding but also by applying edge detectors to gray level images and then converting the results to binary images. Typical objects of interest for visual inspection are:

● Parts whose shape must be inspected, for instance

Screws where the shape of the thread can be determined from a silhouette which is easily obtained from binary images. Typical approaches work with the boundary of the silhouette or some derived representation. An example for the boundary approach is /BATCHELOR '78A/where the boundary lines are transformed into a chain code representation; an example for the second approach is /MUNDY & JOYNSON '77/ where the median curve of the screw silhouette is first derived from the boundary lines and then used for syntactic recognition. Yet another approach works directly with the silhouette with a run length coding from which shape features can be computed /FLÜSCHER & PARTMANN '80/. It may be noted that /MUNDY & JOYNSON '77/ use dedicated hardware and a minicomputer for on-line processing while /FLÜSCHER & PARTMANN '80/ use a general purpose DIA-system (to be described in the next chapter) which also allows on-line computation with high troughput.

Automotive parts where either parts have to be inspected before assembly or where assemblies have to be inspected for completeness. One example for part inspection is /PERKINS '79/ who checks control arm bushings with the aid of shape and spacing of notches that are on the outer rim of those bushings. The system is implemented in PL/I on an IBM 370/168 computer and uses gray level images as input. The circle boundary and the notches are obtained by applying the Sobel-operator for boundary detection. The extracted notches are then matched with those of stored models. As a result of the matching one obtains the class of the bushing as well as its orientation.An example for the inspection of assemblies can be found in /ALBRECHT et al. '77/ who check steering gears. They work with binary images that are transferred to a minicomputer through a TV interface. Here, the authors check the presence of snap rings and similar components - - all checks being based upon shape analysis.

Tablets which must be inspected for roundness; in /NAKAMURA et al. '78/ and /NITTA '80/ we find an example where a DIA-system is applied that performs component labeling, as well as computation of area, perimeter, and centroid coordinates. This system could easily be applied in a number of different applications. The roundness of the tablets is obtained in this particular application through comparison between area and perimeter.

Labels on packages, bottles or other containers that must be inspected for correct size, shape, integrity as well as position and orientation. One early system performs heuristic checks along three selected scan lines that are binarized to verify label alignment /CALLEN & ANDERSON '75/. A more complete analysis is performed in /BROOK et al. '77/, /CLARIDGE & PURLL '78/ who use a linear diode camera for scans in the X-direction and the motion of a conveyor belt for scans in the Y-direction.The obtained binary image is further reduced by edge detection which is performed by special hardware. From the edge image one determines label orientation as well as pattern correctness. Due to the high data reduction high throughput can be reached despite the application of a micro computer for data analysis.

Parts where complex patterns must be inspected such as:

Printed wiring boards or mask patterns where a great many lines must be checked for indentations, protrusions, gaps, distance to neighbouring lines, etc. This application has found a very wide spread interest and 4 basic techniques have been developed for this type of inspection

/JARVIS '80B/.These are: 1) non-reference methods which work with definitions of local shape and size and are the most popular techniques; 2) pixel by pixel comparison methods which are difficult to implement because of alignment and dimension problems; 3) local pattern matching techniques which look for correct or incorrect local patterns; or 4) comparison techniques based on symbolic descriptions. Examples for non-reference methods can be found in: /STERLING '79/, /EJIRI et al. '73/, /GOTO et al. '78/ or /RESTRICK '77/; local pattern matching is performed in /JARVIS '80A/;one example for model driven comparison can be found in /THISSEN '77/78/. Recently, syntactic models that describe mask patterns have found some interest.

Typical examples for the application of DIA-systems for part handling are:

Electrical probing of IC chips which requires to determine the exact position and orientation of the chips on an already assembled component. Based on relational template matching in gray level images the corners of the chip are found and the orientation of the chip is computed. This information allows to position electrical probes into the base and emitter areas of the chip for functional tests/BAIRD '76/, /BAIRD '78/.

Bonding of chips with similar requirements as in electrical probing since here, too, one must determine the exact location and orientation of the chips in order to control bonding. Two examples are: /KASHIOKA et al. '76/ who use local pattern matching for chip positioning; /HSIEH & FU '79/ who scan along vertical and horizontal lines in the gray level image to determine mask orientation and location as well as the location of 2 bonding pads. The first system is partially implemented in hardware and works on-line while the second approach was simulated on a minicomputer.

Sorting of parts according to their type, position and orientation. Part sorting is an important task since for transportation and storage work-pieces are often scattered in bins, boxes or other containers. Visually controlled sorting devices usually consist of 4 components: feeder system, vision system, handling device, and part deposit. It would be most fea-sible to grasp the parts directly from the bin but - with few exceptions - the state-of-the-art is far from a solution of this task. There are a number of set-ups for part sorting. These use bowl feeders, chutes or

conveyor belts as feeding system;vision is performed with dedicated hardware, most often in combination with minicomputers; typical handling
devices are:selective channels, X-Y-tables, turntables, pick-&-place
devices and industrial robots; the parts are deposited either directly
into machines or into magazines or pallets. Let us cite a fex examples.
/CRONSHAW et al. '79/, /CRONSHAW et al. '80/ use a bowl feeder where in an
escapement are mounted 2 linear bundles of fibre optics that provide slit
views of passing objects in two directions. Recognition is based on point
templates that are interactively constructed. In this experimental set-up
no handling is provided.The combination of a bowl feeder and a X-Y-table that
can be rotated is shown in /SARAGA & SKOYLES '76/. Workpieces are fed onto
the table which is in the viewing field of the camera. After location
and orientation of a part are determined the table is moved and rotated
such that the workpiece comes to rest at a fixed site. From there it is
picked and transferred to a second fixed site - the deposit - by a pick-
&-place manipulator. Visual recognition of the workpieces is based on
models that contain features such as area, perimeter, polar radius, etc.

The idea to decouple handling actions into several separate steps is
driven even further in the approach of /HILL & SWORD '80/. The system
consists of a belt or a vibratory feeder, a movable shuttle, an
elevator, a turntable, a vision system and an industrial robot.
Computer-controlled operations of elevator, shuttle and turntable can
bring a part to a desired stable state, location, and orientation such
that it can be grasped by the robot. Undesired stable states can be
changed by pushing the part from the elevator at a predetermined height
('controlled tumbling'); desired orientations are obtained with the aid
of the turntable. The shuttle moves the parts between elevator, turntable and pick-up site from where the robot moves the part to a pallet
that is mounted on a X-Y-table. The set-up uses a vision system (Vision
Module VS 100) that will be described later in this section.

One example for grasping parts from a conveyor belt with a robot is shown
in /ZURCHER '78/. The vision system extracts the contour of the workpiece images, computes the centroid for part location and performs a
polar coding comparison with a reference for part orientation. These
data control the manipulator which grasps the parts from the belt. Another example for grasping of parts from a running conveyor belt will be

explained in chapter 3.

The use of a robot for part handling allows to grasp parts that abut or
rest upon each other. This may happen when parts are fed from a chute
and one example for an experimental set-up is / KELLEY et al.'77/. A
binary image of the workpiece scene is obtained and local image features
are computed from it. From these, feature candidates are selected for
recognition of workpieces. The list of candidates is further refined by
checking relations between features. Once a workpiece and its orientation
are found it is verified whether that part can be grasped. If so, the
robot acquires the part. Obviously this approach leads towards the "grasp
from the bin". This problem is tackled in a different way by two similar
approaches: / KELLEY at al.'79/ use a surface adapting vacuum gripper to
grasp parts form the bin. One camera mounted on the robot arm guides the
gripper by locating smooth surfaces where the gripper can get hold. Once
a part has been grasped in a random position it is presented to a second
camera. Here, the orientation of the part is determined and the robot can
now place the part in a desired stable state at the goal site. A similar
approach was used by /GEISSELMANN '80/ who uses a magnetic gripper instead
of a vacuum gripper and deposits the part in front of the camera.

Assembly tasks are often performed with the aid of tactile sensing, for
instance in bolt fitting to prevent jamming. Yet it seems useful to consider visual sensing as well to guide the manipulator approximately to
the site of fitting. Visual control for assembly tasks has indeed been
studied in a number of approaches. In an experiment where a rectangular
block was inserted into a rectangular hole/TANI et al. '77/ the authors
have mounted fiberscopes to the manipulator for image acquisition. From
the binary image the contours of the bar and the hole are checked until
they are parallel. Here, perspective distortions must be accounted for.
In another approach the camera is mounted directly in the hand of an
industrial manipulator/AGIN '77B/.The assembly task is to insert bolts
into holes. First, an initial gross correction brings the robot arm (and
the camera) from a random position to a position above a hole, then two
fine corrections are performed. A similar assembly task is required in a
related experiment by /McGHIE & HILL '78/. Here, the assembly operation
consists of placing a cover on a compressor housing and fastening them
together with eight bolts. The experimental set-up includes a robot, an

X-Y-table, and DIA-system. The DIA-system analyzes binary images of the top of the compressor housing and commands the X-Y-table to move the compressor housing such that the cover can be placed. After each assembly step the DIA-system also inspects the result of the operation.

Yet another example is the approach of /OLSZTYN et al. '73/ where wheels are mounted by a visually controlled manipulator. In this experiment the DIA-system has to find studs on hubs as well as stud holes in wheels. The DIA-system first determines the center of symmetry of either hub or wheel and then uses this information to perform a circular search to locate the studs and the holes.

While the afore mentioned assembly tasks are rather simple and could be performed with acceptable efforts, the final example shows how difficult complex assembly tasks can be /KASHIOKA et al. '77/. The authors describe a multi-sensory robot which was tested in a vacuum cleaner assembly operation. The robot has two arms (a power arm and a sensor arm) and no less than seven cameras are applied.

From all these examples we see the variety of tasks that exists for DIA-systems. Until now, most often specific solutions of particular tasks have been sought and realized. Sometimes even only simulations or off-line computations were performed. Nevertheless there are some approaches that try to generate systems that provide more generality. These approaches can be grouped into several categories depending on their basic philosophy. These categories are:

1) Software based systems: such systems usually store the image with the aid of a fast interface either directly in the computer or in a dedicated image memory. The complete analysis is performed by accessing the stored data with software. Usually in such systems either micro or mini computers are used. Such systems are highly flexible and it is not surprising that they are used in research institutions that are envolved in basic research /BATCHELOR ' 78B/./BIRK, KELLEY et al. '79 A, B/. Typically, such systems are based on binary image analysis - as for instance /PUGH et al. '78/ - while some systems store gray level images before they convert the picture to binary data /SPUR et al. '78/. At the time of writing only a few systems

are manufactured by the industry and are available commercially. Among the few ,one has to take notice of the VS-100 system which is sold by Machine Intelligence Corporation and is an off-spring of work that was performed at the Stanford Research Institute /AGIN & DUDA '75/, /AGIN '75/, / AGIN '77/ A/, /GLEASON & AGIN '79/,/BOLLES '79B/.This system adapts to several cameras (3 solid state with resolutions varying from 256 x 1 to 240 x 240 and a standard vidicon camera). Its hardware basically consists of a binarization unit, a run length encoder with image memory, and a DEC LSI-11. Its software provides efficient programs for connectivity analysis, the computation of 13 features - such as area, perimeter, centroid coordinates, number of holes, minimal and maximal radii, ... -, nearest neighbour classifiers and a menu driven operation system, as well as I/O-ports for communication with other devices such as controllers for gates, X-Y-tables, industrial robots, etc.. Typical performance times vary from 25 ms to 2.5 sec.

2) Hardware based systems: such systems process the image directly during the image scan. Most often only rather simple operations can be performed during the scan therefore methods such as pointwise template matching or the polarcheck are brought to bear /BRETSCHI '76/, /GEISSELMANN '80/.

3) Mixed systems: Certainly a very promising approach would be to mix software and hardware based approaches by applying hardware whenever many data have to be processed very fast and by applying software when data have to be analyzed in a flexible way. Two examples that use such hybrid approaches are /KARG '78/ and /KARG & LANZ '79/ as well as /ARMBRUSTER et al. '79/ and /MARTINI & NEHR '79/. In the first case a 2-processor system is applied where a LSI-11/2 provides the system management and a bit sclice micro-processor is used for fast access to an image memory. This system binarizes the image data on-line, stores them in 2 image memories and accesses these data through the µP. In 2 processing steps features such as area, centroid coordinates, radii, area as a function of polar distance or polarcheck inter-sections are computed. The second system uses quite similar features; contrary to the first system special hardware is applied to compute area and centroid coordinates of a workpiece in the (binary) image.

4) Light section systems: the use of light section techniques delivers most often stable results - a fact that makes this technique rather feasible for industrial applications. Basically, images that stem from light sectioning

illumination are easily reduced to binary images; therefore these systems are included in our survey. Such systems use either linear or 2-dimensional diode arrays for image acquisition. Examples for the first approach are: the CONSIGHT system /WARD et al. '79/ that uses two strip lights and a linear diode array. Due to the presentation of workpieces on a conveyor belt the system acquires silhouettes of passing objects. These silhouettes are recognized with the aid of shape features such as area, first and second moments, or hole shape features. Much the same approach is pursued by /WOLF '79/ who determines two-dimensional features of the workpiece base as well as three-dimensional features of the workpiece volume (by triangulation). The application of such techniques to object tracking and welding seam following can be found in /AGIN '79/.

Two-dimensional approaches are also used in light sectioning techniques. Two examples are /VANDERBRUG et al. '79/ and /TODA & MASAKI '80/. One essential feature of light sectioning is the fact that the images are easily converted to binary images. Thus, the same image analysis techniques apply. One particular advantage is that three dimensional information can also be obtained from the data.

In concluding it can be stated that existing systems are ready for many practical tasks that one encounters in the industry. At the time of writing the first systems are about to be commercially available and many more are likely to follow. It is generally predicted that these systems will find a wide spread use.

3. S.A.M. -- A SCENE ANALYSIS MACHINE FOR INDUSTRIAL APPLICATIONS

In this chapter we describe a DIA-system that the authors have developed at
the Fraunhofer-Institute for Information and Data Processing (IITB) at
Karlsruhe. The system will be referred to as S.A.M. which stands for
'Sensorsystem for Automation and Measurement'. S.A.M. is commercially available
from Robert Bosch GmbH, TV Equipment Division in Darmstadt, W-Germany.

Let us first explain the basic philosophy that guided our development. As was
pointed out above, there is a wide range of practical tasks for DIA systems.
Tasks with low complexity require simple measurements such as lengths, widths,

etc. Highly complex tasks demand recognition of workpieces with a multitude of
stable positions.Thus there is an extremely broad range of complexity that a DIA
system has to cope with.The same holds for the required processing times: these
vary from tenths of seconds to several seconds. It is obvious that no single
DIA system - as universal as it may be - can cope in an economic way with
these wide ranges of tasks and processing times. There may be simple tasks
with long processing times allowed; here one would best apply a DIA system
that performs the analysis in software from an image memory. On the other hand
there may be difficult tasks that must be solved in a very short time; here,
a lot of special hardware must be applied. Thus the costs of DIA systems also
range from cheap systems to costly ones.

The answer to these problems are modular kits from whose modules DIA systems
can be configurated such that they are cost effectively adapted to the task
at hand. Thus one can always pick the most economic solution. One such modular
kit is S.A.M. which is therefore not a DIA system itself; rather from its
modules DIA systems can be built. S.A.M. consists of a number of hardware and
software modules that perform an extremely fast analysis of binary images.

Fig. 3.-1 : A typical S.A.M. configuration

Typical processing times are between 50 and 500 milliseconds. S.A.M. can be
extended towards simple measurements as well as towards gray level image
processing. From S.A.M. components one can build simple configurations as well
as complex ones. Figure 3.-1 shows an example of a S.A.M. configuration. As
can be seen there is only a keyboard and a panel of buttons for the operation
of the system. With the panel one selects START, STOP as well as the display
of one of four images on a TV monitor (analogue, binary, memory 1, memory 2).
As will be explained later all operating modes of the system are selected with
the aid of a menu driven dialogue. Thus the system can be operated by almost
untrained persons.

We might mention that S.A.M. was developed under the project name 'MODSYS' (for:modular system) and was renamed after completion. Therefore previous publications about our project all refer to MODSYS /FOITH et al. '78/, /FOITH '79/, /FOITH et al. '80/, /RINGSHAUSER ' 80/, /ENDERLE '80/.

3.1 S.A.M. - HARDWARE

The most drastic problem in real-time image processing is the immense amount of data one has to cope with. For economical reasons the use of micro or mini computers is imperative yet if these were put to processing complete images,

cycle times would certainly be outside the required ranges. It is therefore important to reduce the amount of data as much as possible. From our point of view the microprocessor never should get so "see" the complete image but only "interesting" parts of it or - even better - only data that were obtained from the image through dedicated processors. For this reason we have implemented into S.A.M. a number of features that support the reduction of data in various ways. These features make S.A.M. different from most other systems that we are aware of.

The most important features that serve to reduce data are:

● Iterative image processing capability where operators such as shrink, blow or combinations thereof can be applied consecutively to a stored binary image. The amount of necessary hardware is rather small due to a 'ping-pong processing' mode where the image is transferred hence and forth between two image memories. At each transfer the selected operator is applied at TV speed.

- <u>On-line image analysis</u> where the following computations on a binary image are performed in parallel during the TV scan: 1) component labeling, 2) computation of area, 3) computation of perimeter, 4) computation of number of holes, and 5) computation of centroid coordinates. Steps 2) through 5) are performed for each labeled blob in the image (for up to 255 labels).

- <u>Inversion of images from black to white and vice versa</u> allows the computation of the above mentioned features for holes as well with the same hardware. During image analysis black pixels are considered to be figure points and usually one selects the polarity of the binary image such that black points correspond to regions. If one wants to analyze hole features as well, one scans the (stored) image a second time and inverts simultaneously its polarity. As a result, image analysis is now performed on the hole features.

- <u>Suppression of uninteresting blobs</u> can be performed by means of a filtering mode that is implemented within the component labeling module. One specific feature of this module is the fact that the label numbers are not stored pixelwise, in fact they are not stored at all. As will be explained later only the equivalences and the number of assigned labels are stored. If one needs a blob with a specific label one simply repeats the component labeling, only this time with the selected labels flagged. The filtering mode then suppresses all blobs whose labels are not flagged. Since component labeling is done with TV speed it only takes 20 ms for a half frame.

- <u>Logical combinations</u> of an input image with stored images help to reduce the incoming data by setting windows whose size and shape are determinded by blobs from a previous image. One can also combine input images with computer-generated patterns.

The overall structure of the system reflects our basic philosophy about data reduction. Since we intended the design of a modular system,S.A.M. had to be bus-oriented. The S.A.M.-Bus consists of two different subsystems: a video-bus and a processor-bus. If one reads Fig. 3.1.-1 from the left to the right one notices 3 layers of processing units: 1) video circuits, 2) image processing and analysis and, 3) data processing and storage. Video circuits, the image processing and analysis units including image memories share the video bus; image analysis units and image memories share the processor bus with the µP, data memories, and I/O devices. Thus the image processing and analysis layer can be thought of as a reduction stage where the huge amount of image data is reduced to a few data that must then be processed by the data processing stage. In the following we will explain the important modules with greater detail.

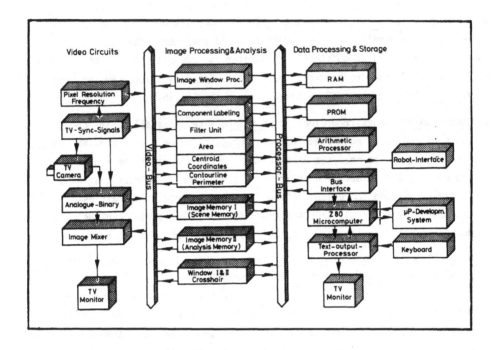

Fig. 3.1.-1: Blockdiagramm of S.A.M. hardware

VIDEO CIRCUITS

Video circuitry consists of Signal Input Processors (SIP) that perform the
binarization and synchronisation of signals from either TV or solid state
cameras. It is possible to read in images from 2 cameras simultaneously. The
polarity of the input images can be selected (black/white or vice versa). The
Pixel Resolution Frequency module determines the resolution along scan lines.
In order to obtain square pixels when working with TV half frames we usually
chose that frequency such that 320 pixels are resolved in one line. The
Analogue-Binary module thresholds the image with a threshold that can be set
by hand. In the future this module will be replaced by a module where threshold
intervals can be set by the μP. The Image Mixer module supports the simultaneous
display of any combination of gray level image, binary image or images from
two image memories. The binary images are coded with different gray levels as
to be able to discriminate between them on the video monitor. In the same way
two image windows and a crosshair are displayed.

IMAGE PROCESSING AND ANALYSIS

The layer of Image Processing and Analysis modules consists of three different groups: image memories (including windowing and crosshair), image processing units, and image analysis units. Although memories are not processing devices they are included here because they play an essential role in the processing and analysis steps.

Image Memories (IM)

There are two types of Image Memories; a half-frame-IM and a run-length-IM. Both IM types can read/write with TV speed. The S.A.M.-Bus allows the application of up to 8 IMs of either type simultaneously.

The half-frame-IM stores the binary image pixel by pixel with a capacity of 256 x 512 x 1 bit. Each pixel is addressed via its X-Y-coordinates. The µP can access every pixel and either read the bit or write it. The µP also commands the half-frame-IM to: 1) start reading in an image, 2) start to output an image, or 3) to invert the image that it outputs. In the output mode the IM generates a binary video signal from the stored image. It is possible to link two IMs such that one outputs an image which the other one reads. Thus 'blob filtering' can be performed in cooperation with the component labeling module; the linkage of two IMs can also be used for the 'ping-pong processing' mode where the image is transferred hence and forth between the 2 memories while at each transfer some binary operation is performed.

The run-length-IM stores the positions of black/white and white/black transitions along scan lines with a capacity of 4K x 16 bit. This IM knows two different types of data words: transition words (TW) and line-number words (LN). Both types of words are 13 bit long. Bit 0 - bit 8 are used for the X-coordinate of a transition or the line number (=Y-position), respectively.Bit 9 specifies the polarity of the transition, bit 10 - bit 12 determine the type of data word (TW, LN, begin 1/2 half frame, end 1/2 half frame). When the run-length-IM reads in an image, it stores at the beginning of a line a line number word,even if the line is empty. Transitions along a line are stored with the corresponding TW. Thus this IM contains data in the following way (for some imaginary image): LN/LN/LN/TW/TW/TW/TW/LN/TW/TW/LN/LN/. The µP can access any stored word and can also write into the memory. Run-length-IM commands are: 1) start reading half frame image, 2) start reading frame image, 3) start to output half frame image, and 4) start to output frame image. In the output mode the IM generates a binary video image from the stored data. This image can be displayed on a TV monitor. The run-length-IM can be applied in much the same way as the half-frame-IM. It is especially useful when run length features must be computed with the µP. A particular feature is the capability to shift the stored image in positive X and Y direction deliberately by setting initial coordinates with one command.

It is not necessary to store always the complete TV images. In order to reduce image size two windows can be set which define the area of the image that is actually processed and stored. Window 1 defines the maximal area which is 256 x 512 pixels. Its left upper corner also defines the origin of all coordinates. This window is positioned by hand and cannot be accessed by the µP. The second window lies within the first and can be set by the µP in size and position. Thus one can restrict the analysis to certain areas that one is interested in. The Window module also contains a crosshair generator. The crosshair is used to mark any position in the image. It can be used by a human operator or be positioned by the µP.

Image Processing with the Image Window Processor (IWP)

Image Processing is performed with the aid of the Image Window Processor (IWP). This module represents a 7 x 7 image window that moves with the TV scan along the image. Binary operators are implemented that process pixels within the window through logical connections. Right now we have realized 8 different operators that can be selected by the µP. These operators are: shrink, double-shrink, blow, double-blow, shrink-and-blow, blow-and-shrink, contourline (= difference between shrink and blow), and finally NOP (= no operation). The IWP can also compare two images via XOR and AND. It can also mix one image into another.

All operations can either be performed on TV-input and/or stored images. Output signals of the IWP constitute a binary video signal that can be routed to one of the image memories. Operators are realized by hardwiring. Any of the operators as well as the direction of the signal flow are determined by commands from the µP that are sent to a data port.

If two image memories (IM) are used, iterative image processing can be performed in the 'ping-pong-processing' mode where the image is transferred hence and forth between the 2 IMs and is processed at each transfer. All IWP-operators work at TV speed. Thus one can apply image transformations many times without

great loss of time. Usually such transforms are to clean the image by suppressing noise, closing gaps, or removing notches. Fig. 3.1.-2 shows an example for
the iterative cleaning of a binary image (B) with the aid of the following
sequence: double-shrink (C), shrink (D), and double-blow (E). The comparison
of (B) with (E) shows that much of the noise has been suppressed while the figure
of interest has kept its original shape. The whole sequence of transformations
takes only about 80 ms (20 ms per transformation and a few ms for µP control).

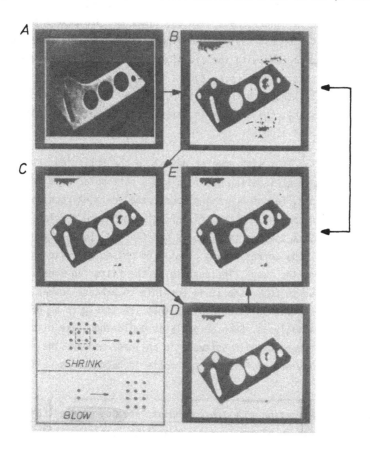

Fig. 3.1.-2 : 'Clean-Up' By Iterated Picture Processing

A - TV Image
B - Binary Image of A
C - Double Shrink of B
D - Shrink of C
E - Double Blow of D

Image Analysis Processors (IAPs)

The Image Analysis Processors (IAPs) are the core of S.A.M.. Basically, they
perform: 1) component labeling, 2) computation of: (i) area, (ii) perimeter,
(iii) number of holes, (iv) centroid coordinates for each labeled blob. It is
the role of the IAPs to perform the necessary data reduction by extracting
shape and position features from the blobs in the binary image. These features
are the data that must be further analyzed by the µP. Let us briefly evaluate
the reduction rate. A binary image with 256 lines and 320 pixels per line has
almost 100.000 bit. Suppose that such a binary image contains about 60 blobs.
Each blob can be described with the aid of the extracted features by approximately 16 byte (cf. section 3.2), i.e. such a binary image can be represented by
less than 1 Kbyte. Although bit and byte operations may not be directly comparable it is obvious that the savings in data processing are tremendous and may
amount to a factor of 1.000.

We will describe the IAPs with greater detail in the following. It may be noted
here that the component labeling module plays a particular role among the IAPs
since it knows two different operating modes: the 'data extraction' mode is the
actual process of labeling and the 'filtering' mode where the labeling process
is repeated, yet this time certain labels are flagged. In this mode flagged
labels (or rather, the corresponding blobs) are passed on while unflagged blobs
are suppressed from the image. The purpose of the filtering mode is, again,
data reduction. Due to this mode it is possible to process images such that the
resulting images contain only those blobs that are likely to be of interest for
a more scrutineous analysis. Such an analysis could then take place either with
more dedicated hardware or with software in an image memory. The filtering mode
is a powerful tool since it helps to cut costs in hardware as well as in software.

During the data extraction mode the <u>component labeling module (CLM)</u> determines
connected components in binary images and assigns labels to these components.
These labels are numbers that correspond to the order of appearance in the TV
image from left to right and top to bottom (TV scan). The principle of connectivity is based on the observation of three consecutive pixels in the previous
line (i.e. we use 8-adjacency) through a 2 x 3 window:

$$\text{Line N-1 :} \quad P \; P \; P$$
$$\text{Line N} \quad : \quad \quad X$$

If there was a label on any of the points P on line N-1 then the same label
holds for pixel X. If not - and if X is a point of a blob - then a new label

is assigned. Such an event corresponds to the beginning of a new blob; the first event corresponds to the continuation of an old blob. There are two more cases that one must take care of: convergences and divergences of branches of blobs. In the case of a convergence, two branches with different labels from the previous lines 'converge', i.e. it turns out that they belong to the same blob. In the case of a divergence one notices that one blob fans out into branches in the succeeding line. Since in this case one knows what is happening one can keep the old label for the new branches. In the case of convergences one must establish rules that determine which of the labels 'survives'. In our design we choose the leftmost label to be dominant over all other converging labels. Fig. 3.1.-3 shows examples for all these cases.

In the literature it is often suggested to store for each pixel the label of the blob to which it belongs. In practice this approach has two disadvantages. Firstly, one transforms a binary image into an 8 bit image (for 256 labels); secondly, if one wants to extract a connected component in a label image one must still search for all equivalent labels. We therefore don't store the labels at all. Instead, we store the binary image together with the equivalence list of labels and the total number of labels and repeat the process of component labeling whenever we are interested in a particular blob (or several blobs).

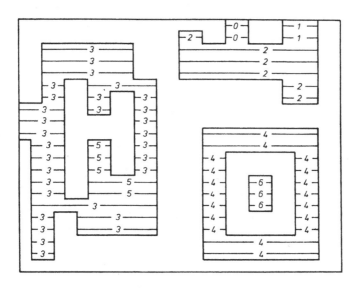

Fig. 3.1.-3 : The Principles Of Component Labeling With Branch Beginnings, Continuations, Convergences, And Divergences

Interesting blobs would typically be selected with the aid of features that were extracted during component labeling in the data extraction mode. The second run of the CLM is then performed in the filtering mode. Since results of the CLM are always obtained by repeating the component labeling we call this approach 'dynamic component labeling'.

Dynamic component labeling requires of course that there are processing units that are capable of computing features during the image scan since this is the only time when the labels are present. In fact, this is just what the IAPs do. As a result we obtain shape and position parameters that can be identified by their label number.

One particular feature of the CLM is the fact that it also determines if a blob is completely inside the image or not. If a blob touches the image window one cannot be sure how complete it is; therefore such blobs are marked and are later ignored in the analysis or treated separately.

The present realization of the CLM permits to assign up to 255 labels and as many convergences. If there are more blobs or branches in the image, then the first 255 are labeled by their corresponding number; the remaining ones are all labeled with label number 256. If the upper borders of blobs are fringed then a lot of labels would be assigned to those blobs. Therefore the CLM smoothes such borderlines by filling all branches that are only one pixel wide. Also, single points as well as holes of one pixel are removed or filled respectively. Due to this cleaning only relevant branches are labeled.

The results of the CLM allow to compute the number of holes of each blob. This will later be explained in the section on software. To conclude, the results that the CLM delivers are:

- the number of all assigned labels   : NAL
- the number of all convergences   : NAC
- the list of convergences   : CONVLIST
- the list of blobs that touch the image window: BORDLIST.

During the component labeling the CLM transmits the active label to the other feature processors such that the features of a blob can be assigned to its label.

The computation-of-area module (CAM) integrates for each label the number of pixels that belong to it. This number A is given by:

$$A = \sum_{y=1}^{M} \sum_{x=1}^{N} B(x,y) \qquad (3.1.-1)$$

where x, y are the pixel coordinates; N, M are the horizontal and vertical extent of the blob, respectively; and

$$B(x,y) = \begin{cases} 1 \text{ for pixels within the blob} \\ 0 \text{ for pixels outside the blob} \end{cases} \qquad (3.1.-2)$$

We assume here without loss of generality that the dimensions of pixels in x and y direction equal 1. The CAM has a counter that is loaded with the intermediate result of summation whenever the image scan moves across a labeled branch. The counter is incremented with the aid of the pixel resolution frequency at each pixel. When the scan leaves that branch on an line the intermediate sum is stored. After the image scan the area of each labeled branch is contained in the area memory. The memory can be accessed by the μP. Since a blob may consist of several branches it is necessary to add up all the partial areas. This is done at a later stage by software.

The computation-of-perimeter module (CPM) detects and counts contour points of blobs. A blob point is said to be a contour point whenever at least one of the neighbouring points belongs to the background. The detection is performed in a 3 x 3 neighbourhood around each blob point. For the computation of the perimeter it is not sufficient to integrate all contour points since the perimeter depends on the orientation of the blob on the grid. Contour points must be weighted according to the number of neighbours outside the blob. Yet, the error that one obtains when rotating a straight contour over the grid may be as high as $\pm$ 6%. This error can be further reduced if direct and diagonal neighbours are weighted differently. The error is minimized to $\pm$ 4% when the ratio between direct and diagonal neighbours is set to 10:7. The CPM is realized with three stages of adders. First direct and diagonal background pixels are added up separately and weighted with multipliers. Then these sums are added in the second layer. This result is added to the perimeter that has been computed up to that point. The result of this adder is finally stored in the perimeter memory. The CPM can also be used to output the contour line simply by issuing all detected contour points.

The computation-of-centroid module (CCM) is the last IAP. For the computation of the centroid coordinates one assumes that each blob point has a mass equal to 1. Centroid coordinates are then:

$$x_c = \frac{\Sigma x \cdot B(x,y)}{\Sigma B(x,y)} \qquad , \quad y_c = \frac{\Sigma y \cdot B(x,y)}{\Sigma B(x,y)} \qquad\qquad (3.1.-3)$$

Since $\Sigma B(x,y)$ is the area of the blob it is already computed by the CAM. It therefore suffices to compute the nominators of (3.1.-3). The division by the area is later performed by software. The CCM works in much the same way as the CAM, the only difference is that coordinates are integrated instead of pixels.

As was already mentioned the CAM, CPM, and CCM receive the actual label number from the CLM and can thus store the results of their computations under the corresponding label number.

DATA PROCESSING AND STORAGE

There are three functional groups of modules in this layer: data processor units, data storage units, and data input/output units.

Data Processors (DPs)

Right now there are two data processor units (DPs). These are a Z-80 Single Board Computer and a fast arithmetic processor (AM 9511) that support the Z 80 in numeric tasks.

The arithmetic processor has an 8 bit bidirectional bus, a data stack, and an arithmetic unit. First the two operands are pushed onto the stack then a command word is transmitted that specifies the operation. A status word signals when the operation is finished. Then the result can be read from the stack. The arithmetic processor performs 16 bit as well as 32 bit integer and floating point operations.

The Z80 is the main controller of all system functions. It can send commands to IAPs. As can be seen from Fig. 3.1.-1 it is not directly linked to the processor bus. This is due to a special feature of the S.A.M.-Bus. When we designed the system we wanted to be able to apply 8 bit processors as well as 16 bit micro processors. We also wanted a lot of address space to be able to store tables, data and programs. The storage of tables can drastically support real-time algorithms by providing fast table look-ups. The processor bus has there-fore a 16 bit wide data bus and a 24 bit wide address bus and a Bus Interface is needed. This interface has two functions: it links the μP to the bus and it provides a paging system for data storage access. It is possible to address

256 memory pages with 32 KByte each. The 64 K address space of the Z80 is
divided (with the aid of the interface) into a direct part with 32 K and a
paging part with the afore mentioned 256 pages of 32 K. The address space of
the paging part is 8 MByte.

Data Memories (DMs)

S.A.M. provides RAMs and EPROMs. EPROM boards offer a storage capacity of 32 K each;
RAM boards have 16 K each. Depending on the S.A.M.-configuration one can use
several boards of both types. All memories can be switched to either direct
or paging access mode. For mass storage a floppy disk drive is used.

Data Input/Output Units (DIO)

Data input/output occurs on two different levels: 1) the human operator must be
able to communicate with the system, 2) the system must send and receive data
from other devices of the workplace. For man-machine communication a commercial
text-output processor was chosen (SGS/ATES VDZ80) that displays alpha-numeric
data on a video monitor and receives alpha-numeric data from a keyboard. Thus
the human operator can communicate with S.A.M. by dialogue driven techniques.
The operator is further supported by a crosshair with which he can point to the
image.

Data communication between other devices and S.A.M. can be performed by using
the Z80 PIO and SIO. Specific data output channels are further: 2 Digital-
Analogue-Converters and a digital Robot Interface. This interface is adapted
for industrial robots such as the Volkswagen R-30 or the KUKA IR-601. It
delivers data for: a 'ready' message, the stable position, location and
orientation of a workpiece; it can receive an acknowledge signal from the robot.

As was pointed out in section 3. these hardware modules can be used to build
configurations of various complexity. Some typical configurations will be
discussed in a later section.

3.2.   S.A.M. SOFTWARE MODULES

Real-time processing of images cannot only be based on the application of
dedicated hardware. It is also necessary to implement algorithms that process
the data as effectively as possible. There is no systematic approach how to

implement real-time processing algorithms. Yet, there are at least two general principles that facilitate real-time implementations: 1) the use of table-look-ups instead of on-line computations; 2) presorting of data into highly organized data structures which are easily accessed. The use of table look-ups is supported in S.A.M. through the huge address space of the system; the organization of data will be explained in this section. Due to the implemented software it is for instance possible to perform a model-driven search in less than 200 ms.

S.A.M. software is implemented in PLZ, a PASCAL-like language with two levels: an assembler type level (PLZ/ASM), and a high level (PLZ/SYS). According to the required speed we have either used PLZ/ASM or PLZ/SYS.

S.A.M. software is organized into a hierarchy of three layers. These layers are:

- basic software
- problem-oriented software
- operator-oriented software.

The first two levels are supposed to be used by the expert programmer who adapts a S.A.M. configuration to a particular problem. The third level is an interactive surface for the untrained operator who performs in-site programming at the workplace.

The basic software itself consists of two levels:

- a microprogramming level for hardware
  and µP control
- a higher level for collection, organization,
  storage, and access of data.

At this level one also finds some high system commands such as text I/O, cross-hair commands or graphic output.

On the second level are implemented routines for nearest neighbour classifiers, polar check, model driven search or other problem-oriented programs. It is at this level that a S.A.M. configuration will be programmed by a system programmer.

The third level finally provides interactive means to operate the system at the workplace - for instance to adapt it to new workpieces. Here, no programming knowledge is required and the user is guided by menu driven dialogues.

BASIC SOFTWARE : MICROPROGRAMS

Let us discuss these levels at some greater detail. The basic software consists of two subsystems: MONSYS and SAMOS. MONSYS is the monitor program for the Z80; SAMOS is the control system for all S.A.M. hardware (besides SAMOS there are some more hardware control commands that are on a higher level then SAMOS commands but are still part of the basic software).

MONSYS commands are grouped into:

- Memory commands such as:

  - DISPLAY.M   : displays the content of a memory whose address range can be specified.

  - SET.M   : sets the content of a memory cell with a value that can be specified.

  - FILL.M   : sets the content of a memory sector with a value that can be specified; also, the range of the memory space can be determined.

  - MOVE.M   : moves the content of one memory sector to another one.

  - LOCATE.S   : locates a string in a given memory sector and outputs its address.

- Register commands such as:

  - DISPLAY.R   : displays the content of register R.

  - SET.R   : sets the value of register R.

- Break commands such as:

  - SET.BREAK.A   : sets a break point at address A.

  - CLEAR.BREAK.A   : clears a breakpoint at address A.

  - CONTINUE.B   : clears a breakpoint, sets a new one, and executes the program from the new breakpoint ('GO').

  - PROCEED.B   : allows to continue a program while leaving the breakpoints where they are.

- <u>Execution commands</u> such as:

  - NEXT.N : executes the next program line(s) and displays the register contents.

  - GO : executes a program whose starting address is specified in the Program Counter.

  - JUMP.A : jumps to address A.

- <u>Floppy Disk Drive commands</u> such as:

  - SET.SECTOR : moves a file to a sector of the floppy disk.

  - GET.SECTOR : transfers a file from the floppy disk to a RAM.

- <u>Port commands</u> such as:

  - OUT.P : transfers data to a port (out of 256 ports).

  - IN.P : gets data from a port.

All S.A.M. hardware modules can be accessed through ports; thus one could program a S.A.M. configuration with the aid of these commands. Yet, this would be rather aukward since there is a special monitor system for the hardware, too : SAMOS.

<u>SAMOS commands are grouped into:</u>

- <u>Initialization commands</u> such as:

  - INIT : initializes the complete system including the filter memory in the component labeling module and all image memories.

  - WINDOW : sets the image window to 'on/off' and - in the 'on'-case - to x_{min}/y_{min} and x_{max}/y_{max}.

  - EXEC : executes a SAMOS command line.

- <u>Data extraction commands</u> such as:

  - READ.I : reads an image while specifying the flow of information: it is determined to which image memory the image is sent and also which IAPs are to be applied.

  - COMP.M : performs the same operation as READ.I, only

in this case the image is already stored in
one of the image memories; therefore one
must specify from which IM the image must
be read.

- <u>Mode selection commands</u> such as:

  - FILTER.B   : filters blobs with the aid of the component
                      labeling module (CLM); one must specify:
                      1) the direction of the image transfer (from
                      memory 1 to memory 2 or vice versa), 2) the
                      desired label numbers must be flagged.

  - PROC.I   : in this mode the Image Window Processor (IWP)
                      is programmed. Again, the flow of information
                      (either from TV, memory 1 or memory 2) as
                      well as the operator sequence must be determin-
                      ed. It is possible to input any sequence of
                      operations; the system completes the sequence
                      always such that the resulting image will be
                      in memory 1.

- <u>Interactive commands</u> such as:

  - XHAIR   : turns the crosshair on or off and also allows
                      to either set it to specific coordinates or
                      read the coordinates of its locations.

  - GET.CHAR   : gets an alpha-numeric character from the
                      keyboard.

  - PUT.CHAR   : puts a character onto the TV-monitor.

  - CONV.H.D   : converts a hex number to a decimal number.

  - CONV.D.H   : converts a decimal number to a hex number.

- <u>Graphic commands</u> such as:

  - LINE   : outputs a line with given direction and
                      coordinates.

  - CIRCLE   : outputs a circle with given centroid and
                      radius.

  - PATTERN   : outputs 6 different pattern (rectangle,
                      diamond, cross, star, point, ...).

  - ASCII   : outputs any ASCII symbol in a white field
                      in an Image Memory.

- <u>Numeric commands</u> such as:

  - PUT.ARI   :   programs the arithmetic processor (ARI) by sending data and the required operation.

  - GET.ARI   :   gets the data from the ARI when its status signal indicates that the operation is finished.

These commands control the complete S.A.M. hardware. As a result one obtains a number of feature data that can be used for a compact description of the binary input image. As was pointed out at the beginning of this section it is feasible to organize these data such that they can be retrieved efficiently. This organization is performed at the second level of basic software.

BASIC SOFTWARE : DATA COLLECTION AND ORGANIZATION

The first step at this level consists of the collection of all feature data into the "Scene Table" (ST) - a data structure onto which all further analysis is based.

After input of an image the Image Analysis Processors(IAPs) have stored the extracted features for all labels that were assigned to blob branches. Since a blob can consist of several branches, the features of the corresponding labels are only partial results. One must therefore determine the set of labels for each blob and combine their feature values into the final values. Let us call this process 'label collection'. It is performed by an algorithm that analyzes the <u>convergence list (CONVLIST)</u> (cf. section 3.1.).

If CONVLIST is empty then all blobs in the image have only one label each and the Scene Table can be generated directly. Otherwise, equivalent labels are grouped together by a fast algorithm in one run through CONVLIST. This algorithm works with a set of stacks into which equivalent labels are pushed. For fast access of the stacks a stack-address field (SA field) is used that contains as many cells as there are labels. The SA field is accessed directly through the label number. Every time a label gets pushed onto one of the stacks, a pointer to that stack is set in the corresponding SA cell.

Let us give an example (cf. Fig. 3.2.-1). Suppose the first equivalent labels (i,j) have been pushed onto stack 1. Then we set $SA(i) = SA(j) = $ 'pointer to stack 1'. If later another label turns out to be equivalent to either i or j,

then it gets pushed onto the same stack and we set the pointer in its SA cell
to that stack. In our example, labels k and 1 end up in stack 1. In general,
every time a pair of labels (i,j) is taken from CONVLIST, one first tests whether
one of the corresponding SA cells already contains a pointer to a stack. The
following cases can occur:

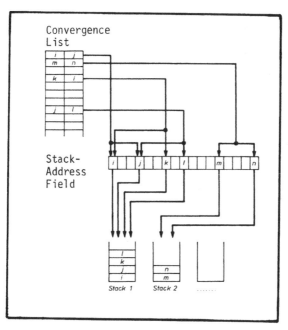

Fig. 3.2.-1 : Label Collection With The Aid Of A Stack-Address-Field

1) None of the labels is in one of the stacks (SA(i) = SA(j) = NONE), then both
   labels are pushed onto the next empty stack X and SA(i) = SA(j) = 'pointer
   to stack X' are set.

2) One of the labels -- say i -- is already in a stack; then j is pushed onto
   the same stack and we set SA(j) = SA(i).

3) The two labels are in different stacks (SA(i) $\neq$ SA(j)); then one of the
   stacks is pushed on top of the other in order to collect all equivalent
   labels. At the same time, all SA cells that pointed to the emptied stack
   must be updated to the common stack and the empty stack is free again.

After one run through CONVLIST, each stack contains a set of equivalent labels.
During label collection it is also noted how often each label appears in
CONVLIST (label frequency is needed for computation of the number of holes in

a blob). Due to the SA field the algorithm for label collection is linear in the sense that it performs with O(NAC) where NAC is the length of CONVLIST.

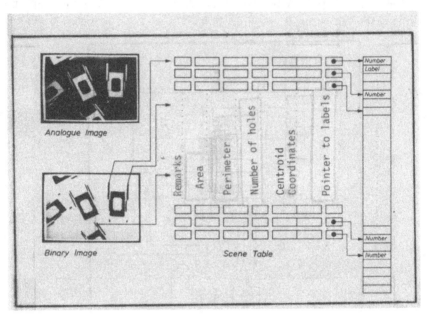

Fig. 3.2.-2 : The Scene Table As A Compact Description Of Binary Images

After label collection it is possible to generate the Scene Table (ST).
Fig. 3.2.-2 shows the structure of this table. The ST is a compact description of the binary image. For each blob there is one line in the ST; blobs are partially ordered from top to down in the order of their appearance during the TV scan. For each blob the ST contains (stored in 16 bytes): 1) a cell for remarks; 2) area; 3) perimeter; 4) number of holes; 5) centroid coordinates (after division of the nominator by area); 6) and a pointer to a separate record that stores corresponding labels.

During construction of the ST one must consider whether a blob has one or several labels. This can easily be determined with the aid of the SA field. We have two cases:

1)   If a SA cell is equal to zero, then the corresponding blob has only one label. Its features can be directly entered into the ST where the number of holes equals zero. Actually, before the entry is made, it is verified that that blob doesn't touch the image window. This is easily done with

the aid of BORDLIST (cf. section 3.1). If the blob touches the window, then no entry is made, i.e. it is excluded from further analysis since it is likely to be incomplete.

2) If the SA cell contains a pointer to a stack (SA (i) $\neq$ o), then we have encountered a blob with several labels. After checking the BORDLIST for these labels we pop label by label from the stack and compute the final feature values by summing up all areas, perimeters, centroid nominators, and label frequencies. If a blob has NL labels with a total label frequency LF then the numer of holes can be computed by:

$$\text{number of holes in a blob} = LF - NL + 1 \qquad (3.2.-1)$$

After all computations, the data are entered in the ST as in case 1).

Instead of suppressing blobs from the ST that touch the image window, it is possible to enter them and mark the ST line especially. Further more, blobs whose area is under a given threshold can also be suppressed form the ST ('software filtering'). During generation of the table total area, perimeter, and number of holes in the image are computed. This computation is performed in the Z80 while waiting for centroid coordinates from the Arithmetic Processor. These total features can be used to determine whether an image is likely to contain reasonable blobs at all.

As was already mentioned, the Scene Table contains blobs in a partial order from top to down. In image analysis one is often interested in two-dimensional range queries such as: "Is there a blob within the area: xmin/ymin and xmax/ ymax?", or "what neighbours does a blob have?" Such queries can support the analysis very efficiently. Due to the partial order of the ST they cannot be easily performed in that table. It was therefore necessary to generate a second data structure which is organized in a two-dimensional way such that range queries are easily performed. We call this second data structure the "Scene Sketch" (SS).

The Sketch is simply a grid of 20x16 square cells that is laid over the image. Each cell covers a 16x16 subimage (given an image with 256 lines and 320 pixels along the lines). With each cell is associated an array of 4 words. Into this array all blobs are written whose centroids fall into the corresponding SS cell. This array is organized in the following way:

        1) number of blobs in the cell
        2) ST line number for first blob
        3) ST line number for 2nd blob
        4) ST line numer for 3rd blob or pointer to an overflow list.

This organization allows efficient storage since there are seldom more than three blobs within the area of a SS cell. If there are more than three blobs in an SS cell, then these can be found in the overflow list.

The address of an SS cell is obtained from the X-Y-coordinates of blobs by setting the high byte to X/16 and the low byte to Y/16. Thus, if one wants to know to what cell a blob belongs to one performs 4 right shifts on its centroid coordinates and adds the results to the basic address of the SS. Elements in the associated array point to the line in the ST where the features of the corresponding blob are stored. The Scene Sketch facilitates a highly organized access of the ST. It is generated from the Scene Table in one run through the table by the program SKETCH.SORT which performs with O(STL) where STL is the length of the Scene Table.
There are three basic search routines that work on the SS. These are:

- SKETCH.SEARCH.C : input are X-Y coordinates;

    output is a list of ST line numbers of those blobs that are in the same SS cell.

- SKETCH.SEARCH.9 : input are X-Y coordinates;

    output is a list of ST line numbers of those blobs that are either in the same SS cell or in any of the neighbouring cells (i.e. 3 x 3 SS cells are searched for blobs).

- SKETCH.SEARCH.W : input are the coordinates of the upper left and lower right corner of a rectangular search window: xmin/ymin and xmax/ymax;

    output is a list of ST line numbers of all those blobs that are in any of the SS cells that the window covers.

With these search routines it is possible to start at some coordinates (not necessarily those of a blob) and find all blobs that are in the neigbourhood. That neighbourhood is either one SS cell, 9 SS cells, or all SS cells covered by the rectangular search window.

Other search routines are based upon the organization of feature data since range queries about feature values are equally important ("Which blobs have an area between value-1 and value-2?", ...). Right now we only sort area values since range queries with this feature are often sufficient to reduce the number of likely candidates in an efficient way.

Area values are organized into a data structure that consists of two substructures: the AREA.KEY-TABLE and the AREA.LIST. The AREA.KEY.TABLE (AK-Table)
allows fast access to the data that are stored in the AREA.LIST (A-List). This
is a technique that we often use: to have an access structure (mostly based
on hash coding techniques) and another structure (mostly a linked list) that
contains the sought data.

For accessing the AK-Table we have divided it into 6 ranges with increasing
widths: 0-255 / 256-1023 / 1024-2047 / 2048-4095 / 4096-8191 / >8192. Each of
these ranges is subdivided into a number of cells; the number of cells varies
in order to represent each range according to its importance. Thus the ranges
have the following cell distribution:

1)   range   0 - 255 :   16 cells with 16 values each;
2)   range 256 -1023 :   24 cells with 32 values each;
3)   range 1024-2047 :   16 cells with 64 values each;
4)   range 2048-4095 :   16 cells with 128 values each;
5)   range 5096-8191 :   16 cells with 256 values each;
6)   range > 8192 :   1 cell for all the remaining values.

We thus have the following structure for the AREA.KEY.TABLE and the AREA.LIST:

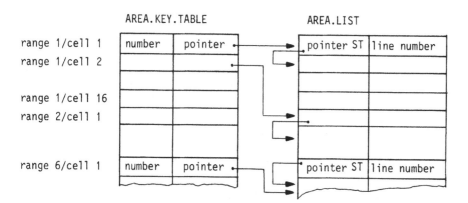

Thus, cells in the AK-Table indicate how many areas belong to that cell and
the pointer indicates the starting address of the corresponding part of the
A-List. A-List elements are then linked together by another sequence of
pointers while the content of an A-List element is the ST line number in which
the corresponding area value can be found. Both data structures are generated
from the Scene Table by a program AREA.SORT which performs with O(STL), i.e.

the structures are generated in one run through the Scene Table.

Based on the organization of area values two search routines have been implemented:

- AREA.SEARCH : input is an area value;

    output is a sequence of ST line numbers where area values of the according range/ cell can be found.

- AREA.SEARCH.TOL : input is a deliberate range of area values: amax and amin;

    output is a sequence of ST line numbers where area values can be found that are within the given range.

Based on the afore mentioned data structures we have implemented several Image Analysis Routines that are rather general in the sense that they perform data queries that are useful in many ways. Of particular interest are:

- PNT.PNT.DIST.DIR : delivers the coordinates of a pixel if given the coordinates of a starting point together with a distance and a direction. input: (x1,y1), distance, direction; output: (x2,y2).

- DIST.P1.P2 : computes the distance between two given points. input: (x1,y1), (x2,y2); output: distance d(P1,P2).

- DIR.P1.P2 : computes the direction between two points P1, P2 where the direction is defined to be the angle between the connection line (P1,P2) and a horizontal line through P1. input: (x1,y1), (x1,x2) DIST; output: $\nleftarrow$(P1,P2).

- FIX.TOL : computes a fixed tolerance for a given value of a feature. input: feature value v, threshold δ; output: vmin, vmax.

- PERC.TOL : computes tolerances in % of a feature value. input: feature value v, % tolerance; output: vmin, vmax.

- SEARCH.WINDOW : determines a square search window of given dimension around a point of given coordinates. input: (x,y), width; output: (xmin/ymin), (xmax/ymax).

XHAIR.SELECT : compares a given crosshair coordinate with entries in the Scene Table; if the centroid coordinates of an entry coincide (within a specific range) then the corresponding ST line number is given. input: x-y coordinates of the crosshair; output: either an ST line number or ERROR.

All these programs constitute the level of basic software onto which the remaining two levels are based. They both make intensive use of these programs, and it should be noted here that it is the basic level whose routines do facilitate real-time processing of the data.

PROBLEM ORIENTED SOFTWARE

Problem oriented software performs the actual recognition tasks -- for instance in workpiece recognition and inspection. At the time of writing we have implemented three programs that can be used for quite a number of applications. For other applications it will be necessary to implement more programs. Due to the software that is available at the basic level, system programming is rather easy. In the following we will describe some procedures as well as the three recognition programs.

The most basic step in recognition programs is the comparison between model features and blob features from the Scene Table. Typically a model determines what features a blob should have and it must be verified whether an actual blob has features that match the description. Since the S.A.M. hardware extracts area, perimeter, and number of holes, the procedure 'FEATURE.VERIFICATION' sequentially compares these features between a given model and all blobs in the Scene Table:

```
procedure     'FEATURE.VERIFICATION'
    begin         GET.MODEL.FEATURES
                  AREA.SEARCH.TOL
              do  AREA.LIST.NEXT
                  PERC.TOL.PERIMETER
                  PERIMETER.COMPARISON

              od
              do  PERIMETER.LIST.NEXT
                  HOLE.COMPARISON
    end       od
```

As can be seen from the listing, the procedure first gets the model features
and performs then AREA.SEARCH.TOL which delivers a list of blobs whose area
values are similar(within a given range) to the model area value (AREA.LIST).
In the next loop this list is checked for blobs whose perimeters are similar
to the model perimeter. As a result one obtains another list (PERIMETER.LIST)
whose elements are compared with a minimal and maximal number of holes of the
model. The result of the complete procedure is a list of all those ST line
numbers that contain blobs with verified features. It may be noted that before calling this procedure in a main program,procedure AREA.SORT must be
applied which organizes area by increasing values.

One application of this procedure can be found in a 'NEAREST-NEIGHBOR-
CLASSIFIER' program that delivers all blobs that correspond to a given set of
input classes. These classes have been learned by the system during a 'Teach-
In' phase that will be described later.

program   'NEAREST-NEIGHBOR-CLASSIFIER'

```
begin      GET.SCENE.TABLE
           AREA.SORT
           GET.INPUT.CLASSES

           do  GET.NEXT.CLASS
               GET.CLASS.FEATURES
               FEATURE.VERIFICATION
           od
           do  CLASS.LIST.NEXT
               ASCII.CLASS.NUMBER
           od

end
```

In the first step the Scene Table is constructed and the areas are sorted. Then
a list of classes that must be found is obtained from a data memory. The procedures GET.NEXT.CLASS and GET.CLASS.FEATURES pass on model features to the
FEATURE.VERIFICATION procedure which delivers a CLASS.LIST for each input class.
Each such CLASS.LIST contains matching blobs. In the final step all recognized
blobs are displayed on a TV monitor together with their class number (ASCII.

CLASS.NUMBER).

Previous to a discussion of the second recognition program 'POLAR.CHECK' we must briefly explain a data structure that is very similar to the AREA.KEY. TABLE/AREA.LIST structure. This structure is called MODEL. ACCESS. STRUCTURE and it is shown in Figure 3.2.-3. Its purpose is fast access to models that contain several blobs as elements.

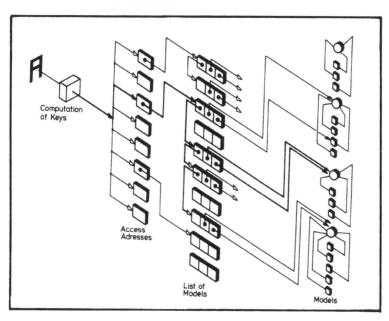

Figure 3.2.-3: The Model.Access.Structure

As in the AREA.KEY.TABLE the MODEL.ACCESS.STRUCTURE is accessed by hash coding of area values - in this case we have chosen a linear coding (division by a constant). The MODEL.LIST differs from the AREA.LIST in the fact that it contains two pointers instead of one. While AREA.LIST pointers refer to ST line numbers, the MODEL.LIST pointers reference a model space. The first pointer refers to the model head, the second points to the corresponding blob directly. The corresponding procedures to AREA.SORT and AREA.SEARCH are the procedures: MODEL.SORT and MODEL.ACCESS. The first procedure generates the MODEL.ACCESS. STRUCTURE, the second procedure delivers a list of model and blob addresses for a given area value. In other words, if one has found a blob in the image with a particular area value, MODEL.ACCESS tells in what models -- and where in the models -- such a blob appears. This information is stored in a queue such that candidates can be worked off sequentially.

The recognition program 'POLAR.CHECK' is based on the assumption that a binary image of a workpiece may well consist of more than one blob. Among those, <u>one</u> blob is said to be the dominant blob (DOM); if there is only one blob it is automatically DOM. In the case of several blobs one should be selected as DOM (in the Teach-In-phase) that is easy to distinguish from the other blobs. All other blobs are called 'satellites' (SATs). The orientation of DOM in the image plane is obtained with the aid of the 'polar.check' which also verifies the features of DOM. This polar.check is an algorithm that scans several circles around the centroid of DOM, determines the intersections of the circles with the contour , and connects these intersections with the centroid. Thus, one obtains a sequence of angles that can be used for recognition and computation of rotational orientation as well (cf. Fig. 3.2.-4).

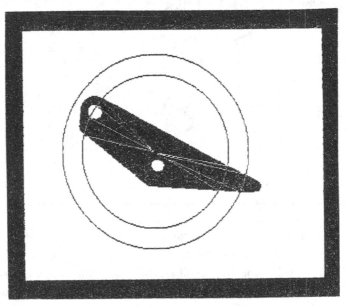

<u>Fig. 3.2.-4</u>: 'Polar.Check' For Workpiece Recognition And
Computation Of Rotational Orientation

```
program    'POLAR.CHECK'
  begin      GET.SCENE.TABLE
             SKETCH.SORT
             AREA.SORT

        do   NEXT.AREA
             MODEL.ACCESS

            do   QUEUE.NEXT
                 FEATURE.VERIFICATION

                do   RESULT.LIST.NEXT
                     FILTER.DOM

                    do   NEXT.CIRCLE
                         ANGLE.SEQUENCE
                         CORRELATION

                    od
                     GET.ROT.ANGLE

                    do   NEXT.SAT
                         PNT.PNT.DIST.DIR
                         SKETCH.SEARCH.9
                         FEATURE.VERIFICATION

                    od
          •      od
            od
        od
  end
```

As can be seen from the listing, the program first generates the Scene Table
and organizes its data through SKETCH.SORT and AREA.SORT. In the main loop,
blobs are selected one by one whose area values indicate that they might be
a DOM. During the Teach-In phase the range of area values of DOMs (amin/amax)
is determined. The procedure NEXT.AREA fetches one area value from the AREA.
LIST and passes it on to MODEL.ACCESS which generates a queue of model and
blob addresses for that area value. QUEUE.NEXT pops one pair of addresses from

that queue and the model features are compared with the features of the actual
blob by the procedure FEATURE.VERIFICATION: In case of a match the corresponding blob is entered into the result list as a hypothetical DOM. Before
scanning circles around that DOM it is necessary to separate it from neighbouring blobs. Otherwise the circles would intersect not only the DOM contour
but also conours of surrounding blobs (see for instance Fig. 3.2-5A where the
triangle shaped DOM in the center has two satellites close by). Therefore the
image is transferred from Image Memory 1 to Image Memory 2 in the filtering
mode where the labels of the DOM are flagged. As a result one obtains an image
that only contains the DOM(Fig. 3.2-5B). Now a circle is drawn around the
centroid of the DOM and the intersections of circle and contour are determined.
The result is a sequence of angles. In the CORRELATION procedure this sequence
is rotated against a stored sequence of the model until both sequences match.
If they do not match that blob is rejected as DOM and the next blob is tested.
In case of a match the correlation delivers the rotational angle in the image
plane. After repetition of the polar.check with other circles the average
rotational angle is computed as final result (GET.ROT.ANGLE).

In many cases it is possible to recognize a workpiece with the aid of just one
blob; yet in many cases it is feasible to continue with the analysis in the
following way. Since location and orientation of the DOM are now known it is
easy to predict where the satellites ought to be provided that the model
contains distance and direction data from DOM to the SATs. This is indeed
given: the model contains for each satellite an entry for: the distance (DIST)
from DOM-centroid to SAT-centroid, the direction (DIR) of that connection line
(in terms of a counter-clock-wise angle that refers to an initial DOM
orientation), and the features of the corresponding blob.

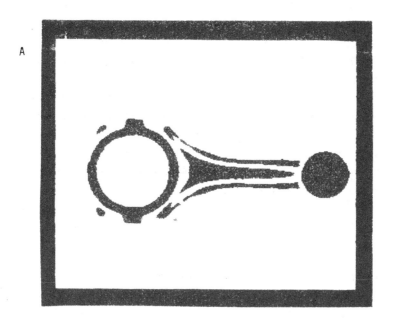

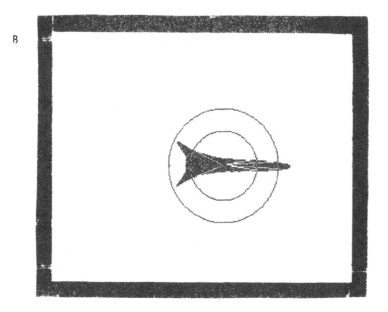

Fig. 3.2.-5: 'Polar.Check' After Filtering the Dominant Blob

By adding the computed rotational angle of DOM to the initial orientation one computes the actual direction where the satellite must be located. The procedure PNT.PNT.DIST.DIR computes that location and SKETCH.SEARCH.9 delivers a list of candidates for that SAT. The procedure FEATURE.VERIFICATION selects that blob that matches best. The search for satellites is repeated until all SATs are found. For a model that contains several SATs see the section on 'operator oriented software' (Fig. 3.2.-8). With the aid of such model it is easy to distinguish between workpieces whose dominant blobs are very similar but whose satellites look different. This is often the case when stable positions of workpieces occur for similar yaw/pitch/roll coordinates of the workpiece (i.e. by slightly turning the workpiece from one stable position into another one). In such cases the binary images resemble each other strongly except for one or two blobs that can be found with the aid of these models.

The idea to store relational information in the models can be taken one step further by eliminating the polar.check and relying completely on relations for the image analysis. Before we explain the recognition programm a few remarks about model driven search are in order. A relational model actually consists of two separate structures: 1) the relational structure that determines which blobs are connected, and 2) a control structure that determines the order in which these blobs are searched for. In order to avoid explosion of our search space not all blobs are treated in the same way. Rather, one blob serves as "access region" (ACR) of a model, i.e. this blob must be found first before the model driven search can start. In this way the ACR plays a similar role as DOM in the polar.check. In order to establish a local orientation a second blob is needed that is also treated differently than the other satellites: SAT1. The connection of the centroids of ACR and SAT1 defines the orientation in the image plane. All other blobs are attached to the ACR in the same way as in the polar.check. Instead of using blobs, holes may also be used as model elements by simply inverting the polarity of the binary image. Fig. 3.2.-6 shows examples for relational models with blobs and holes (mixed models with blobs and holes are also possible if the image is stored and then read from the Image Memory by inverting it).

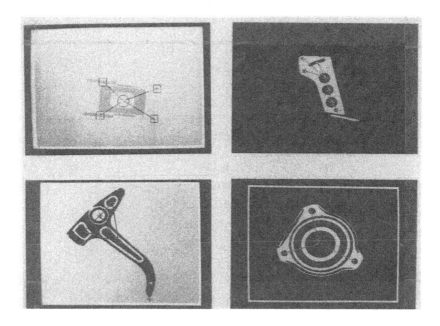

Fig. 3.2.-6: Relational Models Based On Blobs (Left Row)
Or Holes (Right Row)

The star-like models that we are using right now are rather simple
structures but have proven useful in many cases. The investigation
of other structures is the topic of on going research.

Let us now give the program in its present version.

```
program    'MODEL.SEARCH'

  begin    GET.SCENE.TABLE
           SKETCH.SORT
           AREA.SORT
           CHECK.TOTAL.AREA

      do   NEXT.MODEL
           GET.MODEL.FEATURES
           FEATURE.VERIFICATION

          do    RESULT.LIST.NEXT
                SKETCH.SEARCH.T
                FEATURE.VERIFICATION
                CHECK.DIST.ACR.SAT1
                DIR.ACR.SAT1

          od

          do    RESULT.LIST.NEXT

              do    NEXT.SAT
                    PNT.PNT.DIST.DIR
                    SKETCH.SEARCH.9
                    FEATURE.VERIFICATION
                    CHECK.DIST.ACR.SAT
                    CHECK.DIR.ACR.SAT

              od
          od
      od
           GET.GRIP.POINT.DATA
           PNT.PNT.DIST.DIR

    end
```

As in other programs, the data of the Scene Table are organized previous to
the analysis. Before the analysis starts, the total area of the image is checked.
If it is too small then another image is read in. Otherwise the analysis starts
with the search for an ACR. The features of the next model are passed on to
FEATURE.VERIFICATION which delivers a result list that contains likely ACRs and

their corresponding models.

For each such ACR a search is started in a search window whose size is determined by the distance of SAT1 of that model. This is done by SKETCH.SEARCH.T. Blobs
within that window are tested by FEATURE.VERIFICATION for matching features.
In order to be sure that one has really found SAT1 the distance between ACR
and SAT1 is verified. Finally the direction between ACR and SAT1 is computed
(defined as the counter-clock-wise angle of the connection line and a horizontal line through the ACR centroid). The following search for the other
satellites is performed as in the polar.check program. Since in 'MODEL.SEARCH'
the analysis depends mostly on the spatial relations between the blobs, the
exact distances and directions are compared with the model data after the
satellite has been found. This is especially necessary if more than one SAT
was found in the search window.

There remains a final step (that is also incorporated in the polar.check
program): the location of the workpiece is defined by the centroid coordinates
of either DOM or ACR. Yet, most often this is not a point where the gripper
of a robot could grasp the object. It is therefore necessary to define a
"gripping point" and relate it to the workpiece location. This is easily done:
In the model are stored distance and direction of the gripping point from the
DOM/ACR location and orientation. The procedure PNT.PNT.DIST.DIR computes
with these data the location of the gripping point which is the final result.

OPERATOR ORIENTED SOFTWARE

The third layer of S.A.M. software is operator oriented and supports the untrained operator during in-site programming. Such programming is necessary to
adapt the recognition programs to new workpieces or new inspection tasks. All
these software modules are dialogue oriented. Typically, the operator uses a
keyboard and a crosshair for programming. With the keyboard he inputs single
characters that were proposed to him by a menu on a TV monitor. If the operator
needs to input information about the image he simply 'points' with the aid of
the crosshair.

All recognition programs rely on data that had to be programmed into the
system during an instruction phase. It is the purpose of this software layer
to support this instruction phase. In the following, we will explain the
instruction programs for the three recognition programs that were described in

the last section. Basically, they all work in the same way. A workpiece is put in front of the camera and the operator points to certain blobs in the binary image while keying in some information about the meaning of those blobs. Since instruction is performed through 'teaching by showing' we call this type of instruction the 'Teach-In' phase.

Before describing these Teach-In programs it may be noted that S.A.M. can also be used as an interactive system for image analysis -- much like commercial systems that are for instance available for microscope image analysis. Interactive image analysis is important for the application-programmer in order to establish parameters for workpiece models, threshold values, etc.. We have therefore implemented a simple interactive mode that allows to read data that the system computes either by hardware or from the Scene Table. It is obvious that this program can be easily extended to more complex tasks.

```
program    'INTERACTIVE'

    begin    GET.SCENE.TABLE
             GET.CHAR

        if    CHAR

            case    'XHAIR'      then
                                 XHAIR.LOCATION
                                 DISPLAY.XHAIR.COORDINATES

            case    'BLOB'       then
                                 XHAIR.SELECT
                                 DISPLAY.ST.LINE

            case    'RELATION'   then
                                 XHAIR.SELECT.1
                                 XHAIR.SELECT.2
                                 DIST.P1.P2
                                 DIR.P1.P2
                                 DISPLAY.ST.LINE.1
                                 DISPLAY.ST.LINE.2
                                 DISPLAY.DIST.DIR

        fi
    end
```

We have not included in the listing the display of the menu which proposes:

X = CROSSHAIR   B = BLOB   R = RELATION.

Selection of the crosshair allows to read its coordinates from any point in the image. This kind of information may be necessary to design new algorithms. In the 'BLOB' case one marks a blob with the crosshair; the system then displays the corresponding Scene Table line with the extracted features. For the construction of relational models it is important to know distances and directions as well. For this purposes one may select 'RELATION'. Here, the user marks two points or blobs with the crosshair and the system computes distance and direction (from the first point to the second) between the marked points/ blobs. These data are displayed together with the features of the two blobs.

The Teach-In program for the NEAREST.NEIGHBOUR.CLASSIFIER is very simple since we had assumed that each class consists only of one blob. Thus, during Teach-In one must just indicate a particular blob with the crosshair. The corresponding features from the Scene Table are then put into the class list. This way one specifies blob after blob until finished. The input of 'Q' for 'quit' terminates the program. Fig. 3.2.-7 shows an example of the performance of this program.

```
program    'NEAREST-NEIGHBOUR-TEACH-IN'

    begin    GET.SCENE.TABLE

        do    GET.CHAR

            if  CHAR  =  'Q'   then exit fi

            XHAIR.SELECT
            PUT.FEATURES

        od

    end
```

The Teach-In programs for the polar.check and the model search are very much alike. Two particular procedures that are needed in both programs are PUT.SAT and PUT.GRIP.POINT. With PUT.SAT one attaches satellites to either the DOM or the ACR. This is done by pointing to a blob with the crosshair. The system computes the distance and direction and puts these as well as the blob features into the model.

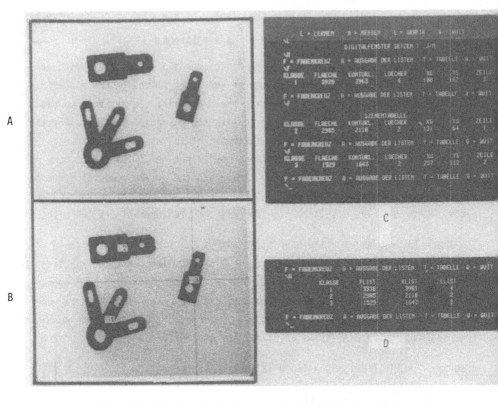

Fig. 3.2.-7: Teach-In Programming With The Crosshair
              A -- Binary Image   B -- Pointing With Crosshair
              C -- Dialogue   D - Class List

procedure   'PUT.SAT'

    begin   do   GET.CHAR

                   if CHAR = 'Q' then exit fi

                   XHAIR.SELECT.SAT.
                   DIST.P1.SAT
                   DIR.P1.SAT
                   PUT.DIST.DIR
                   PUT.SAT.FEATURES

             od

    end

As was already pointed out, the gripping point must not always coincide with the centroid of DOM/ACR. The location of a good gripping point is easily marked with the crosshair. Again, distance and direction to DOM/ACR are computed and put into the model.

procedure   'PUT.GRIP.POINT'

```
begin       XHAIR.SELECT.GRIP.POINT
            DIST.P1.GRIP.POINT
            DIR.P1.GRIP.POINT
            PUT.DIST.DIR

end
```

With these procedures it is easy to understand the two following Teach-In programs. In POLAR.CHECK.TEACH.IN one first selects a DOM whose features are automatically entered into the model. The system then filters DOM from Image Memory1 to Image Memory2. There the user specifies up to four radii. The system scans the corresponding circles, determines the angle sequences, and puts them into the model. Finally, satellites and the gripping point are entered into the model. Fig. 3.2.-8 shows an example.

program   'POLAR.CHECK.TEACH.IN'

```
begin       GET.SCENE.TABLE
            XHAIR.SELECT.DOM
            PUT.DOM.FEATURES
            FILTER.DOM
            PUT.RADII
            CIRCLES
            PUT.ANGLE.SEQUENCES
            PUT.SATS
            PUT.GRIP.POINT

end
```

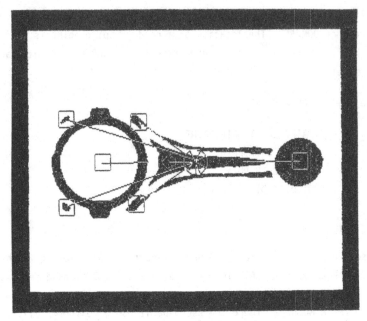

Fig. 3.2.-8: Model For Polar.Check With Satellites

      (DOM is represented by a circle; the SATs by squares;
      the polar.check of the DOM is demonstrated in Fig. 3.2.-5;
      the gripping point coincides with the DOM centroid)

In the MODEL.TEACH.IN the operator marks first the access region ACR and then
SAT1 which determines the local orientation. In both cases the system automatically enters the corresponding blob features into the model (together with
distance and direction data). Then the remaining satellites and the gripping
point are entered into the model. Examples for models are shown in Fig. 3.2.-9.

program   'MODEL.TEACH.IN'

```
begin      GET.SCENE.TABLE
           XHAIR.SELECT.ACR
           PUT.ACR.FEATURES

           XHAIR.SELECT.SAT 1
           DIST.ACR.SAT 1
           DIR.ACR.SAT 1
           PUT.DIST.DIR
           PUT.SAT 1.FEATURES

           PUT.SATS
           PUT.GRIP.POINT
end
```

This concludes our description of S.A.M. software. The given programs should be viewed as examples only, since details may vary from application to application. Especially, many details depend on the type of configuration which is used. We will therefore explain the most important types of S.A.M. configurations in the following section.

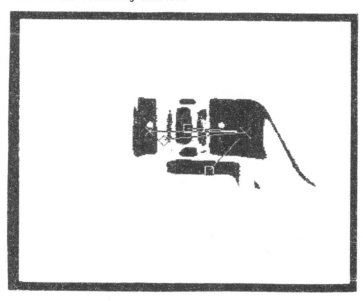

Fig. 3.2.-9: Relational Models
(the diamond represents the gripping point)

3.3 S.A.M. CONFIGURATIONS

S.A.M. hardware was designed such that it can be composed into various
configurations that are adapted to the task at hand. It is obvious that all
kinds of configurations are possible; here, we want to outline the basic types
of configurations. Let us recall that S.A.M. hardware consists of three
different groups of modules:

- video circuits
- image memories (IMs),image processing and
  image analysis processors (IAPs)
- data processors (DPs) and storage.

Video circuits must always be applied; it is possible to synchronize the camera
from S.A.M. or vice versa. Furthermore images from two cameras can be read in
simultaneously into two Image Memories. Other than that, and the choice of an
appropriate threshold for binarization,there are not many possibilities to
modify the front end of S.A.M. configurations. Configurability is mostly given
in the second group of S.A.M. hardware modules, i.e. in the image memories,
image processing, and image analysis processors. The most typical configurations
are:

● The 'Software Configuration' consists of Image Memories and Data Processing
  modules. In this configuration everything is done by software. This is
  certainly the slowest configuration but it is feasible to use it whenever
  long cycle times are .given.

● The 'Image Processing Configuration' consists of two Image Memories, the
  Image Window Processor (IWP), and Data Processing modules. The purpose of
  such a configuration is to process images by operations such as shrink,
  blow, and combinations thereof. Since this configuration includes the
  Software Configuration it is also possible to perform an image analysis
  after processing is finished. During image processing, this configuration
  will typically perform in the ping-pong-processing mode where an image is
  transferred hence and forth between the two IMs. At each transfer one
  transformation is performed. Typical operator sequences are: shrink/shrink/
  shrink/blow/blow; contourline/blow/blow; blow/blow/shrink. Since each
  transformation requires only 20 ms, sequences with up to 5 operations can
  still be executed in about 100 ms.

145

- The 'Real-Time Configuration' consists of Image Analysis Processors (IAPs) and Data Processing Units. This type of configuration performs image analysis in real-time, i.e. during the TV scan. After the image scan data are collected into the Scene Table.The duration of the generation of the Scene Table depends on the complexity of the scene: the more blobs in the image and the more branches in each blob, the longer the time to generate the Scene Table. Time measurements for typical scenes containing several (4-5) workpieces whose silhouettes decompose into several blobs show that the Scene Table can be generated within 40-80 ms; there are of course scenes where it may take several 100 ms to construct the Scene Table. Yet, in general the data are organized for further analysis after about 100 ms.

- Combined Configurations consist of mixtures of all other configurations and are likely to be the most important configurations since they are the ones that are really adapted to particular tasks.

Figure 3.3.-1 shows an example for a configuration that might be called the 'maximal' configuration since it provides all operating modes that S.A.M. is now capable of. In particular, this configuration can perform:

- ping pong processing
- real time data extraction
- filtering.

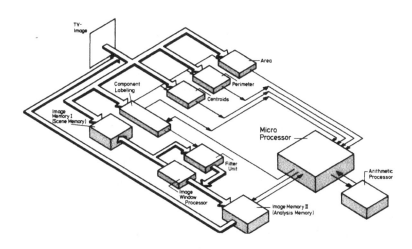

Fig. 3.3.-1: Data Flow In A 'Maximal' Configuration

Let us follow the flow of data in such a configuration. First the image is read
into Image Memory 1. From there it is transferred hence and forth between IM1
and IM2 while the IWP applies some operator to the image (ping pong processing).
After N such operations the image is then routed to data extraction. This is
done by outputting the image from the actual IM onto the bus. All IAPs extract
data from that preprocessed image. These data are then collected by the micro-
processor (with the aid of the arithmetic processor). From the Scene Table are
then selected blobs that are of particular interest. The labels of these blobs
are then flagged in the Component Labeling Module (CLM). After flagging, the
image is once again transferred from one IM to the other one (the system takes
care that this transfer always takes place from IM1 to IM2). During this
transfer the CLM is in its filtering mode where all unflagged labels (and their
corresponding blobs) are suppressed from the image. As a result one obtains a
new image that only contains those blobs that were selected previously. Fig.3.3.-2
shows an example for this filtering. In such a filtered image further analysis
either by hardware or software can be performed much easier than in the
original image.

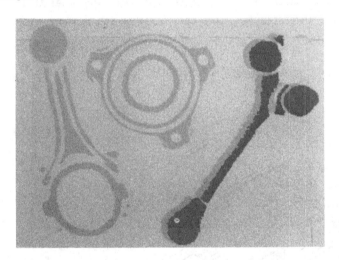

Fig. 3.3.-2: Filtering Of Blobs From Image Memory 1 To Image Memory 2
(gray blobs are in IM1, black blobs are in IM2)

It is possible to perform the analysis of rather complex scenes with such a
configuration in less than 500 ms. There are other configurations; yet, these
examples should suffice to show the processing power of the S.A.M. hardware
and software.

3.4 THE GRIPPING OF PARTS FROM A RUNNING CONVEYOR BELT

The gripping of parts from a conveyor belt has found wide-spread interest. Early solutions suffered from the fact that the belt had to be stopped for image acquisition and analysis as well as for part gripping.

We have chosen this task as a first application of a S.A.M. configuration because here a complex analysis must be performed in a very short time. With a visual field of 30 cm length and a belt running at 30 cm/s, it is necessary to perform the image analysis in less than 500 ms so that parts can be 'seen' at least once when passing through the visual field.

In order to avoid motion blur at this high belt speed, very short image acquisition times are necessary. These can be reached with the use of a flash-light. We have designed an infra-red flashlight which has the following advantages:

1) the light frequencies are adapted to the spectral sensitivity
    of a silicon TV camera;

2) the reflected light can be filtered out in a narrow band,
    thus effects of the surrounding light are eliminated;

3) the light is invisible to the human eye so that the permanent
    flashing does not disturb workers at nearby workplaces.

Fig. 3.4-1 and 2 show the experimental set-up that we are using:

- conveyor belt with path measurement
- flashlight
- camera and S.A.M. configuration (with robot interface)
- robot computer and robot
- pallet.

Details about the robot and its control can be found in /STEUSLOFF '80/. The movements of the conveyor belt are constantly monitored both by the S.A.M. configuration and the robot computer with the aid of a   path measurement. Sensor and robot computer are coupled via the robot interface (cf. section 3.1). The task that has to be solved is to grasp parts from the running belt and put them onto a pallet. Workpieces can be positioned on the belt at random but should not overlap.

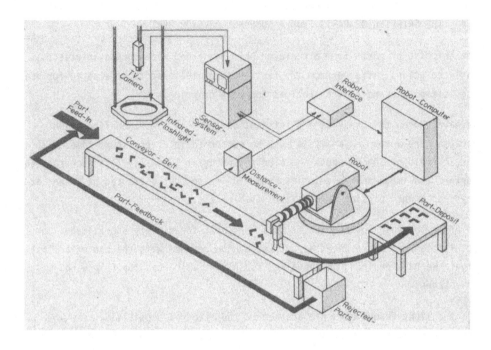

Fig. 3.4.-1: Experimental Set-Up (Diagram)

Fig. 3.4.-2:
Experimental Set-Up
(Photography)

Fig. 3.4.-3 shows a typical scene that the S.A.M. configuration can analyze completely within less than 300 ms. It should be noted here that industrial robots that are available today are not able to grasp fast enough to cope with such high speeds and the multitude of workpieces; for this reason, during the actual handling experiments, there were fewer parts on the belt (as in Fig. 3.4.-3) and the belt was running at a lower speed (12 cm/s). Instead of a robot one could also use a computer controlled gate for part sorting.

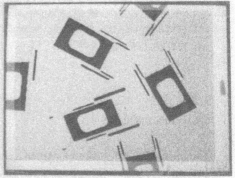

Fig. 3.4.-3: Workpieces On Conveyor Belt
A -- Gray-Level Image   B -- Binary Image

In the handling experiments, the sensor ignites in the beginning flashes contineously and analyzes the image for the appearance of blobs. When the first part enters the image the sensor starts recognition. This will only succeed when all blobs of a workpiece are in the image. Typically it takes 1 - 2 images before this happens. At the time of the flash, i.e. the time of image acquisition, an interrupt signal is transmitted to the robot computer which then starts to integrate the path that the belt covers. After the image analysis, the S.A.M. configuration transmits to the robot interface the positional classes of all workpieces in the image together with their locations (of the gripping point) and their rotational angles. Before transmission, these data are converted from pixel coordinates to metric dimensions (mm).

One problem arises from the fact that the same workpiece may appear in the next image again (somewhat further down in the visual field). If care is not taken then the sensor would compute and transmit the data of that workpiece again, and the robot would try to grasp that part a second time. We therefore need a 'belt description' which contains not only information about workpiece location but which also indicates whether a workpiece has already been 'seen' and transmitted or not. For this reason the S.A.M. configuration integrates the belt path between consecutive images. While reading in a new image the Y-coordinates of the belt description are updated by the belt path. By comparison between the belt description and the coordinates of recognized blobs in the new image one can determine which of the blobs were already transmitted to the robot. Thus, information about each workpiece on the belt is transmitted to the robot computer only once. It may be noted that these data have to be transformed into the coordinate system of the robot. This is done in the robot computer which also determines the path of the robot and performs path control. For details see /STEUSLOFF '80/.

3.5   CONCLUSION

A prototype S.A.M. configuration ('maximal' version) has been up and running now for two years and we have built six more systems in the mean-time. All configurations have proved to be well suited for the required applications. There are two features that we wish to incorporate into the system in the near future: better thresholding techniques (such as an adaptive threshold) and one more Image Analysis Processor: the computation of moments of inertia.

It has often been argued that binary images are too simple to allow an efficient analysis of complex objects. We do not share this belief. As long as binary images can be produced in a reproducible way they suffice for most practical applications (even though these images don't resemble the images that the human observer sees). The reproducibility can be supported by good illumination engineering. Due to model based analysis techniques it doesn't matter that the silhouette of a workpiece decomposes into several blobs, quite the contrary: relations between those blobs provide enough information about the type of workpiece as well as its orientation. Since in most cases these models can be constructed such that they contain only a minimal number of elements, problems with the explosion of the search space can be avoided.

Our future work will be oriented towards two goals: firstly, we want to implement more (and more complex) operators in the Image Window Processor;

secondly, we want to extend the structures of the relational models and investigate methods of automatic model generation.

Let us briefly summarize the basic philosophy that has guided us in the design of the system:

1. Whenever possible, mass data must be reduced as much as possible; most often this is done by dedicated hardware which is the core of our system.

2. Complex computations must be avoided and replaced by table look-ups; since such tables tend to be memory consuming we have facilitated such look-ups by providing an extremely wide address space.

3. Data must always be organized such that they can be easily accessed; this is done by sorting of data as well as providing access structures.

These guidelines have led to a system that shows how the analysis of complex binary images can be performed in real-time with reasonable efforts in software and hardware. Due to the modular concept of S.A.M. specific configurations can easily be built that provide economic solutions for practical tasks.

3.6   ACKNOWLEDGEMENT

S.A.M. has been developed by E. Enderle, C. Eisenbarth (IBAT-AOP, Essen), J.P. Foith, H. Geisselmann, H. Ringshauser,and G. Zimmermann.

The development was supported by the German Minister of Research and Technology (BMFT), the German National Science Foundation (DFG),and several companies. Responsibility for the content of the work is completely with the autors.

4. Literature

/1/   Abbraham, R.G.   "State-Of-The-Art in Adaptable-Programmable
       Stewart, R.J.S.   Assembly Systems".
       Shum, L.Y.   International Fluidics Services Ltd. (Publ.),
                                  Kempston, Bedford, UK, 1977.

/2/   Agin, G.J.   "An Experimental Vision System for Industrial
                                  Applications".
                                  Stanford Res. Lab., Tech. Note 103, Menlo Park,
                                  CA, USA, June 1975.

/3/   Agin, G.J.   "SRI Vision Research for Advanced Industrial
       Duda, R.O.   Automation".
                                  Proc. USA-Japan Computer Conference, Tokyo,
                                  August 1975.

/4/   Agin, G.J.   "An Experimental Vision System for Industrial
                                  Application".
                                  Proc. 5th Int. Symp. on Industrial Robots,
                                  Chicago, Ill., September 1975.

/5/   Agin, G.J.   "Vision Systems for Inspection and for Mani-
       (A)   pulator Control".
                                  Proc. of the 1977 Joint Automatic Control
                                Conference,
                                pp. 132-138

/6/   Agin, G.J.   "Servoing With Visual Feedback".
       (B)   Proc. 7th Int. Symp. on Industrial Robots,
                                Tokyo, October 1977, pp. 551-560.

/7/   Agin, G.   "Real Time Control of a Robot with a Mobile
                                  Camera".
                                  Proc. 9th Int. Symp. on Industrial Robots,
                                  Washington D.C., March 1979
                                pp. 233-246

/8/   Agrawala, A.K.   "A Sequential Approach to the Extraction of Shape
       Kulkarni, A.V.   Features".
                                  Computer Graphics and Image Processing $\underline{6}$ (1977),
                                pp. 538 - 557

/9/   Albrecht, M.   "Teileprüfung im Automobilbau mittels Fernseh-
       Hille, G.   kamera und Prozessrechner".
       Karow, P.   Proc. INTERKAMA 1977, Syrbe, M. & Will, B. (Eds.),
       Schöne, H.   Fachberichte Messen-Steuern-Regeln 1,
       Weber, J.   Springer-Verlag 1977, pp. 107-117.

/10/ Allen, G.R.   "SPARC - Symbolic Processing Algorithm Research
      Juetten, P.G.   Computer".
                        Proc. 'Image Understanding Workshop' Nov. 78,
                        pp. 182 - 190.

/11/ Armbruster, K.   "A Very Fast Vision System for Recognizing Parts
      Martini, P.   and their Location and Orientation".
      Nehr, G.   Proc. 9th Int. Symp. on Industrial Robots,
      Rembold, U.   Washington D.C., March 1979, pp. 265-280.
      Olzmann, W.

/12/ Ashkar, G.P.   "The Contour Extraction Problem with Biomedical
      Modestino, J.W.   Applications".
                        Computer Graphics & Image Processing
                        7 (1978), pp. 331 - 355.

/13/ Batchelor, B.G.   "A Preliminary Note on the Automatic Inspection
      (A)   of Male Screw Threads".
                        Proc. 3rd Int. Conf. on Automated Inspection and
                        Product Control, Nottingham, UK, April 1978,
                        pp. 139-176.

/14/ Batchelor, B.G.   "SUSIE: A Prototyping System for Automatic Visual
      (B)   Inspection".
                        4th Int. Conf. on Automated Inspection and Pro-
                        duct, Chicago, Ill, November 1978, pp. 49-80.

/15/ Baird, M.   "An Application of Computer Vision to Automated
      (A)   IC Chip Manufacture".
                        Proc. 3rd Int. Joint Conf. on Pattern Recognition
                        Coronado, CA, November 1976, pp. 3-7.

/16/ Baird, M.L.   "Sequential Image Enhancement Technique for
      (B)   Locating Automotive Parts on Conveyor Belts".
                        Gerneral Motors Res. Lab. Publ. GMR-2293,
                        CS Dept., Warren, MI, USA, Nov. 1976.

/17/ Baird, M.L.   "Image Segmentation Technique for Locating
                        Automotive Parts on Belt Convevors".
                        Proc. Int. Joint Conf. on Artificial Intelligence,
                        Tokyo, Japan, Aug. 1977, pp. 694-695.

/18/ Baird, M.   "SIGHT-I: A Computer Vision System for Automated
                        IC Chip Manufacture".
                        IEEE Trans. Systems, Man & Cybernetics SMC-8
                        (1978) 2, pp. 133-139.

/19/ Barrow, H.G.
      Popplestone, R.J. "Relational Descriptions in Picture Processing".
                        in: B. Meltzer & Michie, D. (Eds.): 'Machine In-
                        telligence 6', University Press,Edinburgh, 1971
                        pp. 377-396.

/20/ Barrow, H.G.
Ambler, A.P.
Burstall, R.M.
"Some Techniques for Recognizing Structures in Pictures".
in: S. Watanabe (Ed.), 'Frontiers of Pattern Recognition', Academic Press, N.Y., 1971, pp. 1-32

/21/ Birk, J.
Kelley, R.B.
et.al.
"Orientation of Workpieces by Robots Using the Triangle Method".
SME Tech Paper MR 76-612
Univ. Rhode Island, EE Dept.
Kingston, RI, USA, 1976

/22/ Birk, J.
Kelley, R.
Chen, N.
(A)
"Visually Estimating Workpiece Pose in a Robot Hand Using the Feature Points Method".
Proc. IEEE Conf. on Decision & Control,
San Diego, CA, January 1979,
pp. A1-1 -- A1-6

/23/ Birk, J.
Kelley, R.
et al.
(B)
"General Methods to Enable Robots with Vision to Acquire, Orient, and Transport Workpieces".
5th report, EE Dept., Univ. of Rhode Island,
Kingston, RI, USA,
Aug. 1979

/24/ Birk, J.
Kelley, R.
et al.
"General Methods to Enable Robots with Vision to Acquire, Orient and Transport Workpieces".
6th report
EE Dept., Univ. of Rhode Island,Kingston, RI,
USA, Aug. 1980.

/25/ Bjorklund, C.M.
"Syntactic Analysis & Description of Stroke-Based Shapes".
Proc. IEEE Conf. Pattern Recognition and Image Processing, Troy, NY, USA, June 1977, pp. 198 - 202.

/26/ Bolles, R.C.
(A)
"Robust Feature Matching through Maximal Cliques".
SPIE Vol 182 'Imaging Applications for Automated Industrial Inspection & Assembly;Washington, D.C., USA, April 1979, pp. 140 - 149.

/27/ Bolles, R.C.
(B)
"Part Acquisition Using the SRI Vision Module".
Proc. 3rd IEEE Computer Software & Applications Conference COMPSAC-79, Chicago, Ill.,
November 79, pp. 872-877

/28/ Bretschi, J.
"A Microprocessor Controlled Visual Sensor for Industrial Robots".
The Industrial Robot $\underline{3}$ (1976) 4, pp. 167-172.

/29/ Brook, R.A.
Purll, D.J.
Jones, G.H.
Lewis, D.O.
"Practical Experience of Image Processing in On-Line Industrial Inspection Applications".
SPIE Proc. Vol. 130, Automation and Inspection Applications of Image Processing Techniques, London, Sept. 1977, pp. 84-97.

/30/ Burow, M.
Wahl, F.
"Eine verbesserte Version des Kantendetektionsverfahrens nach Mero/Vassy".
'Angewandte Szenenanalyse', J.P. Foith (Ed.), Informatik-Fachbericht 20, Springer-Verlag, Heidelberg, 1979, pp. 36-42.

/31/ Callen, J.E.
Anderson, P.N.
"Checking Labeled Bottles Electro-Optically".
Electro-Optical Systems Designs, July 1975, pp. 44-46.

/32/ Claridge, J.F.
Purll, D.J.
"Automatic Inspection & Gauging Using Solid-Sate Image Scanners".
3rd Int. Conf. on Automated Inspection and Product Control, Nottingham, UK, April 1978, pp. 31-41.

/33/ Colding, B.
Colwell, L.V.
Smith, D.N.
"Delphi Forecasts of Manufacturing Technology".
International Fluidics Services (Publ.) Kempston, Bedford, UK, 1979

/34/ Cronshaw, A.J.
Heginbotham, W.B.
Pugh, A.
"Software Techniques for an Optically Tooled Bowl Feeder".
3rd Int. Conf. on Trends in On-Line Computer Control Systems, Univ. of Sheffield, UK, March 1979, pp. 145-150.

/35/ Cronshaw, A.J.
Heginbotham, W.B.
Pugh, A.
"A Practical Vision System for use with Bowl Feeders".
Proc. ist Int. Conf. on Assembly Automation, Brighton, UK, March 1980, pp. 265-274.

/36/ Davis, L.S.
"A Survey of Edge Detection Techniques".
Computer Graphics and Image Processing 4 (1975) pp. 248 - 270.

/37/ De Coulon, D.
Kammenos, P.
"Polar Coding of Planar Objects in Industrial Robot Vision".
Neue Technik (NT) (1977) 10, pp. 663 - 671

/38/ Dessimoz, J.-D.
"Identification et Localisation Visuelle D'Objets Multiples Par Poursuite de Contour et Codage de Courbure".
Compte-Rendus Journées de Microtechnique, EPF-Lausanne, Suisse, Sept. 1978

/39/   Dessimoz, J.D.   "Recognition and Handling of Overlapping
        Kunt, M.   Industrial Parts".
        Zurcher, J.M.   Proc. 9th Int. Symp. on Industrial Robots,
        Granlund, G.H.   Washington D.C., USA, March 1979,
                        pp. 357 - 366.

/40/   Dodd, G.G.   "Computer Vision and Sensor-Based Robots".
        Rossol, L.   Plenum Press, New York, 1979

/41/   Duda, R.   "Pattern Classification & Scene Analysis"
        Hart, P.   John Wiley & Sons, N.Y. 1973

/42/   Duff, M.J.B.   "CLIP 4 - A large Scale Integrated Circuit
                        Array Parallel Processor."
                        Proc. Int. Joint Conf. Pattern Recognition,
                        Coronado, CA. USA, Nov. 1976, pp. 728-733

/43/   Ehrich, R.W.   "Detection of Global Edges in Textured Images".
                        IEEE. Trans. Comp. C-26 (1977) 6, pp.289-603

/44/   Ejiri, M.   "A Process for Detecting Defects in Complicated
        Uno, T.   Patterns".
        Mese, M.   Computer Graphics and Image Processing (1973)
        Ikeda, S.   2, pp. 326-339.

/45/   Enderle, E.   "Ein Baukastensystem für Bildsensoren zur Sicht-
                        prüfung und Prozeßsteuerung".
                        PDV-Bericht "INTERKAMA'80", W. Hofmann, (Ed.),
                        Kernforschungszentrum Karlsruhe, August 1980,
                        Kfk-PDV, pp. 358 - 365.

/46/   Eskenazi, R.   "Low Level Processing for Real-Time Image Analysis".
        Wilf, J.   Proc. IEEE Comp. Soc. 3rd Int. Comp.- Software &
                        Applications Conference (COMPSAC '79), Nov. 79,
                        Chicago, Ill, USA, pp. 340 - 343.

/47/   Eversole, W.L.   "Investigation of VLSI Technologies for Image Pro-
        Mayer, D.J.   cessing".
        Frazee, F.B.   Proc. 'Image Understanding Workshop',
        Cheek, Jr.J.F.   Palo Alto, CA, USA, April 1979, pp. 159 - 163.

/48/   Feng, H.F.   "Decomposition of Polygons into Simpler Components:
        Pavlidis, T.   Feature Generation for Syntactic Pattern Recog-
                        nition".
                        IEEE Trans. Comp. C-24 (1975) 6, pp. 636 - 650.

/49/ Flöscher, R.   "Sensorsystem zum automatischen Aussortieren
     Partmann, T.   fehlerhafter Kleinteile".
                           Mitteilungen aus dem Fraunhofer-Institut für
                           Informations- und Datenverarbeitung (IITB),
                           FhG-Berichte 2-80, Karlsruhe 1980,
                           pp. 23-25

/50/ Foith, J.P.   "Lage-Erkennung von beliebig orientierten Werk-
                           stücken aus der Form ihrer Silhouetten".
                           Proc. 8th Int. Symposium on Industrial Robots,
                           Böblingen, W.-Germany, May/June 1978, pp. 584-599.

/51/ Foith, J.P.   "A Modular System for Digital Imaging Sensors for
     Geisselmann, H.   Industrial Vision."
     Lübbert, U.   Proc. 3rd CISM-IFToMM Symposium in Theory and
     Ringshauser, H.   Practice of Robots and Manipulators, Udine, Italy,
                           Sept. 1978, Elsevier, Amsterdam, 1980,pp. 399-422

/52/ Foith, J.P.   "A TV-Sensor for Top-Lighting and Multiple Part
                           Analysis."
                           Proc. 2nd IFAC/IFIP Symposium on Information Control
                           Problems in Manufacturing Technology, Stuttgart,
                           Oct. 1979, U. REMBOLD (Ed.), Pergamon Press, Ox-
                           ford, 1979, pp. 229-234.

/53/ Foith, J.P.   "Optischer Sensor für Erkennung von Werkstücken auf
     Eisenbarth, C.   dem laufenden Band - realisiert mit einem modularen
     Enderle, E.   System."
     Geisselmann, H.   in: H. Steusloff (Ed.): "Wege zu sehr fortge-
     Ringshauser, H.   schrittenen Handhabungssystemen", Messen - Steuern -
     Zimmermann, G.   Regeln Band 4, Springer-Verlag, Berlin 1980,
                           pp. 135-155.

/54/ Frei, W.   "Fast Boundary Detection: A Generalization and
     Chen, Ch.-Ch.   A New Algorithm".
                           IEEE Trans. on Comp. C-26 (1977) 10, pp. 988-998

/55/ Fries, R.W.   "An Empirical Study of Selected Approaches to the
     Modestino, J.W.   Detection of Edges in Noisy Digitized Images".
                           Proc. IEEE Conf. on Patt. Rec. & Image Processing,
                           Troy,N.Y. USA, June 1977, pp. 225 - 230

/56/ Geisselmann, H.   "Griff in die Kiste durch Vereinzelung und
                           optische Erkennung."
                           in: H. Steusloff (Ed.): 'Wege zu sehr fortge-
                           schrittenen Handhabungssystemen',
                           Fachberichte Messen-Steuern-Regeln Band 4,
                           Springer-Verlag, Berlin 1980, pp. 156-165

/57/   Giralt, G.   "Object Identification and Sorting with an
        Ghallab, M.   Optimal Sequential Pattern Recognition Method".
        Stuck, F.   Proc. 9th Int. Symp. on Industrial Robots,
                             Washington, D.C., USA, March 1979,
                             pp. 379 - 389

/58/   Gleason, G.J.   "A Modular Vision System for Sensor-Controlled
        Agin, G.J.   Manipulation and Inspection."
                             Proc. 9th Int. Symp. on Industrial Robots
                             Washington D.C., March 1979,
                             pp. 57 - 70.

/59/   Goto, N.   "An Automatic Inspection System for Mask
        Kondo, T.   Patterns".
        Ichikawa, K.   Proc. 4th Int. Joint Conf. on Pattern
        Kanemoto, M.   Recognition, Kyoto, 1978
                             pp. 970-974

/60/   Haralick, R.M.   "Decomposition of Polygonal Shapes by
        Shapiro, L.G.   Clustering".
                             Proc. IEEE Conf. Pattern Recognition and
                             Image Processing '77,
                             Troy, N.Y., USA, June 1977,
                             pp. 183-190

/61/   Hasegawa, K.   "On Visual Signal Processing for Industrial
        Masuda, R.   Robot".
                             Proc. 7th Int. Symposium on Industrial Robots,
                             Tokyo, Japan, Oct. 1977,
                             pp. 543-550

/62/   Heginbotham, W.B.   "The Nottingham 'Sirch' Assembly Robot".
        et al.   Proc. 1st Conf. on Industrial Robots
                             Nottingham, UK; 1973
                             pp. 129 - 142

/63/   Hill, J.W.   "Programmable Part Presenter Based on Computer
        Sword, A.J.   Vision and Controlled Tumbling".
                             Proc. 10th Int. Symp. on Industrial Robots,
                             Milan, Italy, March 1980, pp. 129-140

/64/   Holland, S.W.   "A Programmable Computer Vision System Based on
                             Spatial Relationships".
                             General Motors Res. Lab. Publication GMR-2078
                             CS Dept., Warren, MI, USA, Feb. 1976

/65/ Holland, S.W.   "CONSIGHT-I: A Vision Controlled Robot System
     Rossol, L.   for Transferring Parts from Belt Conveyors".
     Ward, M.R.   in: 'Computer Vision and Sensor-Based Robots',
                        G.G. Dodd & L. Rossol (Eds), Plenum Press,
                        N.Y., 1979,
                        pp. 81 - 97

/66/ Hsieh, Y.Y.   "A Method for Automatic IC Chip Alignment
     Fu, K.S.   and Wire Bonding".
                        Proc. IEEE Conf. on Pattern Recognition and
                        Image Processing, Chicago Ill., August 1979,
                        pp. 101-108

/67/ Hueckel, M.H.   "An Operator which Locates Edges in Digitized
                        Pictures".
                        Journal of the ACM 18 (1971) 1, pp. 113-125.

/68/ Iannino, A.   "A Survey of the Hough Transform and its
     Shapiro, S.D.   Extensions for Curve Detection".
                        Proc. IEEE Conf. on Patt. Rec. & Image Pro-
                        cessing, Chicago, Ill, June 1978,
                        pp. 32-3C

/69/ Jarvis, J.F.   "A Method for Automating the Visual Inspection
     (A)   of Printed Wiring Boards".
                        IEEE Trans. Pami-2 (1980) 1, pp. 77-82.

/70/ Jarvis, J.F.   "Visual Inspection Automation"
     (B)   IEEE Computer May 1980, pp. 32-38

/71/ Kamin, G.   "Der Geometrie Computer".
                        rme 40 (1974) 3, pp. 105 - 109

/72/ Karg, R.   "A Flexible Opto-Electronic Sensor".
                        Proc. 8th Int. Symp. on Industrial Robots,
                        Stuttgart, W.-Germany, May/June 1978,
                        pp. 218-29

/73/ Karg, R.   "Experimental Results with a Versatile
     Lanz, O.E.   Optoelectronic Sensor in Industrial Appli-
                        cations".
                        Proc. 9th Int. Symp. on Industrial Robots
                        Washington D.C., March 1979,
                        pp. 247-264.

/74/ Kashioka, S.   "A Transistor Wire-Bonding System Utilizing
     Ejiri, M.   Multiple Local Pattern Matching Techniques."
     Sakamoto, Y.   IEEE Trans. on System, Man, and Cybernetics
                        SMC-6 (1976) 8, pp. 562-570

/75/ Kashioka, S. "An Approach to the Integrated Intelligent
Takeda, S. Robot with Multiple Sensory Feedback:
Shima, Y. Visual Recognition Techniques".
Uno, T. Proc. of 7th Int. Symp. on Industrial Robots,
Hamada, T. Tokyo, October 1977, pp. 531-538

/76/ Kelley, R.B. "Algorithms to Visually Acquire Workpieces".
Birk, J. Proc. 7th Int. Symp. on Industrial Robots,
Wilson, L Tokyo, Japan, Oct. 1977,
pp. 497-506

/77/ Kelley, R.B. "A Robot System which Feeds Workpieces
Birk, J. Directly from Bins into Machines".
Martins, H. Proc. 9th Int. Symp. on Industrial Robots,
Tella, R. Washington D.C., March 1979, pp. 339-355

/78/ Korn, A. "Segmentierung und Erkennung eines Objektes
in natürlicher Umgebung".
in: E. Triendl. (ED.): 'Bildverarbeitung und
Mustererkennung',DAGM-Symposium Oct. 78,
Informatik-Fachberichte Band 17,
Springer Verlag, Berlin, 1978,
pp. 265-274

/79/ Kruse, B. "A Parallel Picture Processing Machine".
IEEE Trans. Comp. C-22 (1973) 12,
pp. 1075 - 1087

/80/ Levialdi, S. "Finding the Edge".
Proc. NATO Advanced Study Institute on Digital
Image Processing and Analysis, June 23 - July 4,
1980, Bonas, France, publ. by INRIA, Le Chesnay,
pp. 167-208

/81/ Löffler, H. "Meßverfahren der Bildanalyse zur Fertigungs-
Jäger, J. kontrolle feinmechanischer Präzisionsteile
oder elektronischer Bauelemente".
messen + prüfen/automatik, Oct. 79,
pp. 755 - 758

/82/ Martelli, A. "Edge Detection Using Heuristic Search Methods".
Computer Graphics & Image Processing 1 (1972)
pp. 169-182.

/83/ Martini, P. "Recognition of Angular Orientation of Objects
Nehr, G. with the Help of Optical Sensors".
The Industrial Robot (1979) June, pp. 62-69.

/84/ McGhie, D.   "Vision Controlled Subassembly Station".
     Hill, J.W.   Society of Manufacturing Engineers (SME)
                         Paper No. MS78-685, 1978

/85/ McKee, J.W.   "Computer Recognition of Partial Views of
     Aggarwal, J.K.   Curved Objects".
                         IEEE Trans. Comp. C-26 (19-7) 8,
                         pp. 790-800

/86/ Mero, L.   "A Simplified and Fast Version of the Hueckel
     Vassy, Z.   Operator for Finding Optimal Edges in Pictures".
                         Proc. IJCAI '75, Tbilisi, USSR, 1975

/87/ Milgram, D.L.   "Region Extraction Using Convergent Evidence".
     (A)   L.S. Baumann (Ed.), Proc. 'Image Understanding
                         Workshop', Science Applications, Inc.
                         Arlington, VA, April 1977, pp. 58 - 64

/88/ Milgram, D.L.   "Progress Report on Segmentation Using Convergent
     (B)   Evidence".
                         L.S. Baumann (Ed.), Proc. 'Image Understanding
                         Workshop', Science Applications, Inc., Arlington
                         VA, Oct. 1977, pp. 104-108

/89/ Milgram, D.   "Clustering Edge Values for Threshold Selection".
     Herman, M.   Computer Graphics and Image Processing 10 (1979),
                         pp. 272-280

/90/ Montanari, U.   "On the Optimal Detection of Curves in Noisy
                         Pictures".
                         Communications of the ACM 14 (1971),
                         pp. 335-345.

/91/ Mori, K.   "Design of Local Parallel Pattern Processor for
     Kidode, M.   Image Processing".
     Shinoda, H.   Proc. AFIPS, Vol 47, June 1978, pp. 1025-1031.
     et al.

/92/ Mundy, J.L.   "Automatic Visual Inspection Using Syntactic
     Joynson, R.E.   Analysis".
                         Proc. IEEE Conf. on Pattern Recognition and
                         Image Processing, Troy, N.Y., June 1977,
                         pp. 144-147.

/93/ Nakagawa, Y.   "Some Experiments on Variable Thresholding".
     Rosenfeld, A.   CS Report TR 626, Univ. of Maryland, College
                         Park, MD, January 1978

/94/ Nakagawa, Y.
Rosenfeld, A.
"A Note on Polygonal and Elliptical Approximation of Mechanical Parts".
Pattern Recognition 11 (1979), pp. 133-142.

/95/ Nakamura, K.
Edamatsu, K.
Sano, Y.
"Automated Pattern Inspection Based on 'Boundary Length Comparison Method'".
Proc. 4th Int. Joint Conf. on Pattern Recognition Kyoto, 1978.

/96/ Nawrath, R.
"LEITZ-T.A.S., neue Möglichkeiten der Bild-analyse".
LEITZ-Mitteilungen Wiss.- u. Techn, Band VII (1979) 6, Wetzlar, pp. 168-173

/97/ Nevatia, R.
Babu, K.R.
"Linear Feature Extraction and Description".
Proc. 6th Int. Joint Conf. on Artificial Intelligence, Tokyo, Auf. 1979, pp. 639-641

/98/ Nitta, Y.
"Visual Identification and Sorting with TV-Camera Applied to Automated Inspection Apparatus".
Proc. 10th Int. Symp. on Industrial Robots Milan,Italy, March 1980, pp. 141-152

/99/ Nudd, G.R.
Nygard, P.A.
Erickson, J.L.
"Image Processing Techniques Using Charge-Transfer Devices".
Proc. 'Image Understanding Workshop'. Palo Alto, CA.USA, Oct. 1977, pp. 1-6

/100/ Nudd, G.R.
Nygard, P.A.
Fouse, S.D.
Nussmeier, T.A.
"Implementation of Advanced Real-Time Image Understanding Algorithms".
Proc. 'Image Understanding Workshop', Palo Alto, CA. USA, April 1979, pp. 151-157

/101/ O'Gorman, F.
"Edge Detection Using Walsh Functions".
Artificial Intelligence 10 (1978), pp. 215-223.

/102/ Ohlander, R.
Price, K.
Reddy, D.R.
"Picture Segmentation Using a Recursive Region Splitting Method".
Computer Graphics and Image Processing 8 (1978), pp. 313 - 333.

/103/ Olsztyn, J.T.
Rossol, L
Dewar, R.
Lewis, N.R.
"An Application of Computer Vision to a Simu-lated Assembly Task".
Proc. 1st Int. Joint Conf. on Pattern Recognition, Washington D.C., Oct./Nov. 1973, pp. 505-513

/104/   Panda, D.P.   "Image Segmentation by Pixel Classification
        Rosenfeld, A.   in (Gray-Level, Edge Value) Space".
                            IEEE Trans. Comp. C-27 (1978) 9, pp. 875-879

/105/   Pavlidis, T.   "Structural Pattern Recognition:
                            Primitives and Juxtaposition Relations".
                            in: S. Watanabe (ed.) "Frontiers of Pattern
                            Recognition,
                            Academic Press, N.Y., 1972
                            pp. 421-451

/106/   Pavlidis, T.   "Structural Pattern Recognition".
                            Springer Verlag, Berlin, 1977.

/107/   Pavlidis, T.   "A Review of Algorithms for Shape Analysis".
                            Computer Graphics and Image Processing $\underline{7}$
                            (1978) pp. 243-258

/108/   Perkins, W.A.   "Model-Based Vision System for Scenes Containing
                            Multiple Parts".
                            Proc. Int. Joint Conf. on Artificial Intelligence,
                            Tokyo, Japan, Aug. 1977,
                            pp. 678-684

/109/   Perkins, W.A.   "Computer Vision Classification of Automotive
                            Control Arm Bushings".
                            Proc. IEEE 3rd Int. Computer Software & Appli-
                            cations Conference COMPSAC 79, Chicago,
                            Ill., November 1979,
                            pp. 344-349

/110/   Perkins, W.A.   "Area Segmentation of Images Using Edge Points".
                            IEEE Trans. PAMI-2 (1980) 1, pp. 8-15.

/111/   Prager, J.M.   "Extracting and Labeling Boundary Segments in
                            Natural Scenes".
                            IEEE Trans. PAMI-2 (1980) 1, pp. 16-27.

/112/   Prewitt, J.M.S.   "Object Enhancement and Extraction".
                            in: B. Lipkin, A. Rosenfeld (Eds.).
                            'Picture Processing and Psychopictorics'.
                            Academic Press. 1970, pp. 75-149

/113/   Pugh, A.   "A Microprocessor-Controlled Photo-Diode
        Waddon, K.   Sensor for the Detection of Gross Defects".
        Heginbotham, W.B.   Proc. 3rd Int. Conf. on Automated Inspection
                            and Product Control, Nottingham, UK, April 1978,
                            pp. 299-312.

/114/   Restrick III, R.C.   "An Automatic Optical Printed Circuit In-
                              spection System".
                              Proc. SPIE Vol. 116 'Solid State Imaging
                              Devices', 1977, pp. 76-81

/115/   Ridler, T.W.   "Picture Thresholding Using an Iterative
         Calvard, S.   Selection Method".
                              IEEE Trans. SMC-8 (1978) 8, pp. 630-632

/116/   Ringshauser, H.   "Digitale Bildsensoren für industrielle An-
                              wendungen in Sichtprüfung, Handhabung, Ablauf-
                              steuerung und Prozeßregelung".
                              LEITZ-Symposium "Quantitative Bildauswertung
                              und Mikroskopphotometrie, Wetzlar, Sept. 79,
                              Sonderheft MICROSCOPICA ACTA, Hirzel Verlag,
                              Stuttgart, 1980, pp. 298-302.

/117/   Riseman, E.M   "Computational Techniques in the Visual Seg-
         Arbib, M.A.   mentation of Static Scenes".
                              Computer Graphics and Image Processing $\underline{6}$ (1977)
                              pp. 221 - 276

/118/   Riseman, E.M.   "Segmentation of Natural Scenes".
         Hanson, A.R.   in: HANSON & RISEMAN (Eds.): 'Computer Vision
                              Systems', Academic Press, N.Y. 1978, pp. 129-163

/119/   Roberts, L.G.   "Machine Perception of Three-Dimensional Solids."
                              in: J.Tipett, D. Berkowitz, L. Clapp, C. Koester,
                              & A. Vanderbrugh (Eds.),
                              Optical and Electro-optical Information,
                              M.I.T. Press, 1965, pp. 159-197

/120/   Robinson, G.S.   " A Real-Time Edge Processing Unit".
         Reis, J.J.   Proc. of IEEE Workshop on 'Picture Data Des-
                              cription and Management', Chicago, Il., U.S.A.,
                              April 1977, pp. 155-164.

/121/   Robinson, G.S.   "Detection and Coding of Edges Using Directional
                              Masks".
                              Opt. Engr. $\underline{16}$ (1977) 6, pp. 580-585

/122/   Rosen, C.   "Exploratory Research in Advanced Automation".
         Nitzan, D.   5th Report, Stanford Research Institute,
         et al.   Menlo Park, CA, USA, Jan. 1976

/123/   Rosen, C.A.   "Machine Vision and Robotics:
                              Industrial Requirements".
                              in: 'Computer Vision and Sensor-Based Robots'
                              G.G. Dodd & L. Rossol (Eds.), Plenum Press,
                              N.Y., 1979, pp. 3-20

/124/   Rosenfeld, A.   "Edge and Curve Detection for Visual Scene
        Thurston, M.   Analysis".
                                       IEEE Trans. Comp. C-20 (1971),
                                       pp. 562-569

/125/   Rosenfeld, A.   "Digital Picture Processing".
        Kak, A.   Academic Press, N.Y., 1 76

/126/   Rosenfeld, A.   "Interactive Methods in Image Analysis"
                                       Proc. IEEE Conf. on Pattern Recognition &
                                       Image Proc. Troy, N.Y.,
                                       June 1977
                                       pp. 14-18

/127/   Rosenfeld, A.   "Scene Labeling by Relaxation Operations".
        Hummel,   IEEE Trans. SMC-6 (1976),
        Zucker, S.   pp. 420-433

/128/   Saraga, P.   "An Experimental Visually Controlled Pick
        Skoyles, D. R.   and Place Machine for Industry".
                                       Proc. 3rd International Joint Conf. on Pattern
                                       Recognition, Coronado, CA, November 1976,
                                       pp. 17-21

/129/   Schärf, R.   "Untersuchungen zur mehrkanaligen Bildverar-
                                       beitung und Objektseparierung".
                                       Proc. 'Digital Image Processing',
                                       GI/NTG conference, March 1977, Munich,
                                       H.-H. Nagel (Ed.), Informatik-Fachberichte 8
                                       Springer-Verlag, 1977, pp. 280-294

/130/   Shapiro, L.G.   "A Structural Model of Shape".
                                       CS Dept. Tech. Report CS 79003-R,
                                       Virginia Polytechnic Institute & State Univ.,
                                       Blacksburg, VA, USA
                                       April 1979

/131/   Slansky, J.   "Image Segmentation and Feature Extraction".
                                       IEEE Trans on Systems, Man, and Cybernetics
                                       SMC-8 (1978) 4, pp. 237-247.

/132/   Shirai, Y.   "Recognition of Real-World Objects Using Edge
                                       Cues".
                                       in: Hanson, A. & E. Riseman (Eds.): 'Computer
                                       Vision Systems', Academic Press, N.Y., 1978,
                                       pp. 353-362

/133/   Spur, G.   "Optisches Erkennungssystem mit Halbleiterbild-
        Kraft, H.-R.   sensoren zur Steuerung von Industrierobotern".
        Sinning, H.   ZwF 73 (1978) 7, pp. 363-366.

/134/   Steusloff, H.   "Wege zu sehr forgeschrittenen Handhabungs-
        (Ed.)   systemen". Fachberichte Messen-Steuern-Regeln,
                            Band 4, Springer-Verlag, Berlin, 1980

/135/   Sterling, W.M.   "Automatic Non-Reference Inspection of Printed
                            Wiring Boards".
                            Proc. IEEE Conf. on Pattern Recognition and
                            Image Processing, Chicago, Ill., August 1979,
                            pp. 93-100

/136/   Stockman, G.C.   "Equivalence of Hough Transformation To
        Agrawala, A.K.   Template Matching".
                            'Interactive Screening of Reconnaissance Imagery'
                            L.N.K. Corp., AMRL-TR-76-15
                            Silver Spring, Md
                            June 76
                            pp. 105-114

/137/   Tani, K.   "High Precision Manipulator with Visual Sense".
        Abe, M.   Proc. 7th Int. Symp. on Industrial Robots,
        Tanie, K.   Tokyo, October 1977, pp. 561-568.
        Ohno, T.

/138/   Tenenbaum,J.M.   Proc. Int. Joint Conf. on Artificial Intelligence,
        Kay, A.C.   D.A. Walker & L.M. Norton (Eds. 1969)
        Binford, T.   pp. 521-526 a.
        Falk, G.
        Feldman, J.
        Grape, G.
        Paul, R.
        Pingle, K.
        Sobel,I.

/139/   Thissen, F.L.A.M.   "Ein Gerät für die automatische optische Kontrolle
                            von Verbindungsleiterbahnmustern für integrierte
                            Schaltungen".
                            Philips Technische Rundschau $\underline{37}$ (1977/78) Nr. 4,
                            pp. 85-96.

/140/   Toda, H.   "Kawasaki Vision System -- Model 79A".
        Masaki, I.   Proc. 1oth Int. Symp. on Industrial Robots,
                            Milan, Italy, March 1980,
                            pp. 163-174

/141/   Tokumitsu, J.   "Adaptive Binarization Using A Hybrid Image Pro-
        Kawata, S.   cessing System".
        Ichioka, Y.   Applied Optics $\underline{17}$ (1978) No. 16, Aug.,
        Suzuki, T.   pp. 2655 - 2657

/142/   Tropf. H.   "Analysis-by-Synthesis Search to Interpret
Degraded Image Data.
1st International Conference on Robot Vision
and Sensory Controls, Stratford-on-Avon, UK.
April 1-3, 1981

/143/   Vanderbrug, G.J.   "A Vision System for Real Time Control of
Albus, J.S.   Robots".
Barkmeyer, E.   Proc. 9th Int. Symp. on Industrial Robots,
Washington D.C., March 1979
pp. 213-231

/144/   Veillon, F.   "One Pass Computation of Morphological and
Geometrical Properties of Objects in Digital
Pictures".
Signal Processing $\underline{1}$ (1979) 3, pp.

/145/   Ward, M.R.   "CONSIGHT: A Practical Vision-Based Robot
Rossol. L.   Guidance System".
Holland, S.W.   Proc. 9th Int. Symp. on Industrial Robots,
Dewar, R.   Washington D.C., March 1979
pp. 195-211

/146/   Wedlich, G.   "Serienreifes Gerät zur lokaladaptiven Video-
signalverarbeitung".
IITB-Mitteilungen 1977
Fraunhofer-Gesellschaft, Karlsruhe,
pp. 24-26

/147/   Willett, T.J.   "CCD Implementation of An Image Segmentation
Bluzer, N.   Algorithm".
Proc. 'Image Understanding Workshop',
Science Applications,
Palo Alto, CA, USA, 1977,
pp. 9-11.

/148/   Willett, T.J.   "Relaxation, Systolic Arrays, and Universal
Brooks, C.W.   Arrays".
Tisdale, G.E.   Proc. Image Understanding Workshop' Palo Alto,
CA, USA, April 79, pp. 164-170

/149/   Wolf, H.   "Optisches Abtastsystem zur Identifizierung und
Lageerkennung dreidimensionaler Objekte".
Feinwerktechnik & Messtechnik 87 (1979) 2,
pp. 86-88.

/150/   Yachida, M.   "A Knowledge Directed Line Finder for Analysis
Ikeda, M.   of Complex Scenes".
Tsuji, S.   Proc. IJCAI '79, Tokyo, August 79,
pp. 984-991

/151/   Zamperoni, P.   "Darstellung von Binärbildern mit Hilfe von dilatierten Kernen" in: J.P. Foith (Ed.): 'Angewandte Szenenanalyse', Informatik-Fachbericht 20, Springer-Verlag, Berlin, 1978, pp. 124-128.

/152/   Zucker, S.W. Hummel, R.A. Rosenfeld, A.   "An Application of Relaxation Labeling to Line and Curve Enhancement". IEEE Trans. Comp. C-26 (1977) 4, pp. 394-403

/153/   Zurcher, J.M.   "Conception D'Un Systeme De Perception Visuelle Pour Robot Industriel". Compte rendus des Journées de Microtechnique, Ecole Polytechnique Federale, Lausanne,1978, pp. 175-193.

/154/   Zurcher, J.-M.   "Extraction de contours en traitment électronique des images II: Processeur spécialisé pour signal vidéo". Bull. ASE/UCS (Switzerland) 70 (1979) 11, 9 juin, pp. 532-536

CPO-2/K-202:

A UNIVERSAL DIGITAL IMAGE ANALYSIS SYSTEM

by

Zenon KULPA, Janusz DERNAŁOWICZ,
Henryk T. NOWICKI[*], Andrzej BIELIK

Polish Academy of Sciences
Institute of Biocybernetics and Biomedical Engineering
Department of Picture Recognition and Processing
00-818 WARSAW, Poland

[*] Presently at:
Monument-Hospital "Center of Child's Health"
Department of Genetics
WARSAW-MIĘDZYLESIE, Poland

Abstract

Great universality and flexibility of an automatic picture analysis is most easily reached by the use of a computer-based picture processing system. A digital picture processing system designed, built up and utilized in the Institute of Biocybernetics and Biomedical Engineering is an example of such a system. It is very useful as a research tool to investigate methods of an analysis of pictures as well as it is used for many practical applications of this methods in science and technology.

The CPO-2/K-202 system consists of a minicomputer system and a special picture input/output device. The special pictorial peripheral, named CPO-2, for digital image conversion and for input/output of pictures to/from the computer system contains: a TV-camera and TV monitors, A/D and D/A converters, and an image buffer memory. The computer system comprises Polish K-202 minicomputer, a standard set of I/O peripherals and an appropriate software system for image processing. The software includes an assembler, a large library of image processing subroutines called PICASSO, and a PICASSO-SHOW family of interactive programming languages for picture processing.

Several application programs were written for the system, e.g. for analysis of pictures of leukemia cells, radar cloud covers, chromosome banding patterns as well as for measurement of limb joints angles for locomotion research.

1. Introduction

Great universality and flexibility of an automatic picture analysis is most easily reached by the use of computer-based picture processing systems. From the theoretical point of view, any picture processing algorithm can be realized by some program for a universal digital computer. A digital picture processing system designed, built up and utilized in our Institute in Department of Picture Recognition and Processing since 1974 represents an example of such a universal and flexible system [1-5]. It serves as a very useful research tool to investigate methods of picture analysis [23-29] as well as it can be used for many practical applications of these methods in science and technology [16-23, 33].

As the input information to the system any kinds of pictures can be given: natural scenes, photographs, drawings, negatives, diapositives, microscope pictures, and so on. As a picture processing tool serves a digital picture processing system based on a minicomputer with I/O devices augmented by a digital image converter. Results of picture processing can be of several types:

- qualitative results: selection, filtration, feature extraction,

recognition, comparison, data compression;
- quantitative results: measurements of length, area and size of picture objects, counts of their number, and other computable features (e.g. shape factors);
- processes on picture data banks: collection, searching and retrieval, etc.

All elements of the CPO-2/K-202 system can be grouped into two main groups:
1) the special peripheral, named CPO-2, for digital TV image conversion and for input/output of TV pictures to/from the computer system;
2) the computer system comprising the Polish K-202 minicomputer, a standard set of I/O peripherals and an appropriate software oriented for programming of picture processing algorithms.

2. System hardware

The block diagram of the system structure is shown in Fig. 1 (see also [1, 5]). Main operations and processes performed in the CPO-2 unit are:
1) _Conversion_ of a physical image into an electrical video-signal by means of a standard TV-scanning process using a professional vidicon TV-camera.
2) _Quantization_ of the video-signal into digital form and its coding to fit a computer-word format. The quantization process runs with the same speed as TV-scanning. It quantizes:
   - the value of gray intensity during every picture line into 16 levels (by the use of fast A/D converter), and
   - every picture line into 512 picture elements (by sampling the quantized video-signal at appropriate time intervals).
3) _Storage_ of the digitized picture in a buffer core memory. The memory operates both as a refreshing memory for a TV-monitor and as a picture data store for the computer system.
4) _Display_ of the picture, for visual inspection purposes, on two TV-monitors (black/white and colour). On the first monitor either the direct picture output from the TV-camera, or the signal after gray-levels quantization, or the digital picture from the buffer memory is shown in black and white, whereas on the second monitor the digital picture from the buffer memory is shown in artificial colours. For monitoring of inter-

172

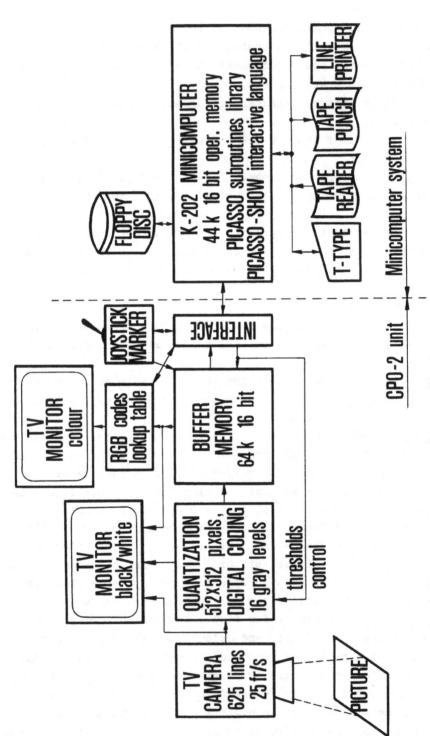

Fig. 1. The CPO-2/K-202 system structure

mediate stages of processing, any pictures can be send from
the computer system to the buffer memory, so that they could
be seen immediately on the screen.

5) <u>On-line communication</u> with the computer system.

The pictures inputted by the CPO-2 device have resolution of
512×512 picture elements: a square picture area is divided into
512 lines (a part of the standard 625-line TV-frame is taken) and
then every line is divided into 512 picture elements (by appropriate sampling). The number of distinguished gray levels of each
picture element is 16. The quantization parameters, i.e. the position of the lowest level within the whole video-signal range
(from black to white) and the distances between the levels can be
changed either manually or from the computer, and set to one of
256 possible values. The computer can also read the actual values
of these parameters.

The fast A/D converter, providing the quantization of a video
-signal with the speed of TV scanning has been based on a set of
differential comparators working parallelly. Their input thresholds are controlled by the above-mentioned quantization parameters. The 15-line output, corresponding to 16 gray levels (including 0-level), feeds an encoder.

In the encoding process the value of gray intensity of every
point is expressed by a four-bit binary number. Then, the digitized video-signal is sampled and every block of 16 successive picture elements, lying along a scan line, is represented by a group
of four 16-bit computer words. The bits placed at the same position in every word of the group represent the 4-bit code of gray
intensity of the corresponding picture element. Schematically,
the quantization process, encoding and sampling are shown on the
block diagram in Fig. 2. This method of picture encoding ensures
convenient operation with the picture in one of its 16-, 8-, 4-,
or 2-gray levels versions, simply by taking into consideration
only 4, 3, 2, or 1 word(s) from the group, corresponding to the
most significant bits of the picture element code.

During the scanning of a new picture, the groups of words can
be stored in the buffer memory one by one in such a manner that
every word of a group is placed in a separate memory block. There
are four such blocks in the memory, corresponding to the four
words in each group. That is, in one memory cycle four 16-bit

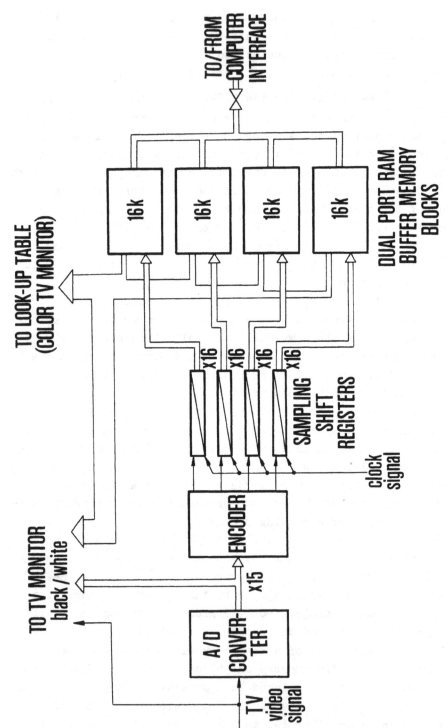

Fig. 2. Image quantization, encoding and storage in the system

words are stored or fetched simultaneously. Within a time interval of a single TV-picture frame (1/25s), the whole digitized picture is stored in the memory. Storage of a new picture can be made on the request of an operator (pushing an appropriate button) or on the signal from the computer, without necessity of the operator intervention.

The capacity of memory sections is of 16k words each. It corresponds to the number of picture elements (512 lines × 32 groups of 16 elements). In effect, the total storage capacity is equal to the amount of information contained in one 16 gray-levels picture (4 blocks × 16k words = 64k words = 1 048 576 bits).

Additionally, the CPO-2 unit is equipped with the joystick point marker, which allows either some intervention into the contents of picture information (correction, drawing of some picture elements, lines, etc.) or pointing to the computer program the position of objects chosen by the operator in a processed picture. A point marker (black or white) of the shape of a right angle corner pointing to the upper left is superimposed on a digital picture shown on the screen of the TV-monitor. The movement of the marker across the picture and its setting to some required position is usually done by hand, using a joystick manipulator. Depending on the operation mode, either every position of the marker and its trace can be memorized (in the buffer memory), changing therefore the picture contents, or the coordinates of its position can be send to the computer, as an answer to its request. The computer can also place the marker at any given position, sending the coordinates of its position to the marker.

The second TV-monitor of the system is a colour one. The quantized picture signal from the buffer memory can be seen on the monitor screen in "artificial colours". The correspondence of colours to different picture elements codes is determined by the look-up memory of RGB colour components, updated by the computer, so that to every individual gray-level code different combination of RGB signals may correspond. Every colour component (R, G or B) can be set individually into one of 16 levels. In effect, there is theoretically available 16^3 = 4096 different colours to represent every picture element code.

The 16 bit Polish K-202 minicomputer performs all image analysis programs on appropriate fragments (windows) of the input

picture, transmitted for this purpose into the operating memory
from the CPO-2 image buffer. The minicomputer operating core memory (1.5μs cycle time) has two blocks of 16 bit words: the first
(12k words) contains the operating system, and the second (32k
words) contains user's programs and processed picture fragments.
The instruction list includes about 90 basic instructions and
programmed floating-point arithmetic. The standard set of peripherals consists of a teletype, paper tape reader/punch (ISO-7
code) and a line printer. A floppy-disc memory is being connected
presently.

3. System software

The software for image processing in the CPO-2/K-202 system
consists of the following parts:
1) Operating system SOK-1/CPO-2.
2) Assembler ASSK-3.
3) Library of basic picture processing subroutines PICASSO
   [1-6, 14].
4) A family of interactive languages PICASSO-SHOW [1-9, 14].
5) Application programs (usually written in one of the PICASSO-
   -SHOW languages) [16-22].

The operating system presently in use is rather primitive -
it is the standard SOK-1 system of the machine, augmented with
a few subroutines to handle the CPO-2 device. It does not make
use of the disc memory. The new operating system is under development. It is called COSMOS (COnceptually Simple Modular Operating System) and will be used with the floppy-disc memory being
connected to the minicomputer (Fig. 1). Its structure will be
based in part on the structure of the PICASSO-SHOW language interpreter and it will integrate into a single whole the functions
of the operating system, the assembler and the PICASSO-SHOW interpreter.

The ASSK-3 assembler is also the standard assembler of the
K-202 minicomputer. The library of picture processing subroutines
PICASSO is written in assembly code, to achieve the highest possible efficiency of execution of these basic processing subroutines.

The PICASSO library and PICASSO-SHOW language will be described in some detail below (Sections 3.1 and 3.2). Some application

programs will be briefly described in Section 4.

A new high-level language for image processing (called PAL - Picture Analyzing Language) has been designed also [11-14] and will be implemented on the system. Meanwhile, some its ideas and parts of its compiler have been incorporated in the PICASSO-SHOW 3 language [8-10].

3.1. The PICASSO subroutines library

The PICASSO (PICture ASSembly-programmed Operations) package is a rather large set of subroutines for basic operations on pictures [1-6, 14]. It counts now about 170 operations. All operations assume the same structure of processed data items - numbers, pictures and number vectors. They are written so as to achieve maximal efficiency in execution time.

The program listings are standardized in order to become self-documented. Every subroutine is preceded by a standardized "comment header", summarizing all informations needed in order to use properly the subroutine in some program. The header describes parameters, results, non-local variables and subroutines called by the given one, machine register usage, error conditions and signals, and a form of the call. Within a subroutine body several standard conventions are also usually observed (e.g. in formation of variable and label names, program structuring) in order to enhance readability and facilitate modification and maintenance of the library. The fact that the library is included into the PICASSO-SHOW languages (see Section 3.2) is another reason for this standardization.

The most important convention adopted here is the form of basic data structures, namely pictures. The pictures are rectangular matrices of pixels, and to achieve greatest flexibility, they can have any dimensions and any number of bits of pixel values representation. In the memory, every picture is preceded by a header including the following parameters:

XO, YO: coordinates of the lower left corner of the picture (in some absolute coordinate system),

M, N: width and height of the picture (in pixels),

S: the number of bits per pixel,

L: the length of picture representation (in memory words).

Every picture operation uses this header to organize appropriately its processing of the picture.

Two different representations of pictures in memory are used, namely so-called "packed" and "stacked" representations. For the packed representation, all S bits representing the pixel value are stored in S consecutive bits of the same memory cell; one such cell contains usually several pixels. For the stacked representation, the picture is stored as S binary "planes", each containing a single bit of the representation of all pixels of the picture. Every memory cell in the plane contains the given bit of W consecutive pixels (along a row) of the picture, where W is the machine word length. The S bits of representation of some pixel are stored in S different memory cells, placed in the same positions of different planes. A binary picture (S=1) is a special case of a stacked picture, and consists of a single plane.

Utilizing the above packing of pixels into words and the fact that computers usually perform most operations with a single instruction over the whole word (bit-parallel), many PICASSO subroutines implement a semi-parallel processing method, gaining significantly in speed and efficiency over more serial processing requiring individual access to every single pixel.

Most of PICASSO picture operations are written in two versions, one for packed and one for stacked arguments. Some of them also have simplified versions operating on binary pictures. There are also operations processing only binary pictures (e.g. many propagation operations). The whole library is actually divided into 14 groups which are summarized (with examples of the most important operations in every group) in the table below. The greek letters α and β occuring in some names of operations stand for letters S or P (for α) or B, S or P (for β). These prefixes distinguish similar operations differing only by types of their arguments (i.e. Binary, Stacked, or Packed pictures, respectively).

1) <u>CPO-2 device input/output</u>

SCAN, DISP	input/output of a picture window,
SPOINT, DPOINT	input/output of single pixels,
COMPR, ENLARG	input/output of windows with linear scaling,
PUT, NEG	putting to a given value or negating windows in image buffer,

2) <u>Changing picture form in memory</u>

    TOSTACK, TOPACK, PACK   changes between stacked and packed
                                        form of pictures,

    αSCAL, αMOV   changes gray value scale of a picture,

3) <u>Single-pixel operations</u>

    αREAD, αWRITE   read/write of single pixel,

    SFIPO, SLIST   finding and listing of pixels with given
                                          values,

    SLINE & NEXPLI   ⎫
    CIRC & NEXPCIR   ⎪ generate discrete lines, circles, rings
    RING & NEXPRI   ⎬   and arcs (point by point) [24-26],
    ARC & NEXPAR   ⎭

    BAPROX   approximate binary contour with discrete
                                          straight line segments,

4) <u>Input/output operations</u> (to/from paper tape, to printer)

    αDUMP, αLOAD   print/load: a number of different versions
                                  depending on the form of pictures on
                                  external medium,

    HIST   print a histogram (also many versions),

5) <u>Global features calculation</u>

    αWEIGHT, αCENTER   sum of gray values and center of gravity,

    αHIST   gray level histogramming,

    BAREA, BPERIM, ⎫
    VARPER   ⎬ area and perimeter (corrected [24]) of blob,

    BAXIS   main axis of inertia,

    BWDOW   minimum window containing a blob,

    NORMHI, MOMHIS   histogram normalization and moments,

    FACSBL, FACSMA, ⎫
    FACSDA, FACSHA   ⎬ different global shape factors [18-20, 27],

    HIMA, HIPMA, WYMA   determination of local masks for texture
                                          filtering [28],

6) <u>One-argument (pointwise) operations</u>

    αPUT   put all pixels to a given value,

    αNEG   negate a picture,

    αCOPY   copy a picture,

    SDIVC   divide all pixel values by a given number,

    STHRC   thresholding,

7) <u>Two-argument (pointwise) operations</u>

 βOR, βAND, βDIF   logical,

 βADD, βSUB, βDIV arithmetic,

 STHR   thresholding with pointwise different
           thresholds [18, 19],

8) <u>Picture shifts</u>

 αSHIFT, SSH1D, SSH1X

9) <u>Tests</u>

 αEQ   are two pictures equal?

 αVAL, αBLACK, αWHITE have all pixels the specified value?

 BORD0, BORD1   does the white/black component touch
           the boundary of a picture?

10) <u>Local operations</u> (3×3 neighbourhood usually)

 BCLEAN   "salt & pepper" noise removal,

 BCONT   contour extraction,

 BLINEND, BLICOS   line ends and intersections extraction,

 SAV   local averaging,

 BCURV   local line curvature determination,

11) <u>Propagation operations</u> (on binary pictures)

 BPRO4, BPRO8, ⎫
 BPRO48, BPRO84 ⎬ basic propagation operations,

 BCON, BCCOM, ⎫
 BCOMPS & NEXCOM ⎬ connected components extraction,

 BFILL, BFILLG   hole filling,

 BTOUCH   extraction of components touching
           a boundary,

 BLOB, BLOBC1, BLOBR blob extraction [18, 19],

 BTHINL   thinning (ACL algorithm [30]),

 BARC, BLIC & NEXLI extraction of discrete arcs,

12) <u>Object extraction operations</u>

 HUECK   simplified Hueckel operator [31, 32],

 HITHR, LOCTHR, THR dynamic thresholding [18, 19],

 SFILTT   extraction of objects of a given texture
           [28] (see operations in 5th group),

13) Object-generation operations

BFRAM, SZER, SMAX	setting values on the boundary,
SCIRC	circular disk generation [25, 26],
BLINSEG	straight lines drawing [24],

14) Correction operations

CORSHW, CORSHB	additive shading correction.

3.2. The PICASSO-SHOW languages

The PICASSO-SHOW languages comprise a family of interactive, command-oriented picture processing languages for a minicomputer--based picture processing systems. Earlier languages of the family, called PICASSO-SHOW [1, 6, 7], PICASSO-SHOW 1.5 and PICASSO--SHOW 1.6 [2-5, 14] have been working for about 4 years as a basic programming tools for the CPO-2/K-202 picture processing system. Basing on experience gained with these versions, design principles of the new version, called PICASSO-SHOW 3 [8, 9, 14] have been developed (the PICASSO-SHOW 2 version has been proposed also, although not implemented).

The PICASSO-SHOW 3 language is oriented towards picture processing operations from the PICASSO library [1-6, 14]. Individual operations can be executed in the way of interaction between a human operator and the interpreter, or they can be grouped into programs, stored in the operating memory and run there. The former mode of work is called interactive one. The latter one comprises two distinct modes, oriented either toward convenient program development and debugging (the so-called interpretative mode) or towards fast running of debugged programs (the program mode).

The set of operations of the PICASSO-SHOW 3 language is not fixed. Any user-defined subroutine can be appended to the language as its normal operation and any subset of the PICASSO library can be selected as the set of PICASSO-SHOW 3 operations.

3.2.1. The PICASSO-SHOW 3 language

Basic executable units of the language are called statements. In the interactive mode, the statement is executed immediately after it has been written. Under the interpretative mode, a sequence of statements (optionally preceded by label declarations) constitutes a program. A labeled statement can be executed under interactive mode as well - in this case the label declaration has no result. Generally, all statements are legal under all modes, though sometimes there are minor differences in their results.

Statements of the language are of three types: declarations, instructions and assignments. A declaration generates some object the instructions are to deal with, supplying the interpreter with parameters of the object (e.g. size). An instruction evokes, via the system vocabulary of operations, some operation from the system library, passes to it its parameters and starts its execution. An assignment fixes the numerical value of a symbolic number of an object.

Objects processed by the PICASSO-SHOW 3 instructions are of five general types: pictures, numerical vectors, numerical variables, atoms and vectors of atoms.

The structure of pictures in memory is the same as that accepted by the PICASSO subroutines library (see Section 3.1). Besides "stacked" and "packed" types of pictures, a "binary" type is introduced which corresponds to pictures of two possible gray levels (black or white only). Pictures of these three types have different names. As a parameter of PICASSO operation, a binary picture is a special case of a stacked one; the distinction is made because some PICASSO subroutines operate on binary pictures only, what should be made visible in program texts.

Numerical vectors are one-dimensional sequences of memory cells. Their elements can be interpreted also as numerical variables of any numerical type.

Numerical variables are of three types: integer, long integer and real. There is ten predefined standard numerical variables for every type - they need not be declared.

Atoms are sets of fields (dynamic records). Fields are ordered pairs consisting of a field selector (see below) and a field value. A field has a type attached to it, which determines the type of its value. An atom as a whole has also a type assigned to it. Atom types are significant only when the atom is used as a field selector (see below), otherwise the atom type has no significance at all. The atom type allows building hierarchical data structures of any complexity, for structural picture description and processing. The atom concept has been borrowed from the PAL language [9, 11-14].

Objects used as instruction arguments are referred to by names. Only some fixed set of object names can be used and their form is also standard. Generally, there exist ten different names for objects of every type, e.g. ten different static numerical variables of every numerical type, ten numerical vectors, ten stacked pictures, etc. For numerical variables and atoms this restriction does not limit a programmer because appropriate vector elements can be used as well. For other objects the restriction on the number of the object names does not affect the number of the objects themselves. An object can exist without a name as a value of some atom field (where it is accessible by a name of the field), or as an auxiliary parameter of an instruction (where it is created by a "generator", see below). By a field name the object may be referenced to in atom-dealing instructions, but it must be assigned to an object name before it is used in other instructions.

The fixed form of object names simplifies argument reading subroutines, which is important especially when working under interactive or interpretative modes (no need for any identifier tables). It also simplifies manual translation of PICASSO-SHOW 3 programs into assembly code and makes the programs more "semantically legible", because standard object names indicate immediately their types.

An object name consists of a letter (specifying the type of the object), a digit (specifying the number of the object) and, eventually, a vector element index (if needed). The digit may be replaced by a symbolic number (a single letter). The use of this device simplifies linking of different program fragments, because all used object numbers may be symbolic, so that changing the number requires only changing appropriate assignment (see below) instead of changing many names.

A declaration generates an object, allocates a space for it in operating memory and assigns to it a name. The declaration consists of a list of names of generated objects and a list of parameters of the objects. Objects generated in the same declaration must be of the same type (except for stacked and packed pictures which may be declared together). The parameters may be written explicitly or by a reference to some existing object of the same type. E.g. the stacked picture S3 may be declared in two ways:

   *S3: (100, 200, 128, 64, 4), or

   *S3: S5,

In the first case the size of the generated picture is given explicitly by the parameter list (in parentheses), while in the second one the parameters of the existing S5 picture are used. Another examples, in this case of the atom declaration:

   *AI1: (FIO1:5, FS21:S3),

   *AR2: A1,

The parameters of an atom define the initial set of its fields. Field selectors consist of the letter F, the type indicator, and a pair of digits.

    An object without a name can be also generated. The form of such an "object generator" is similar to that of a declaration, but it does not contain the object name, and it can be used only as argument of an instruction. The aim of using the generator is to provide an instruction with an auxiliary object, some intermediate results of the instruction can be kept in. The contents of such auxiliary objects are not important before and after the execution of the operation, so there is no need of assigning any names to them. Examples of possible forms of generators of auxiliary packed pictures are:

   *P(10, 50, 100, 100, 2)   < a picture with given parameters >

   *P3   < the same parameters as in the P3 picture >

    Instructions perform operations on objects. The operation is defined by a subroutine attached to the instruction in the instruction module of the system library (see below). Instruction name is a typical alphanumerical character sequence. As arguments of an instruction, objects, arithmetical expressions and texts can be used. In order to avoid unnecessary declarations of temporary arguments or to shorten the notation of some arguments, two additional conventions were introduced: generators (described above) and "windows".

    When working under interactive mode, one often encounters the need of executing a sequence of operations consisting of scanning an image from input device, performing some image operation (e.g. from PICASSO package) and displaying the result immediately on the screen. The "window" allows to condense the notation of this sequence of actions into one statement. A window is a picture name placed as an instruction argument together with a command for transmitting the picture to/from the image buffer memory. In the following example, one instruction with windows replaces four normal instructions. The upward-pointing arrow symbol denotes "display" command while the left-pointing arrow denotes "scan" command. The window may also contain some parameters, describing the place in the buffer (coordinates on the screen) to/from where the transmission would take place. For instance:

    AND, S1←, S2←, S3↑,

is equivalent to the sequence of instructions (simplified):

    SCAN, S1,
    SCAN, S2,
    AND, S1, S2, S3,   < the result is on the picture S3 >
    DISP, S3,

After that instruction the result of the AND operation is immediately seen on the TV-monitor screen.

Arithmetical expressions may be used anywhere as numerical arguments. Four arithmetical operators are allowed as well as parentheses (with arbitrary nesting). Two-argument operators deal with pairs of operands of the same type (integer, long integer, or real). To convert an operand to appropriate type, conversion operators are used.

An object name consists of a letter and a digit. The letter defines the type of the object and the digit - its number. However, it is often convenient to use symbolic names of objects. In a symbolic name, the digit is replaced by a letter. The letter obtains its value by means of an assignment, having the form:

    letter = digit,

Using actual values of letters (as defined by assignments) the interpreter (in the course of loading a program) changes all symbolic names into explicit ones.

Labels are of two kinds: global and local. Label denotations consist of the symbol "$" and a name. The names of global labels have the same form as instruction names. Local labels names consist of two digits. Global labels are accessible everywhere in a program while the scope of local labels is restricted to the program segment between pairs of consecutive global label declarations.

Comments, having the form of strings of characters enclosed in angle brackets "<" and ">", can be placed anywhere, even within instruction names.

3.2.2. Instructions repertoire

The set of instructions available in the language consists of the so-called "system instructions" and any set of other instructions (usually a subset of the PICASSO library, see Section 3.1) chosen by a programmer in the phase of assembling "instruction modules" into the system vocabulary (Section 3.2.3).

The system instructions are permanently resident in the system. They can be classified into the following groups:
- jumps and testing instructions,
- loop organization instructions,
- subroutines organization instructions,
- editing instructions,
- execution control instructions,
- list processing instructions,
- other.

Each jump instruction has a label as an argument. For conditional jumps there is another argument (sometimes implicit) which decides whether the jump is to be performed or not. There are six jump instructions:

GOTO (unconditional); GOKEY (if some key is on);

GOL, GOE, GONE, GOG (if the value of the IO variable is less, equal, not equal or greater than O, respectively).

Closely connected with jumps is a set of testing operations. This set contains arithmetical comparison instruction COMP and some PICASSO operations of the same character. They set the variable IO to -1, O or +1, depending on the fulfilment of some conditions. The IO variable is accessible for a programmer as any other variable, and can be set to any value with the SET instruction as well.

Loops in a program are organized by using pairs of BEGLOOPi - - ENDLOOPi instructions, where the letter "i" denotes a digit. The digit is a number of the loop. The full form of the BEGLOOPi instructions is:

BEGLOOPi, an1, an2, an3,

where an1, an2, are numerical arguments setting boundaries of the

loop counter of standard name Ki, and the an3 numerical argument
is the step of the counter. Thus the BEGLOOPi instruction is
roughly equivalent to the ALGOL 60 construction:

for Ki := an1 step an3 until an2 do begin

and the ENDLOOPi instruction is equivalent to the end instruction
closing the loop body. An important difference is that the body
is always executed at least once. Loops can be nested, but then
they must have different numbers.

Subroutines are implemented by means of two operations: the
operation CALL that puts on a stack a return address (of the statement following the CALL) and jumps to some label (starting label of the subroutine), and the operation RETURN that pops up the
stack and jumps to the statement the popped stack element was an
address of. Thus recursive calling of subroutines is possible.
Nevertheless, there is no special mechanism for passing arguments
to and results from the subroutine - they have to be transferred
within global variables and objects. It should be explained that
the subroutine on the language level has nothing in common with
the instruction subroutine realizing some language instruction.
The latter is written in assembly language as a part of some instruction module (see the next Section). For example, the PICASSO-
-SHOW 3 program below computes recursively the factorial of a
number given in the variable L1, puts the result into L2, then
prints it out and returns to the interactive mode:

```
    SET, L2, L1,
    CALL, $1,
    PRL, L2,
    DO, 3,  < EXIT TO INTERACTION WITH TELETYPE >
$1:  < A FACTORIAL SUBROUTINE >
    SET, L1, L1-1,
    COMP, L1, 1,   GOL, $2,
    SET, L2, L2 * L1,
    CALL, $1,  < RECURSIVE CALL OF FACTORIAL >
$2: RETURN,
```

To execute this program, one should place a number into L1
(say, the number is 5) by writing on the teletype:

```
    SET, L1, 5,
```

and activate the program:

```
    DO,,
```

After a while the system responds with the factorial of the number 5:

120

and waits for the next command to be written on the teletype.

The LOAD instruction reads the text of a program from an input device, places it in the system memory and numbers its lines. The PRINT instruction outputs the required fragment or the whole program to an output device. The INS and REPL instructions insert or replace fragments of a program respectively.

The DO instruction switches the mode of work between interactive and interpretative modes. The COMPILE instruction translates a program to the intermediate code allowing its fast interpretation, and the RUN instruction runs this code, i.e. sets the program mode.

The STOP instruction halts program execution if a special key is on, otherwise it has no result. To restart a program after the STOP or other interruption (e.g. an error), the GO instruction can be used.

The ON instruction changes the reaction of the interpreter after an error has been detected in a program. The standard reaction is the printout of an error message and halting the program, i.e. returning to the interactive mode. Once the ON instruction has been executed, the interpreter does not halt the program after an error message (of the error specified by the parameter of the ON instruction), but resumes its execution from the point marked by a label given by another argument of the ON instruction.

List processing instructions allow dynamic extension and compression of vectors (either numerical vectors or vectors of atoms) and access to atom fields. The dimension of a vector is changed by the ALTER instruction. Access to a field of an atom is given by instructions OF (reading) and ASSOC (assigning); with the latter instruction a new field can be also added to the atom, whereas the FREE instruction removes a field from it. The ISF instruction tests the existence of a given field in an atom.

There are some other system instructions, e.g. input/output ones (dealing with numbers, characters and texts), CPO-2 device control, etc. Some of them are closely dependent on the hardware of the system, others are more general and rather typical for many programming languages.

3.2.3. Structure of the interpreter

The main concept of the interpreter is the idea of operation vocabulary. The vocabulary consists of entries describing all instructions legal in the system. Instructions are organized into "instruction modules". A module of a single instruction (or a set of closely related instructions) consists of a subroutine (or subroutines) performing the operation (or several related operations), some entries of the operation vocabulary, and possibly some entries of the linker vocabulary (if the subroutine calls another subroutines). The modules are constructed in such a way that instruction can be added to the system library with the use of a special linker as well as with the standard assembler.

An entry of the operation vocabulary consists of a sequence of characters (the six initial characters of the instruction name), an address of an entry point in the subrotine body, an address of the next vocabulary entry, a sequence of descriptions of arguments (operation parameters) and the end marker. Because argument descriptions simply name subroutines to be activated for the arguments reading and setting, the entry provides a "procedural" description of types of arguments and their sequence.

Every argument reading subroutine reads an argument of a defined type, checks it for its correctness, changes to the form of a parameter of the main subroutine which performs the operation, and passes it to that subroutine. Some subroutines which appear in the operation vocabulary entries do not read any arguments but perform some auxiliary actions. For example, the HELP subroutine, used in order to facilitate a dialogue with an uninitiated user, prints on the monitor any prescribed text, giving the user additional informations, e.g. about the type and meaning of subsequent arguments to be written. There is also a set of subroutines controlling checking of argument parameters, e.g. which pictorial arguments should have the same size.

All PICASSO-SHOW 3 declarable objects as well as some tables of the interpreter (e.g. the table of global label names) are administered by the SETSYS dynamic storage allocation system [10]. The SETSYS is an autonomous system of storage allocation procedures, and its use in the PICASSO-SHOW 3 interpreter is one of its possible applications.

Basically, SETSYS consists of two levels: semantic (or user)

level and memory (or implementation) level. The user level essentially coincides with the list processing capabilities of PICASSO-
-SHOW 3. I.e., it allows:
- creation and deletion of objects,
- attachment and detachment of elements to/from objects,
- getting and putting values from/to elements of objects.

There are four types of objects: simple, vector, atom, picture. Simple objects correspond roughly to PICASSO-SHOW variables
except that they may contain references to other objects and are
dynamic (may be deleted from the computation). Vectors behave
like double-ended queues and, additionally, indexed access to
their elements is possible. Atoms are sets of named values which
can be freely accessed, added to and deleted from the atom by
means of their names. Picture is a problem-oriented data type.
Elements of composite objects (vectors, atoms) are of simple type.

Morphology of the above objects and operations on them is
realized in terms of memory level of SETSYS. The memory level operates on the so-called "sets". Sets are blocks of consecutive
memory cells placed in a predetermined pool of memory cells,
called a heap. A set consists of the useful part (used for storing elements of objects it represents) and the spare part (used
for eventual future extensions).

Possible operations on sets are: creation, deletion, extension and contraction. Deletion simply releases block of cells
occupied by the set, which thereafter becomes the so-called hole.
Contraction of the set reduces the number of its elements, adding
the cells occupied by them to the spare part of the set. Creation
and extension in their turn both consist of allocating new free
storage (in the case of extension, the possibility of using the
spare part of the set to be extended is tried first). If the
spare part was not sufficient to complete the required extension,
a sufficiently large hole is searched for and the sets and holes
between the extended set and the found hole are shifted in order
to use the hole to enlarge the set. Similarly, for creation of
a new set, the multistage strategy of acquiring necessary amount
of free cells is adopted. In each subsequent stage the complexity
of the algorithm increases, until the success is achieved:
1) try to seize a hole,
2) try to allocate free storage from the heap,

3) **repeat** (2) after hole merging,
4) repeat (2) after spare parts retrieval and merging,
5) perform garbage collection (i.e. recovery of sets which are not referred to by any other set accessible directly or indirectly from the actual program).

Conceptually, SETSYS is an elaborated version of the so--called MINIPAL/SET system [15]. It was initially intended for use in the PAL language compiler [10-14].

4. Applications

The CPO-2/K-202 image processing system has been used for several practical applications. Application programs (mostly written in PICASSO-SHOW language) have been used for processing of various kinds of pictures, mainly biomedical. More important realized programs include:
a) calculation of blood vessels width ratio in eye-fundus photographs [2, 17],
b) calculation of areas and shape descriptors of the optic disc and cup in eye-fundus images [2, 16, 17],
c) ERG curves digitization [23],
d) analysis of copper ore samples,
e) blood groups precipitation data recognition,
f) quantitative measurement of shape changes of moving leukemia cells [18-20],
g) measurements of radar pictures of cloud covers,
h) calculation of limb joints angles for animal locomotion research [21-23],
i) determination of banding profiles of chromosomes [33],
j) muscle tissue analysis.

One of the most elaborated programs is that for cells shape changes measurement ((f) above). The program (strictly speaking, several its versions, called CSC-1, ..., CSC-4) has been used in investigations of leukemia cells motility and adhesiveness properties (in connection with cancer research [20]). The time-lapse films of a cell culture have been analyzed off-line, frame by frame, on the CPO-2/K-202 system. In every frame usually several cells were analyzed. Various quantitative features (about 20 different quantities) have been measured for every cell image. Preliminary analysis of the biological significance of obtained parameters has been attempted in [20].

The first stage of analysis is aimed for extraction of cell outline from the background (Fig. 3a-e). The image, quantized into 16 gray levels by the CPO-2 device, is then binarized by dynamic thresholding method [18, 19]. By this method, the image is thresholded with different thresholds in different parts of the image. These local thresholds are determined from analysis of gray-level histograms calculated for small windows of the image. If the histogram is markedly bimodal, the threshold is set to the gray level value corresponding to the minimum between the modes. Otherwise, the threshold is undetermined for this window, and it receives its default value by some iterative interpolation process involving thresholds of nearest "good" windows. The binary picture thus obtained (Fig. 3c) is then filtered out to remove the background components touching the boundary and filling holes within the cell component (Fig. 3d). In this stage, the image can be edited by the operator (using the joy-stick point-marker of the system, Fig. 1), e.g. in order to cut off eventual "bridges" joining the cell component to the background (due to minute cell contour imperfections). The main component representing the cell is then extracted and subjected to some boundary-smoothing operation and its contour is extracted finally (Fig. 3e).

The second stage consists of measuring various quantitative features of the extracted cell. Among others, the program calculates:

- coordinates of the center of gravity,
- area and perimeter,
- various global shape factors (see [18-20, 27] for details),
- direction of main axis of inertia,
- length (along the axis) and width (perpendicular to the axis),
- cross-sections for several positions along and perpendicular to the axis.

Then, the cell is decomposed into the cell body and extensions. The body is extracted by iterative circular propagation with the center shifted after every iteration to the center of extracted "candidate body" [18, 19, 25, 26]. Usually from 2 to 4 iterations suffice to obtain the final result, as in Fig. 3f. Parts of the

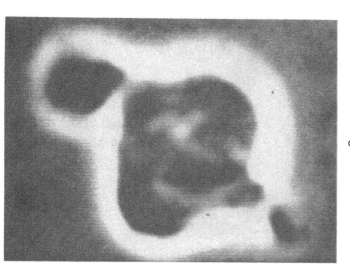

(a)
cell image from
the camera

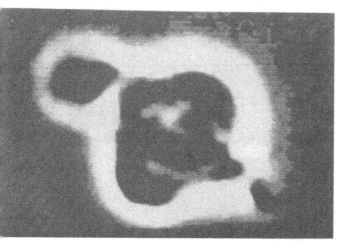

(b)
cell image after
quantization
(16 gray levels)

Fig. 3. Leukemia cells analysis example

(c)
cell image binarized
by dynamic thresholding

(d)
cell image after gap-
-filling & border-
-touching component
removal

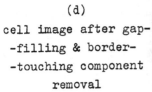

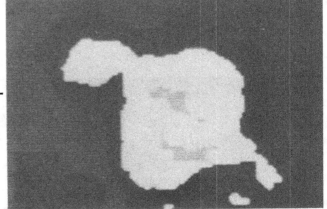

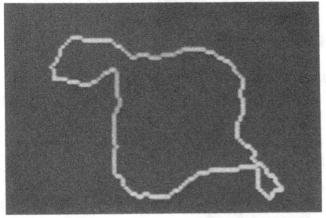

(e)
final cell image
(contour)

Fig. 3. (continued)

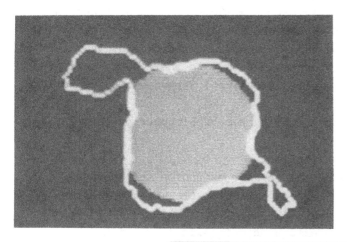

(f)
cell body
extraction

(g)
five candidate
extensions

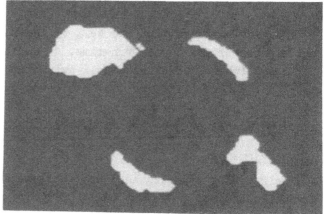

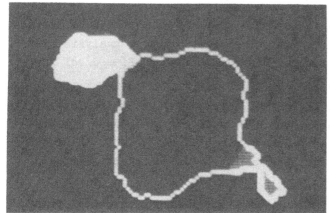

(h)
two true extensions
superimposed
on the contour

Fig. 3. (continued)

cell protruding from the body (Fig. 3g) are then examined as eventual extensions. True extensions are distinguished by the dimensions (should be large enough) and the percentage of that part of their perimeter which touches the body to their whole perimeter (Fig. 3h). Several so-called structural features are then calculated, among others:

- radius of the body (the number of circular propagation steps),
- number of true extensions,
- ratio of areas of the largest extension and the body,
- position of the largest extension (relation of centers of gravity of the body and the extension),
- direction of the extension main axis (also with relation to the cell axis).

The whole analysis of the cell by the CSC program takes several minutes of the system run-time, depending on the quality of the image (which affects the cell-extraction process) and complexity of the cell structure (which affects the decomposition process). The programs written for the system were (and still are) used to process and analyze many thousands of pictures.

Acknowledgments

The research reported here was supported by the Research Programme No. 10.4.

References

1. Z. Kulpa, J. Dernałowicz, H.T. Nowicki et al., System cyfrowej analizy obrazów CPO-2 (CPO-2 digital pictures analysis system, in Polish), Institute of Biocybernetics and Biomedical Engineering Reports, Vol. 1, Warsaw 1977.

2. Z. Kulpa, J. Dernałowicz, M. Raczkowska, M. Piotrowicz, Digital picture processing system CPO-2 and its biomedical applications, In: Selected Papers of the 1st Natl. Conf. on Biocybernetics and Biomedical Engineering, Polish Scientific Publ. (PWN), Warsaw 1978.

3. Z. Kulpa, J. Dernałowicz, Digital picture processing system CPO-2 and its biomedical applications, Proc. BIONIKA'77 Conf., vol. 3, Bratislava, Sept. 1977, 288-293.

4. Z. Kulpa, M. Sobolewski, Obrabotka i raspoznavanye izobrazhe-
   nyi s pomoshchyu universalnoy systiemy CPO-2/K-202 (Image
   processing and recognition using universal system CPO-2/K-202,
   in Russian), Proc. BIONIKA'78 Conf., vol.1, Leningrad, Oct.
   1978, 182-192.

5. Z. Kulpa, J. Dernałowicz, Digital image analysis system
   CPO-2/K-202, general hardware and software description, Proc.
   IV Polish-Italian Bioengineering Symp. on "Pattern Recognition of Biomedical Objects", Porto Ischia/Arco Felice, Oct.
   1978.

6. Z. Kulpa, H.T. Nowicki, Simple interactive picture processing
   system PICASSO-SHOW, Proc. 3rd Inter. Joint Conf. on Pattern
   Recognition, Coronado, Calif., Nov. 1976, 218-223.

7. Z. Kulpa, H.T. Nowicki, Simple interactive picture processing
   system PICASSO-SHOW, Proc. Inter. Seminar on "Experiences of
   Interactive Systems Use", Szklarska Poręba, Oct. 1977, Wrocław Tech. Univ. Press, Wrocław 1977, 101-115.

8. H.T. Nowicki, Interactive picture processing language PICASSO-
   -SHOW 3 and its interpreter, as in [5].

9. Z. Kulpa, Propozycja podjęzyka przetwarzania list do systemu
   PICASSO-SHOW (A proposal of a list-processing sublanguage for
   the PICASSO-SHOW system, in Polish), Institute of Biocybernetics and Biomedical Engineering Internal Reports, Warsaw 1978.

10. A. Bielik, Z. Kulpa, System dynamicznej rezerwacji pamięci i
    przetwarzania listowego SETSYS/K-202 (Dynamic storage alloca-
    tion and list processing system SETSYS/K-202, in Polish),
    ibid.

11. Z. Kulpa, An outline description of the picture analyzing lan-
    guage PAL, Proc. 9th Yugoslav International Symp. on Informa-
    tion Processing (INFORMATICA'74), Bled, Oct. 1974.

12. Z. Kulpa, Język analizy obrazów graficznych PAL (A graphic
    pictures analyzing language PAL, in Polish), Institute of Bio-
    cybernetics and Biomedical Engineering Internal Reports,
    Warsaw 1977.

13. Z. Kulpa, Konstrukcja języka programowania algorytmów cyfrowego przetwarzania złożonych obrazów wizualnych (Design of a programming language for digital processing algorithms of complex visual images, in Polish), Ph. D. Thesis, Institute of Computer Science, Warsaw 1979.

14. Z. Kulpa, PICASSO, PICASSO-SHOW and PAL - a development of a high-level software system for image processing, Proc. Workshop on High-Level Languages for Image Processing, Windsor, June 1979; Academic Press, 1981 (in press).

15. Z. Kulpa, System dynamicznego przydziału pamięci i przetwarzania listowego MINIPAL/SET 1204 (A dynamic storage allocation and list processing system MINIPAL/SET 1204, in Polish), Institute of Biocybernetics and Biomedical Engineering Internal Reports, Warsaw 1973.

16. K. Czechowicz-Janicka, K. Majewska, L. Prządka, M. Raczkowska, Surface and shape of the optic disc in healthy subjects in various age groups - application of computer picture processing, Ophtalmologica, 674, 1977, 1-4.

17. M. Rychwalska, M. Piotrowicz, Analysis of the eye fundus using digital image processing system CPO-2, Proc. BIONIKA'77 Conf., vol. 2, Bratislava, Sept. 1977, 192-195.

18. Z. Kulpa, A. Bielik, M. Piotrowicz, M. Rychwalska, Measurement of the shape characteristics of moving cells using computer image processing system CPO-2, Proc. Conf. BIOSIGMA'78, Paris, April 1978, 286-292.

19. A. Bielik, Z. Kulpa, M. Piotrowicz, M. Rychwalska, Use of computer image processing in quantitative cell morphology, as in [5].

20. K. Lewandowska, J. Doroszewski, G. Haemmerli, P. Sträuli, An attempt to analyze locomotion of leukemia cells by computer image processing, Computers in Biology and Medicine, vol. 9, 1979, 331-344.

21. Z. Kulpa, A. Gutowska, Measurement of limb movement coordination in cats using universal computer image processing system CPO-2, In: A. Morecki, K. Fidelius, eds., Biomechanics VII, Proc. VIIth Inter. Congress of Biomechanics, Warsaw, Sept. 1979, Polish Scientific Publ. (PWN), Warsaw 1980, 459-465.

22. Z. Kulpa, A. Gutowska, Limb movement coordination in cats measured by universal computer image processing system CPO-2, Proc. EUSIPCO-80 Conf., Lausanne, Sept. 1980 (Short Communication and Poster Digest), 85.

23. Z. Kulpa, Errors in object positioning with "centre of gravity" method, The Industrial Robot, vol. 5, Nr.2, 1978, 94-99.

24. Z. Kulpa, Area and perimeter measurement of blobs in discrete binary pictures, Computer Graphics and Image Processing, vol. 6, Nr.5, 1977, 434-451.

25. Z. Kulpa, On the properties of discrete circles, rings and disks, Computer Graphics and Image Processing, vol. 10, 1979, 348-365.

26. M. Doros, Algorithms for generation of discrete circles, rings and disks, Computer Graphics and Image Processing, vol. 10, 1979, 366-371.

27. Z. Kulpa, M. Piotrowicz, Shape factors of figures in discrete pictures, In: Selected Papers of the 3rd Natl. Conf. on Biocybernetics and Biomedical Engineering, Polish Scientific Publ. (PWN), Warsaw 1980.

28. M. Młodkowski, Texture discrimination using local masks, as in [5].

29. M. Młodkowski, S. Vitulano, Some experiments with two-dimensional C-transform applied to texture analysis, as in [5].

30. C. Arcelli, L. Cordella, S. Levialdi, Parallel thinning of binary pictures, Electron. Letters, vol. 11, Nr. 7, 1975.

31. M. H. Hueckel, An operator which locates edges in digitized pictures, J. ACM, vol. 18, 1971, 113-125.

32. L. Mérő, Z. Vassy, A simplified and fast version of the Hueckel operator, Proc. 4th Inter. Joint Conf. on Artificial Intelligence, Tbilisi, 1975, 650-655.

33. M. Piotrowicz, Z. Kulpa, Determination of profiles of banded chromosomes using computer image processing system CPO-2, Proc. EUSIPCO-80 Conf., Lausanne, Sept. 1980 (Short Communication and Poster Digest), 83-84.

THE GOP PARALLEL IMAGE PROCESSOR

Goesta H. Granlund

Picture Processing Laboratory
Linkoeping University
581 83 LINKOEPING
Sweden

ABSTRACT

Images contain a great deal of information which requires large processing capabilities. For that purpose fast image processors have been developed. So far they have mainly dealt with processing of binary images obtained by thresholding gray scale images. For segmentation of images having more subtle features such as noisy lines or edges, texture, color, etc. more elaborate procedures have to be used.

A new type of image processor, GOP (General Operator Processor), has been developed. It can work on gray scale or color images of any size, where it uses a combination of local and global processing which makes it possible to detect faint lines or edges. It also produces texture descriptions which can be integrated in the processing to enable segmentation based upon textural features. The processor can be used for classification and segmentation using simultaneously up to 16 different transforms or representations of an image. Feedback controlled processing and relaxation operations can also be implemented with the processor.

The GOP processor can be connected to any system for picture processing where it speeds up the processing by a factor of 200-1000, dependent upon the situation. Processing of a 512x512 image with a 3x3 operator takes approximately 0,5 seconds in the processor.

INTRODUCTION

Grayscale and color images with a reasonable resolution contain great amounts of information. Analysis of such images takes excessively long time and requires large processing capabilities. For that reason fast special purpose image processors have been developed [1-10]. Most of these processors are oriented towards use of logical operations on binary images.

A common procedure is to use thresholding on an image to create a binary image where objects can be separated and described using topological transformations. Generation of a reduced representation of an image, e.g. a binary image, gives a large compression of the amount of information, but it also gives a great loss of information. For that reason the method can be utilized in a very limited number of situations.

In fact, most situations where we would like to employ image analysis involve images with characteristics given by subtle variations in gray scale or color. We may have different regions described by various textures, and it is often required to detect the borders of such texture regions.

The GOP processor has been designed to perform computations within the General Operator framework. However, the processor is by no means limited to this class of operations, but it can perform most arithmetical and logical operations suggested in an efficient way. In order to give some background to the choice of architecture we will review some aspects of the General Operator concept.

THE GENERAL OPERATOR CONCEPT

If we are working with gray scale or color images and we want a quantitative description of image information, there is a problem of how to represent image information and to determine what operations should be performed on an image.

In this context we have made two fundamental assumptions concerning representation of image information.

1.   Image information can be described as locally
      one-dimensional structures.

2.   Information about orientation of structures is
      extremely important, and it has to be integrated
      in processing.

These assumptions have important consequences for the definition of operations on image information. We will not go into a discussion of the relevance of, these assumptions as they are outside the scope of this paper. These matters have been discussed in more detail earlier [11-13]. Briefly it can be said that these assumptions have proved valid and useful for defining image operations.

The preceding assumptions have provided the basis for definition of a particular operator described earlier [3]. The effect of the operator is to generate a transformed image of a given input image.

The given input image is generally considered to be complex valued, that is, every picture point is represented with two numbers. We can represent an ordinary black and white scalar image by using only one of the numbers in the complex value; setting the other one to zero. We can represent images with more than two components using a set of complex images.

An operator field of a certain size, say 5x5 elements, scans the input image step by step. For each position of the operator field a complex value is computed for the corresponding position in the transform image or output image. See Figure 1.

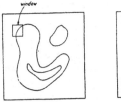

Figure 1

Illustration of the basic function of the operator. (a) original image; (b) contribution from window to transformed image.

The complex value computed for a local region has two components:

1.   A magnitude reflecting the amount of variation within the window,
      e.g. step size of an edge.

2.   An angle determined by the orientation in which we find the largest
      magnitude component according to 1.

In the computation of the amount of variation within the image region, the image content is matched with a combination of edge and line detectors for a number of different orientations, e.g. eight.

Mask correlations

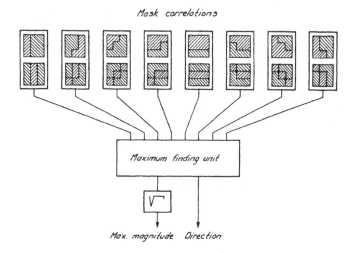

Maximum finding unit

Max. magnitude   Direction

Figure 2
Simplified structure of output vector computation

Every combination of edge and line detector gives a particular output for a particular local region of the image. The outputs for all eight orientations are
now compared and the largest output is taken to represent the neighborhood. See
Figure 2. A vector is determined by the orientation of the operator set giving
the largest output.

If we were to just take the direction of maximum variation we might obtain a result like in Figure 3.

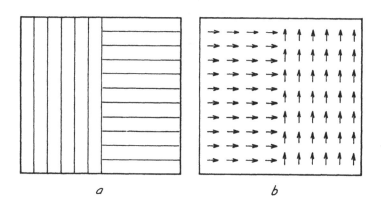

a   b

Figure 3
A stylized image (a) with its transform (b)

Such a definition of orientation of structure and direction of vector would give rise to a number of ambiguities and problems:

1. Orientation of a line or a boundary is not uniquely defined.

2. Such a definition produces a vector that uses only 180° of the angular spectrum.

3. Structures maximally different in terms of orientation do not give opposing vectors, something that we would appreciate intuitively.

The reason for this ambiguity is the fact that orientation of a border or of a line is not uniquely defined.

These problems can be resolved by rescaling with a factor of two the relationship between vector direction and orientation of dominant structure. See Figure 4.

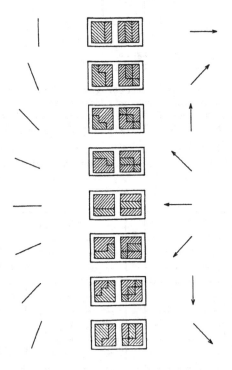

CORRESPONDENCE BETWEEN DIRECTIONALITY AND VECTOR ORIENTATION

Figure 4

Relationship between orientation of structure, line and edge mask giving maximum output, and direction of produced output vector

We can see that in this case perpendicular orientations of the structures, e.g.
lines, give vectors that are opposing. If we use this convention for orientation
the output from a transformation of a disc will appear as in Figure 5.

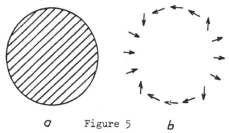

a　　Figure 5　　*b*

Image of disc (a) with its transform (b)

The preceding is an intuitive description of the function of the operator. More
specifically, the operator computation goes as follows: See Figure 6.

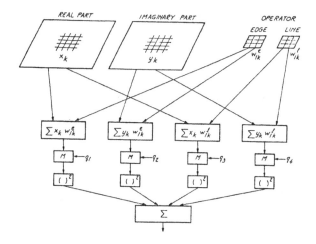

Figure 6

Illustration of computation of edge and line content in one direction.

We have seen earlier that the transform image is complex. As the operator is
intended to work hierarchically on previous transform products, this means that
the input to the operator generally is a complex valued image.

Let us denote the n picture points of the real part image within the window at
some position (ξ, n)

$$x_k \qquad k = 1, \ldots, n$$

and corresponding points of the imaginary part

$$y_k \qquad k = 1, \ldots, n$$

Let us denote the weights of the n points of mask number i

$$w_{ik}^e \qquad k = 1,\ldots,n$$

$$w_{ik}^\ell \qquad i = 1,\ldots,m$$

where m is typically 8, as we have edge and line masks for each one of 8 directions. Edge and line masks are designated by ^{e} and $^\ell$ respectively. In this case

w_{ik}^e and w_{ik}^ℓ can be positive as well as negative.

A multiplication with the mask and a summation is performed for each one of the windows which gives 4 product sums

$$X_i^e = \sum_k w_{ik}^e x_k \qquad Y_i^e = \sum_k w_{ik}^e y_k \qquad k = 1,\ldots,n$$

$$X_i^\ell = \sum_k w_{ik}^\ell x_k \qquad Y_i^\ell = \sum_k x_{ik}^\ell y_k \qquad i = 1,\ldots,8$$

As indicated in [11] these sums bear a strong resemblance to Fourier expansion sums. Using this as an argument, we can define the amplitude content in direction i

$$Z_i = \sqrt{(q_1 \, X_i^e)^2 + (q_3 \, X_i^\ell)^2 + (q_2 \, Y_i^e)^2 + (q_4 \, Y_i^\ell)^2} \qquad i = 1,\ldots,8$$

The parameters q_1 to q_4 can normally be considered as having value one.

By selecting other values, however, it is possible to emphasize the edge operator to the line operator or to emphasize one image component to the other one.

The preceding discussion refers to the case of one complex input image. Often, however, we can have an input to the operator consisting of several complex images.

This may be the case when we have as input a three color image plus a complex transform image. If we denote the magnitude component Z_i from image s by Z_{is} we obtain the magnitude from all image components

$$Z_i = \sqrt{\sum_s Z_{is}^2} \qquad s = 1, 2,\ldots s_{max}$$

In relation to the simplified discussion with regard to Figure 2 we perform a comparison to find the maximum value Z_{max} of Z_i

$$Z_{max} = \max_{i=1,\ldots,8} (Z_i) = \max(Z_i,\ldots,Z_8)$$

We now define an output vector $\underline{Z}$ where $\underline{Z} = Z_{max} \cdot e^{j(i_m-1)\frac{\pi}{4}}$ and i_m is the direction corresponding to the one giving maximum output.

This gives a relationship between orientation of structure, line and edge mask giving maximum output, and direction of produced output vector, according to Figure 4. The design of operator weights for this purpose is described elsewhere [15,16].

An important property of the operator is that it can be used repeatedly upon earlier transform products to detect structure and to simplify the image. This property of the operator can be used to describe texture, and to discriminate between textures [14]. Two steps of transformation of a stylized image appear in Figure 7.

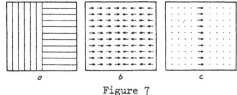

Figure 7

Result of two transformations. (a) Original image; (b) First order transformation; (c) Second order transformation.

The hypothetical example conveys the idea that the structural content in the original image is transformed into a slowly varying field. A second transform gives the boundary between the two fields. An interpretation in image analysis terms is the following:

a)   Original image with two different texture regions.

b)   First transform giving a description of the textures in terms of variation content and orientation.

c)   Second transform giving the border between the textures.

A more realistic example is given in Figure 8. In the texture image of skin from unborn calf from Brodatz book on textures [17], a patch of the skin to the left has been turned 90°. Between the first and second transformations, an angular average of the first transform has been computed.

It is unfortunate that this and the following photographic illustrations can not be printed in color as the vector fields were originally displayed on a color TV monitor with the luminance controlled by the magnitude and the color by the angle of the vector. Some of the information in the original displays is consequently lost in the black and white reproductions.

It is apparent that the procedure gives a very good delineation of the border between the two texture regions. It should be pointed out that the difference in average density over the border has not been used for discrimination, although this is the discrimination feature that is most apparent to the eye in certain parts of the border.

The operator gives a description of the texture in terms of something like variation content and orientation. As we will see in the next section there is no need to tune the frequency characteristic of the operator to that of the pattern as a set of operators with different frequency characteristics is used, and information will be picked up by one operator or another.

An important aspect is that we after the first transformation obtain a slowly varying field which does not contain the high frequency components existing in the texture but only a description of the structural properties of the texture and how these properties vary.

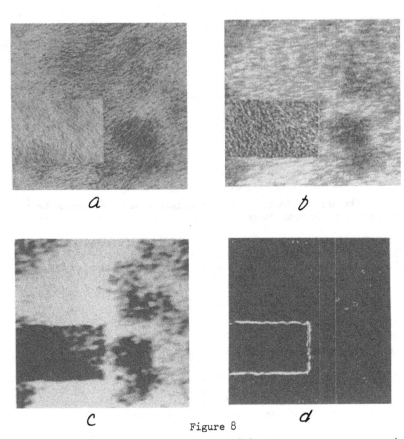

a

b

c

Figure 8

d

Processing of calf skin. (a) Original image; (b) First order transform; (c) Angular average of first order transform; (d) Second order transform of angular average.

An important property of the operator is its ability to detect structure as opposed to uniformity, whatever structure and uniformity may imply at a certain level.

This relates to the function of the operator to describe variations in the image. These variations may relate to edges, lines, texture or some other feature. Edges and lines will retain their identity as local events, while a more global event like texture will assume the description as a slowly varying field. A second order transform will now try to detect variations in the variations displayed in the first order transform.

It has been shown earlier that it is possible to extract most of the information in a picture by analyzing the content in local regions of varying size, [11]. We have also seen some of the effects of sequences of transformations, each with a certain window size giving the information within a limited frequency band. The question now arises: What type of structure can combine these two effects in a useful way?

It has been found useful that the windows become increasingly wider on higher transformation levels. One effect of the transform is that it gives a simplification of the pattern. In order to contain the same average amount of information the window must become wider at higher levels of transformation. After every transformation only higher level features remain, and these features have to be related to other features on the same level. Thus the width of the operator field or the window must be increased.

The organization suggested for a system combining several levels of transformations is indicated in Figure 9. At the bottom left is the first-order transformation covering the highest frequency band around r_1 and consequently having the smallest window size. The window size and thus the sampling frequency are indicated by a grid pattern on this and other picture functions. The transformation gives as a result the complex function $f_{r_1}(1) (x,y)$. In accordance with the earlier discussion, this transformed picture function has a lower feature density and ought to be sampled at a lower density and within a lower frequency band. This is indicated by the grid pattern of lower density for $f_{r_1}(1) (x,y)$.

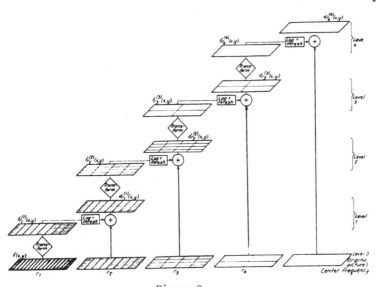

Figure 9

A hierarchical structure of transformations.

According to the earlier discussion we should proceed with another transformation of $f_{r_1}(1)(x,y)$. It has been found, however, that a better result is obtained if we threshold the function and take the log function of it. This procedure removes low-level noise and gives a compression of the range of values of $f_{r_1}(1)(x,y)$ emphasizing the middle amplitude range. It may be interesting to observe that this amplitude characteristic is similar to certain stimulation-response characteristics of the visual system.

In order for us to obtain information within lower-frequency ranges, the original picture has to be processed using wider windows and a lower center frequency $r_2 < r_1$. From Figure 9 it is apparent that the transformed and rescaled picture is combined with the original picture to form a picture function $d_{r_1}(1)(x,y)$ which is transformed further. The combination operator is denoted $\oplus^1$ and could in general be addition, multiplication, or something else. In our experiments it has been found that a form of addition gives appealing results.

As we deal with a logarithmic representation of the transform, an addition of transforms will imply multiplication of the pictures. It might be argued that we do not perform any logarithmic rescaling on the original image; however, many media for picture input, such as photographic film, do in fact exhibit logarithmic characteristics.

As the next transformation is done around a lower center frequency, r_2, only a band around that frequency will be taken from the original image. This is indicated by the lower resolution grid imposed upon the original picture function for that frequency.

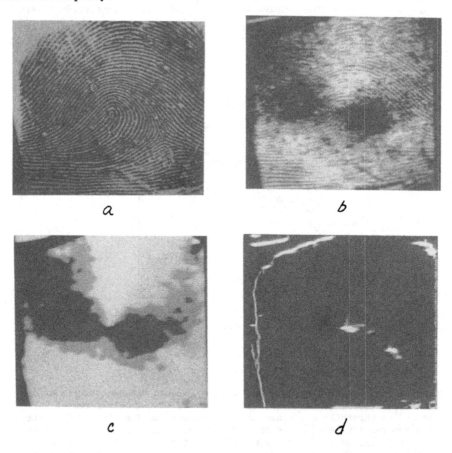

Figure 10

Processing of fingerprint. (a) Original image; (b) First order transform; (c) Angular average of first transform; (d) Second order transform of angular average.

The combined picture function $d_{r_1}^{(1)}(x,y)$ is now transformed into a function $f_{r_2}^{(2)}(x,y)$, which is rescaled logarithmically and thresholded and combined with the original picture giving a picture function $d_{r_2}^{(2)}(x,y)$, and so on for each level analogously to the previous discussion.

The number of transformation levels to use is still an open question, and will have to be determined after further experiments have been performed.

An example of description of structure is given in Figure 10. In a fingerprint pattern we have regular as well as irregular features.

We can see how structural irregularities appear in the second order transform indicating the principal points of the fingerprint. It should be noted that these features are not indicated by any differences in density, only in structure.

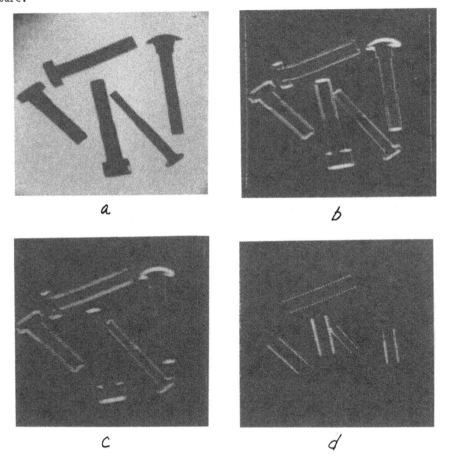

Figure 11

Processing of bolts. (a) Original image; (b) First order transform using high frequency operator; (c) First order transform using medium frequency operator; (d) Combination of the preceding two first order transforms

There are a number of ways in which structures can be discriminated between, using different combinations of transforms. In Figure 11 we have an example where the use of two first order transforms with different frequency characteristics makes it possible to discriminate between thread and cylinder of a bolt. Again, the limitation to gray scale in the images makes them less informative.

We can see that different transforms extract different structural properties.

This ability of the structure to employ information from operators of different sizes is extremely important. One of the attractive features is the reduction of noise that can be obtained in a way similar to the function of the operator described by Rosenfeld [18]. Let us consider a "one-dimensional" image as in Figure 12.

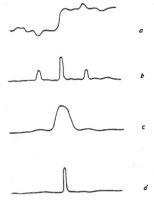

Figure 12

Combination of transform products in a one-dimensional image. (a) Noisy edge in image; (b) First order transform, small operator; (c) First order transform, larger operator; (d) Product between transforms

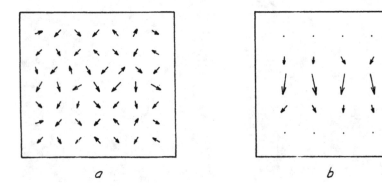

Figure 13

Transformations of a hypothetical noisy edge. (a) First order transform giving edge candidates; (b) Second order transform combining edge candidates having consistent orientations.

The idea conveyed in this figure is that a small operator gives a noisy output well defined in position, while a large operator gives an output with less noise but also less well defined position. A combination of both outputs suppresses noise but preserves position of edge. This combination of operator products is obtained implicitly in the structure given in Figure 9.

Operations on angular information are even more important and efficient than those on the magnitude in filtering operations, because we can detect consistency in directionality which is the feature that distinguishes it from noise. Figure 13 illustrates the transforms of a hypothetical noisy edge.

The operator automatically takes the orientation of edge elements into account, which makes it possible to suppress the noise efficiently and to get a good definition of the boundary line. If we use feedback processing, as will be discussed later, we can obtain an even more precise definition of the boundary.

THE GOP IMAGE PROCESSOR

The GOP (General Operator Processor) image processor implements in hardware the operations described earlier, as well as most other operations suggested for image processing. The processor can be attached to a standard computer system used for image processing. A typical configuration is the one given in Figure 14 [19-20].

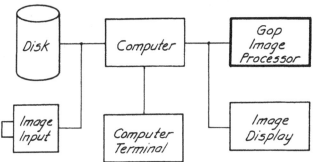

Figure 14
Typical configuration of image processing system using the GOP image processor.

The GOP processor speeds up the processing by a factor of 200-1000 dependent upon the situation. The processor is designed to provide maximum speed with maximum flexibility in a cost-effective manner. This is achieved by having the processor divided into two parts where processing speed and flexibility are interchanged. Processing of a 512x512 image with a 3x3 operator takes approximately 0.5 seconds in the processor.

The processor cummunicates with the rest of the system on the DMA channel. This normally gives a good balance between transfer speed on the DMA channel and the speed of the processor, as every picture point in general is used several times.

The operations that we have found to be of primary interest in image processing and analysis are of type:

$$f = f(\alpha, \beta, \gamma, ..., \underbrace{\underbrace{\Sigma \Sigma \, x_{ij} \, a_{ij}, \Sigma \Sigma \, x_{ij} \, b_{ij}, ...}_{I}}_{II})$$

where f is the output element computed from a neighborhood containing image elements x_{ij}.

This very general form includes operations of arithmetical as well as logical type. The output is partly a function of a number of product sums which may be convolutions between mask functions and neighborhoods of the image. The computations of these product sums are generally very time-consuming as they contain a great number of products for each sum. However, the computation is very straightforward and needs very little flexibility.

The output is also a function of a number of parameters α, β, γ.... These parameters enable a high degree of non-linearity in the procedure. The parameters are typically functions of pictures or picture transforms which means that their value varies from one point of the image to another. The parameters can either be combined with the product sums to form any function, or they can point to different subroutines in the micro-program memory. Thus any degree of flexibility can be obtained. The parameters can e.g. imply a variable threshold function or a dominant orientation for non-isotropic filtering.

The two types of computations described earlier require two different architectures to be performed efficiently. This gives a structure according to Figure 15.

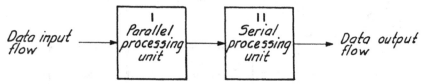

Figure 15
Simplified block diagram of system architecture.

A more detailed block diagram of the processor is given in Figure 16.

Part I of processor

Part I of the processor is a reconfigurable pipelined parallel processor, where data from the image segment memory and weights from the mask memory are combined in four parallel pipelines.

Image segment memory:

Capacity 16K words of 16 bits. Can be restructured to fit the current processing situation, such that up to 16 input images can be involved in processing simultaneously. Software in the external computer determines the allowable length of the image segment, and moves data to the processor one line at a time. There it substitutes the oldest line in a "rolling" fashion. E.g. we can simultaneously have 4 input image segments of size 512x8 pixels. The definitive arrangement of the image segments is determined by the number of images and the mask size.

Data modes:

The image segment memory contains 16-bit words. Due to a selection and rescaling facility at the input of the pipelines there is a great deal of flexibility in the choice of data representation. Among the most commonly used are the following data modes:

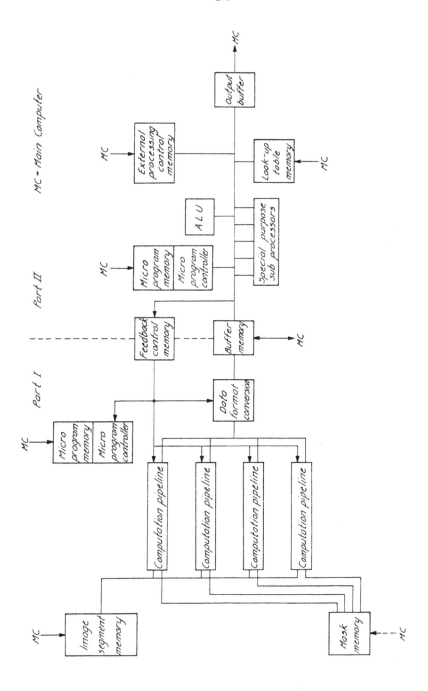

Figure 16
Block diagram of GOP image processor.

Complex data: The 16-bit data word is divided into two parts; one for magnitude and one for angle, generally 8+8 bits.

Two-image data: The 16 bits are divided into two words of arbitrary length, e.g. two images with each 8 bits. These two images can either be processed independently or their contributions can be combined.

16-bit data: The 16 bits can represent just one word of data. This can be used e.g. in classification procedures.

Binary image data: The 16-bit word contains data representing binary images. The desired binary image can be selected. This gives the processor simultaneous access to up to 256 binary images input.

Mask memory:

The mask data is stored in a memory of size 16K words of 20 bits. This storage can be restructured in a number of ways.

The normal configuration is that the mask memory is divided into four sections, one section providing each pipeline with weight coefficients. In parallel with the first section is another memory of 4K words of 14 bits. The content of this later memory points to the image segment memory selecting data points to be processed. This means that points can be picked arbitrarily within the 16K image segment memory to form a neighborhood of up to 4096 points sampled in any order or arrangement. This allows e.g. masks of different sizes to be used on different input image planes.

The mask memory can be organized to contain up to 4096 different masks with any distribution of size within the limits of the size of the mask memory itself. These masks can be freely combined in up to 256 different mask sets. Which one of these mask sets to use can be determined by part II, e.g. in response to image data intended to control the processing.

Data modes:

As is the case with the image segment memory, there is a great deal of flexibility available in the choice of data representation in the mask memory due to a selection and rescaling facility at the input of the pipelines. Among the most commonly used data modes are the following:

Complex data: The 20-bit data word is divided into two parts; one for magnitude and one for angle, generally 10+10 bits.

16-bit data: Each word stores 16 bits of data in the least significant positions. Is used e.g. in classification procedures.

Data format conversion:

In order to allow fast computation, part I of the processor uses fixed point arithmetic. However, great care has been taken not to cause errors due to overflow or underflow. Consequently, at the end of the pipeline there is a dynamic range of 27 bits.

Before data enters part II of the processor it is converted to either of three data modes: 16 bit fixed-point data, logarithmic data or floating-point data. Data converted in this fashion is then stored in the buffer memory between part I and part II. The data mode can be selected with respect to demands on accuracy and speed in the computation in part II.

16-bit fixed-point data:

The 27 bits are converted to 16-bit fixed-point data using a resettable binary rescaling. Overflow check is provided. This mode is useful for procedures giving results with small and predicted dynamic range.

Logarithmic data:

The 27 bits of fixed point data are converted to a signed-magnitude logarithmic representation of 16 bits. Computations with logarithmic data are very useful in many image analysis procedures, where relative magnitudes are of importance. This type of data can also be handled very fast in part II of the processor.

Floating point data:

The 27 bits of fixed point data are converted to a floating point representation consisting of a 16-bit mantissa and a 8-bit exponent. This data mode is useful where high accuracy in computations is needed.

Buffer memory

The communication from part I of the processor to part II is done over a dual memory of $2 \cdot 4K$ words of 16 bits. Part I can write into one half of this memory at the same time as part II reads from the other half.

Part II of processor

Part II of the processor has an entirely different architecture. After processing in part I, the amount of information is reduced considerably. Now a high degree of flexibility is required to combine intermediary results derived by part I. These combinations are usually highly nonlinear operations, determined from one point to the other by some particular transform of the image to process.

Part II is consequently a serial, special purpose processor. The central parts are a microprogram controller 2910 and an arithmetic logic unit 2901 B. A fast microprogram memory (access time 55 nsec) of size 2K words of 64 bits (expandable to 4K words of 80 bits) gives a cycle time of 150 nsec for the processor. All units communicate over a 16-bit bus. A special work memory of 2K words (expandable), with possibilities of indirect addressing facilitates programming.

In order to obtain fast processing of complicated algorithms, a 16K word memory area can be used for look-up tables. A memory area of 4K words is available for external processing control. In this memory lines from up to 4 images can be stored to control the processing point by point.

On the main bus are attached a number of special purpose processing units. They perform operations such as fast multiplication, scaling and shifting (up to 16 steps in one cycle), floating point operations, etc.

The computation within the processor can be performed using fixed-point 16-bit representation, logarithmic 16-bit representation or floating-point representation, or any desired mix of these during a particular procedure.

Common features

Part I is controlled by part II regarding what operations to perform, but does not interfere during the computations set up for a neighborhood. However, the configuration of the pipeline can be changed after the computation, and an entirely different configuration can be set up instantaneously for a different type of computation on the same (or different) neighborhood. This allows maximal flexibility in conjunction with high speed.

In normal processing the pipelines remain in the same mode for the whole image. Parts I and II run simultaneously at maximum speed with data exchanged over the twin buffer.

A typical operation step where maximal flexibility is needed, may go as follows:

The appropriate element from the controlling image is fetched from the memory. This data is processed in some way to determine which one of a number of predetermined actions to take. This particular action leads to an address of the micro-controller, which goes through a procedure to activate the desired preset mode, to determine what set of masks to use and to give part I permission to start. Part I goes through the micro-program sequence determined by part II, thereby performing e.g. convolution within a particular mask, and returning the result to the buffer memory. Part II may now analyze this result and decide that it wants a different operation performed on a different input image (of which there may be up to 16) using a different size neighborhood, although the computation is performed with relation to one particular output pixel. The same type of prcedure is performed over again. The action decided leads to a different adress in the micro-controller, which points out a different mode, a different micro-program procedure and different masks to use for part I.

The preceding procedure may sound very complicated but the computations can be performed very fast, as most possible actions can be prepared for, using look-up tables. We also have a speed of the whole procedure which is dependent upon the complexity of the procedure.

All this flexibility would be extremely demanding, if it were not that assembler and macro-languages have been developed for both parts of the processor. Thus macro-routines are available for most common processing tasks, and use of these macros to develop new routines is not too demanding.

One of the cards of the GOP processor handles all the communication with the host computer, and this is the only part that is specific for the particular environment in which the processor is going to operate. Interface cards will be developed for most of the common computers used for image processing.

SOFTWARE

In order to obtain an easily workable system with a processor as flexible as the GOP, it is necessary to have a good software system. For that reason an extensive, interactive program system has been developed. The goal has been to provide program routines for most commonly occurring processing tasks, as well as to provide an attractive environment for the researcher who wants to investigate new algorithms and develop his own programs.

The program system is built around several levels of languages. The intention has again been that the program system should be easily transportable between different computers.

The highest level language is a highly portable, interactive language INTRAC. This language is implemented on at least 5 different computers, and the package is written in FORTRAN. Its purpose is to give an easy, interactive way of combining precoded application modules with automatic variation of parameters. This is done through the use of MACRO command files that are created and invoked by commands entered from a terminal.

The medium level language is FORTRAN, in which the bulk of the application modules are written. The intention is that the user should be able to create his own particular application modules without too much difficulty.

The low level language is the assembly language of the computer used, which is only utilized in very few I/O drive routines. These routines are, however, very close to the standard form for other DMA peripherals of the computer used.

As mentioned earlier, there are also assembly languages available for the creation of microprograms for part I and part II for the processor. As a rule, the average user will never have to worry about this, and he will use available modules for different modes of operation. Still, he will be able to employ the flexibility available, by specifying switches and parameters in the modules.

There are also hardware checkout program modules available. The module of main interest to the user is one that checks every function of the processor on test data, as well as the communication with the main computer. An error message is printed out in the case of error. This testprogram can be activated at the beginning of each work period to insure proper operation.

Another set of available program modules can be used to create synthetic images, which is of great value in evaluation of algorithms. Programs are also available for creation and optimization of filter functions with desired properties, and various types of mask functions.

MODES OF OPERATION

Most of the software available is for work in image processing and analysis. Software for the most common problems has been developed, and further software is under development.

In the following section it will only be possible to mention some of the modes of operation for which the GOP processor can be used.

Filtering

A real or complex valued image of any size can be convolved with a real or complex valued filter function with a size of up to 128x128 elements. Filtering using a mask of this size (if ever needed) on a 512x512 image will take approximately two and a half minutes to process.

The filtering can also be performed using various non-linear functions. Non-linear scaling functions can easily be specified and stored in look-up tables for fast access.

The non-linear filtering procedure can be made very specific, in that it can be image-content dependent. This means that we can employ different filter functions (or in general any operation) from one point to another of the processed. This gives limitless possibilities to guide the process from some processed version of the image. One framework for such experiments, that has proved successful, is within the General Operator information representation.

The filtering procedures can also be used for image interpolation and optimal shrinking of an image.

Edge and line detection

Most suggested types of edge and line detectors can be implemented in the GOP. Most of the software available, however, implements various forms of the General Operator. Routines are available for edge element connection, contour thinning, masking of weaker contours next to stronger, etc.

Texture description

Most local texture description operators can be implemented using the GOP. While the General Operator has proved quite useful for texture description and discrimination between different textures, a specific, more sensitive texture operator has been developed within the GOP information representation framework. This gives a texture description that can easily be integrated in the classification procedure.

Higher-order feature detection

A number of higher order feature or structure operators have been developed. These include operators for curvature, endpoints, symmetry and other higher order features which have proved useful in image analysis.

Segmentation and labeling

The processor can be used to implement various labeling and segmentation algorithms.

Relaxation procedures and feedback processing

The structure of the processor makes it attractive for applications in relaxation procedures and in feedback processing. The high flexibility makes it possible to perform image-dependent operations and to store the restriction rules to be employed.

The feedback provision makes it possible to have the information of a number of image transformations determine the processing to be performed, to a complexity that is limited only by imagination and the effort to define the operations. The guiding information transformation products can determine the set of restriction rules to invoke for at particular subset of the image.

Classification

Classification is most easily done using linear discriminant functions, which well adapt to the GOP structure. Classification can be done point by point, e.g. for multispectral images of which there can be 16 real valued or complex input images. Classification can also be performed using contextual information over increasingly global regions. One way of doing this is using the GOP transforms, which form a natural, hierarchical structure of higher-order and global features.

Again, we can include information from up to 16 representations or transformations of the image, to classify different regions for labeling or segmentation.

Quadric or other discrimination functions can also be implemented, although with less speed.

Logical operations

Logical operations on binary images can be performed with neighborhood sizes up to 3x4 elements. This allows classical operations such as erosion, dilation, labeling, skeletonizing, etc. Even in this case it is possible to determine the operation to perform on a particular neighborhood using some earlier image transform.

Content-dependent translation

Apart from translations with a fixed step size, it is possible to obtain a content-dependent translation of image elements. This gives possiblities to produce controlled distortions of the image, as well as to correct existing geometric distortions.

EXAMPLE OF PROCESSING - CONTENT DEPENDENT IMAGE FILTERING

As one example of the many uses of the GOP image processor we will look at how it can be used for content dependent image filtering in a feedback mode.

An important feature of the processing system around this operator is its hierarchical structure with higher and lower levels as indicated earlier. There we suggested a hierarchy with processed information going from lower to higher levels. We also have a local feedback effect to low levels, due to the fact that the information concerning orientation of a structure is indicated in every single element belonging to this structure. This feature is most important because it makes it possible to use some very efficient filtering procedures to enhance and suppress various features.

An important use of the hierarchical structure is to introduce feedback from higher levels to the operation of the system at a lower level. This can be used for a number of purposes such as relaxation procedures [21].

The architecture of the processor allows such a processing to be performed, as a set of images can be used to control the operations to be performed from one neighborhood to another. Se Figure 17.

This architecture makes the processor in effect an MIMD (Multiple Instruction stream - Multiple Date stream) machine.

One use of feedback processing is for image-content dependent filtering. In this case a structure like the one in Figure 18 can be used.

From the original image a controlling transform is computed. In the simplest case the controlling transform may be an ordinary first order transform giving the dominant orientation of structures in the images.

The original image to be filtered is now brought into an iteration loop. The image is convolved with a filter function to form a filtered image. One interesting case is when the filter function is rotationally non-isotropic, and the controlling transform determines the axis of symmetry of the filter. Figure 19 gives an example of such an interative non-isotropic filtering of a fingerprint.

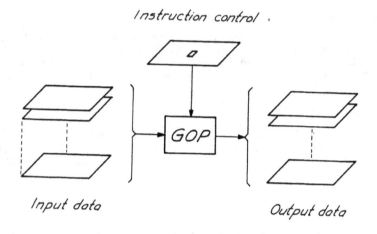

Figure 17
Input-Output structure of GOP Processor.

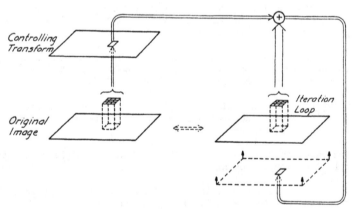

Figure 18
Feedback structure for content dependent image filtering

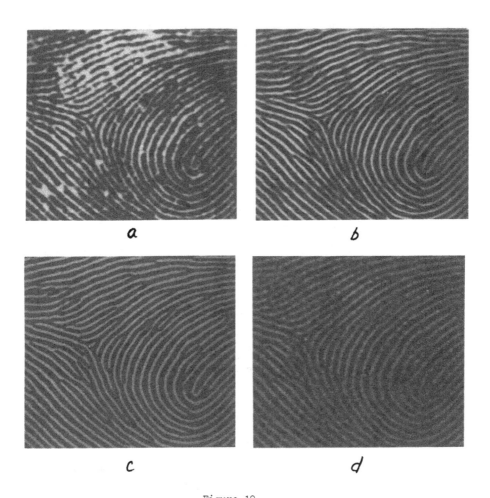

Figure 19
Non-isotropic filtering of fingerprint (a) Original image (b) Results after one
interation (c) Results after two interations (d) Comparable isotropic filter

Another example of feedback processing is for contour detection and masking. Figure 20 illustrates the structure used.

The original image is processed with the General Operator producing a transform
containing essentially contours. In general the first order transform is sufficient for this purpose. In the case where different regions are defined at least
partly by different textures, it may be necessary to produce a second order
transform which will then give borders between different textures [14]. The
first and second order transform can then be combined which will give optimal
definition of existing boundaries.

From the contour transform a controlling transform is produced. The controlling
transform is a function of the contour transform. In the simplest form it may
consist of the contour transform or a low pass filtered version of the contour

transform. The controlling transform thus displays the direction of the dominant variation within the neighborhood.

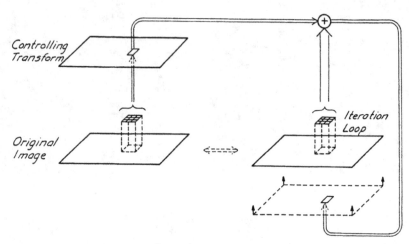

Figure 20
Feedback structure for contour detection and masking

The contour transform is now brought over to the iteration loop. A specially designed operator is used here, which performs a nonlinear differentiation in one direction and an integration in the perpendicular direction. The directions for differentiation and integration are determined for every point by the controlling transform.

Figure 21 shows an example of the processing that can be performed. We can see that there is a fairly efficient thinning of the main contours. Another important property of the processing is the one of masking, implying that weak contours are suppressed next to strong ones.

These structures described and the results given are very preliminary indications of the potential of the method. In the cases given, the controlling property is simply the dominant direction found within the local region under consideration. In general it is possible to have more elaborate properties of the image content to control the operations on the image. This gives very flexible and powerful procedures for filtering and for detection.

This procedure can also be formulated in relaxation terms, where the controlling transform determines which compatibility relations to employ in a particular part of the image. This discussion is however outside the scope of this presentation.

ACKNOWLEDGEMENTS

This research was supported by The National Swedish Board for Technical Development. The author also wants to express his appreciation of the enthusiastic work by the GOP group: Dan Antonsson, Anders Ekdal, Martin Hedlund, Hans Knutsson, Kenneth Lundgren and Bertil von Post.

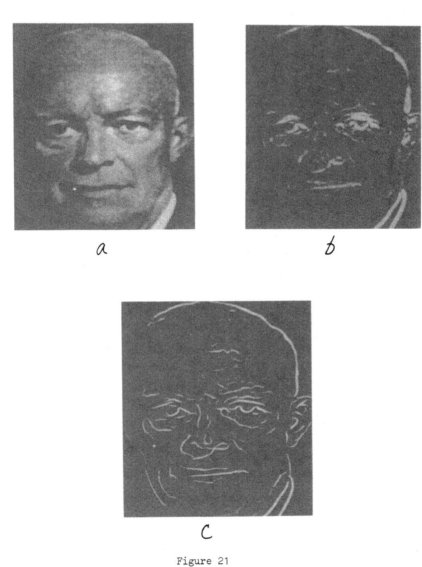

Figure 21

Example of processing in contour detection and masking (a) Original image (b)
First order transform (c) Interatively processed image.

REFERENCES

1. Kidode M, Asada H, Watanabe S:
    Local Parallel Pattern Processor, PPP
    Toshiba Review No. 125, 1980.

2. Lougheed R.M, McCubbrey D.L, Sternberg S.R:
    Cytocomputers: Architectures for Parallel Image Processing.
    Environmental Research Institute of Michigan
    Ann Arbor, Michigan, 1980.

3. Kruse B:
    System Architecture for Image Analysis
    Structured Computer Vision
    Eds S. Tanimoto and A. Klinger
    Academic Press 1980, pp 169-212.

4. Gemmar P, Ischen H, Luetjen K:
    FLIP: A Multiprocessor System for Image Processing.
    Report from Forschungsinstitut fuer Informationsverarbeitung
    und Mustererkennung.
    Karlsruhe, Germany, 1980.

5. Gerritsen F.A, Aardema L.G:
    DIP-1: A Fast, Flexible and Dynamically Microprogrammable
    Pipelined Image Processor.
    Report from Delft University of Technology, Delft, Netherlands,
    1980.

6. Briggs F.A, Fu K.S, Hwang K, and Patel J.H:
    PM^4 - A Reconfigurable Multiprocessor System for Pattern Recog-
    nition and Image Processing.
    AFIPS-Conference Proceedings, Vol. 48, 1979.

7. Van Daele I, De Roo J, Vanderheydt L, Oosterlinck A, Van den
    Berghe H:
    Image Computer Configuration with Video Rate Processing
    Capabilities.
    Proc. First Scandinavian Conference on Image Analysis,
    Linköping, Sweden, 1980.

8. Reeves A.P:
    A Systematically Designed Binary Array Processor.
    IEEE Trans. Comp, Vol. C-29, No. 4, 1980.

9. Duff M.J.B:
    Review of the CLIP Image Processing System.
    AFIPS Conference Proceedings, Vol. 47, 1978.

10. Reddaway S.F:
    The DAP Approach.
    Infotech State of the Art Report on Supercomputers, Vol. 2,
    1979.

11. Granlund G.H:
    In Search of a General Picture Processing Operator,
    Computer Graphics and Image Processing, Vol. 2, pp 155-173,
    1978.

12. Granlund G.H:
    On One-dimensional Representation and Filtering of Image
    Information.
    Proc. International Conf. on Digital Signal Processing,
    Florence, Italy, 1978.

13. Granlund, G.H:
    An architecture of a Picture Processor Using a Parallel
    General Operator.
    Proc. from the Fourth International Joint Conference on
    Pattern Recognition, Kyoto, Japan, 1978.

14. Granlund G.H:
    Description of Texture Using the General Operator Approach.
    Proceedings of the 5th International Conference on Pattern
    Recognition, Miami, Florida, 1980.

15. Knutsson H, von Post B, and Granlund G.H:
    Optimization of Arithmetic Neighborhood Operations for Image
    Processing. Proceedings of the First Scandinavian Conference
    on Image Analysis
    Linköping, Sweden, 1980.

16. Knutsson H, and Granlund G.H:
    Fourier Domain Design of Line and Edge Detectors.
    Proceedings of the 5th International Conference on Pattern
    Recognition, Miami, Florida, 1980.

17. Brodatz P:
    Textures
    Dover, New York, 1966.

18. Rosenfeld A, and Thurston, M:
    Edge and Curve Detection for Visual Scene Analysis
    IEEE Tr on Computers, C-20, pp 562-569, 1971.

19. Granlund G.H:
    GOP, A Fast Parallel Processor for Image Information.
    Proceedings of the First European Signal Processing Conference
    Lausanne Switzerland, 1980.

20. Granlund G.H:
    GOP, A Fast and Flexible Processor for Image Analysis.
    Proceedings of the 5th International Conference on Pattern
    Recognition. Miami Beach, Florida, 1980.

21. Rosenfeld A, et al:
    Scene Labelling by Relaxation Operations
    IEEE Tr. Systems, Man & Cybernetics
    SMC-6, pp 420-433, 1976.

OBJECT DETECTION

IN INFRARED IMAGES

David L. Milgram*
Azriel Rosenfeld**

The support of the Defense Advanced Research Projects Agency and
the U.S. Army Night Vision Laboratory under Contract DAAG-53-76C-
0138 (DARPA Order 3206) is gratefully acknowledged, as is the help
of Kathryn Riley in preparing this paper.

* Lockheed Palo Alto Research Labs, D52-53, B204,
   3251 Hanover Street, Palo Alto, CA 94304.
**Computer Vision Laboratory, Computer Science Center, University
   of Maryland, College Park, MD 20742.

ABSTRACT

This paper describes algorithms for detecting and classifying objects such as tanks and trucks in forward-looking infrared (FLIR) imagery. It summarizes research conducted in the course of a two-year project in the areas of image modeling, pre- and post-processing, segmentation, feature extraction, and classification.

1. Image models

The work on image modeling conducted under this project was concentrated in three main areas:

1) Modeling of the joint (gray level, edge value) statistics of FLIR scenes, as a basis for defining threshold selection techniques.

2) Modeling of thresholding and edge detection responses to background regions, as a basis for predicting false alarm rates.

3) Modeling edges in images as a basis for defining optimal edge detection operations and for evaluating edge detector output.

This work is briefly summarized in the following subsections. References are given to earlier project reports [1-4] in which detailed treatments can be found.

1.1 Model-based threshold selection

An approach to modeling FLIR imagery has been developed, based on the simplifying assumption that targets appear as homogeneous hot regions within a homogeneous cooler surround. This model describes the joint probability density of gray level and edge strength in such images, for various edge-detecting operations [1,2]. In brief, the model predicts that for low edge values (corresponding to points in the interiors of objects and background), there should be two relatively well separated probability peaks, of different sizes, representing the gray levels of object and background interiors, respectively. For higher edge values, corresponding to points on object/background borders, these peaks should merge together and become a single peak representing the border range of gray levels.

The model just described can be used as a guide to segmenting
FLIR images by thresholding. At low edge values, it should be
easy to pick a threshold at a gray level in the valley between the
two probability peaks, since these are relatively well separated.
At high edge values, the peak gray level value itself, or perhaps
the mean gray level, should be a good threshold, since this represents the "center" of the edges. For intermediate edge values,
one can compromise between these two thresholds in various ways.
A comparative study of threshold selection schemes based on this
approach has been conducted [5]. This work will be discussed
further in Section 4.

1.2 Operator response prediction

a) Predicting results of thresholding

Thresholding images is a common process and much work has been
directed towards selecting the correct value at which to threshold
and estimating the expected error. Normally, one thresholds only
images which contain some signal. Thresholding pure noise is to
be avoided when possible. Since there may be occasions when
thresholding noise is unavoidable (e.g., a poor threshold was
chosen), it is important to predict the expected results. The
expected number of above-threshold regions that result when noise
is thresholded is useful in planning for data structure storage
allocation and in predicting false alarm rates. When a bad
threshold "breaks up" an object, knowledge of the expected sizes
and shapes of noise regions can be used to help discriminate
object fragments from noise. No methods currently exist for predicting the number of connected components of thresholded spatially
correlated signal (or noise). However, it has been found possible
[6] to estimate the moments of regions, the density of border
points, and lower bounds on the number of connected components in
thresholded noise images. The input grayscale image is modeled as
a two-dimensional random process (stationary random field) characterized by its mean and power spectrum. Tests with both synthetic
data (smoothed noise) and actual data were conducted to compare
the predicted and measured responses. The predictions are worst
for thresholds at or near the mode of the noise distribution, but
in general, the comparison showed reasonable agreement between the

predicted and measured values.

   b)   Predicting edge detector response

Statistical response prediction for edge operators can be used
to determine the nature of further processing of the response.
If edge detector output is to be thinned or thresholded, the false
alarm and false dismissal rates depend on the statistics of the
operator responses. A study has been conducted [7] which discusses the statistical properties of the outputs of some edge
detectors operating on a general class of images.

The image model considered is the same as in (a) just above;
this model is appropriate for predicting the response of edge
detectors to background noise. The edge detectors analyzed are
the Laplacian and its absolute value, and the absolute difference
of averages over adjacent 2x2 and 4x4 neighborhoods. The response
features which were measured are the mean edge response at each
point, the variance, the auto-covariance, and the cross-covariance
of gray level and edge value at a number of displacements. In
addition, the density of the local maxima of edge values was computed. Tests using a set of synthetic background images showed
good conformity to the predicted features.

1.3 Edge modeling

   a)   Optimal edge detection

Many optimality criteria have been proposed for edge detection. Among the most well known is that devised by Hueckel [8,9].
It involves fitting an ideal parameterized step edge to the image
data so as to minimize the mean squared error. A new optimal
detector has been designed [10] that simplifies several assumptions associated with the Hueckel detector and thereby solves an
easier optimization problem. Specifically, by assuming that the
local mean is zero and the local variance is unity, two Hueckel
parameters can be eliminated. Further simplifications follow if
the operator can be applied at each point with the edge assumed
to pass through the center (or not to exist at all). The resulting
formulation can be tuned to favor edges with known a priori
probabilities. The computational effort involved in applying the
operator may be reduced by solving the associated cubic equation
using a simple iterative approximation, such as Newton's formula.
Testing on actual data has verified that this approach provides

greater sensitivity than a previously proposed [11] simplification of the Hueckel operator.

b) Evaluation of edge operators

The Hueckel operator defined in [9] has been found to incorporate a theoretical flaw leading to eccentric behavior in textured images. An operator which is conceptually similar but apparently more dependable has been defined [12]. Comparative tests have been made of this and several other operators (including Hueckel's [9], its simplification [11], and the new optimal operator defined in [10], as well as the very simple Sobel operator), to evaluate their adequacy in obtaining the magnitude, direction, and reliability of the edge response at some set of image points, for both ideal and distorted images. The performances of these operators were, in general, closely related to their sizes (and hence, to their computational costs). All of the local operators were able to detect the directions of distorted edges on small (6x6) domains to an accuracy of about 10°, and their magnitudes to within about 10%. On larger (9x9) domains, angular resolution was improved, but ramps became significant as a source of spurious responses. The Sobel operator was judged to perform better than the operator of [11]. The operator of [10] was better able to reject ramps on larger domains, but it is more expensive to apply than the other local operators. The regional operators of [9] and [12] performed similarly; the latter was less affected by the presence of imperfections.

2. Preprocessing

Preprocessing refers to those transformations applied to the raw image data for the purpose of correcting, simplifying, and regularizing the imagery. The resulting images should therefore be more amenable to further processing and more alike in certain properties essential to subsequent algorithms. Thus, for example, sampling and windowing reduce the size of the image to be processed. Histogram transformation and requantization convert all image quantization levels to a range which facilitates feature extraction. Smoothing reinforces regional uniformity and decreases the effects of certain kinds of noise.

Preprocessing steps are best justified by the problem environment itself. A knowledge of the sensor characteristics and geometry will suggest various kinds of radiometric and geometric corrections. For example, with FLIR data, the image is best understood as an array of thermal measurements. If these measurements reflect the ground truth, then much more subtle distinctions can be made; recognizing that a particular temperature is beyond the normal range for a vehicle can, perhaps, indicate that the vehicle is on fire. Similarly, a range map converting pixels to actual size/area measurements can allow a viewer or a program to gauge the size of a particular region and thereby discern its identity more reliably.

In the problem environment at hand it was not possible to acquire substantial information concerning the sensor or the imaging situation, due to classification problems. Thus the "intelligent" corrections of the previous paragraph were impossible. However, several preprocessing steps do make sense. The following subsections describe them.

2.1 Sampling

According to the sampling theorem, the spacing of the data points should be half the size of the smallest feature to be detected. Thus, to detect objects of one meter on a side, pixels should correspond to one half meter on a side. In practice, however, the presence of noise demands that the data be redundant to increase the reliability of the extraction process. A finer resolution can often provide this redundancy. Naturally, the price must be paid in additional processing time. This tradeoff is difficult to model analytically especially since many different features are extracted from an image and their relative importance is difficult to assess.

Two processes for region extraction are paramount for our work -- thresholding for whole region extraction and edge detection for region border verification. Of these two, edge detection is more sensitive to noise. The degree of sampling allowable for the image data set should therefore not be so great that reliable edge extraction is compromised. A 2-to-1 size reduction (eliminating every other row and column) was found to be compatible with reliable edge detection. In the unsampled images, the average edge ramp cross-section was found to be about 5 pixels wide; thus a 2-to-1 reduction gave about a 3-pixel edge ramp which was consistent with the need to localize edges fairly accurately.

An alternative approach attempted to reduce high frequency noise by extracting windows based on 2x2 averaging rather than sampling. Thus, instead of discarding every other row and column, each pixel in the sampled image was the average over a (disjoint) 2x2 neighborhood in the original image. A smooth, less noisy image was produced and row dropouts were partially eliminated. However, the images seemed to have less constrast. Sampling followed by smoothing appears to be better than smoothing followed by sampling.

A major emphasis in the project has been the detection of small or faint targets. For this reason, the sampled images were also windowed so as to capture the target regions and to further reduce the computational load. Naturally, one must avoid techniques which assume that each window contains exactly one target in its central region. This dilemma asserts itself in subtle ways. Statistical properties of the window, e.g., histogram, central moments, etc. are good predictors of object presence, threshold, etc. However, they cannot be employed in practice unless window size is correctly estimated and window border situations are handled. Our approach does not depend on window size (or frame size) and therefore windowing is an appropriate preprocessing step. Note, however, that estimates of the false alarm rate cannot be reliably derived solely from target windows. For this reason, small noise windows (containing no targets) and large windows (consisting mainly of background clutter) were also processed.

2.2 Histogram transformations and adaptive quantization

Sensor output is related to actual phenomena according to physical laws. If this correspondence is well understood beforehand, it is possible to correct and transform the data to improve subsequent processing. Thus if FLIR data could be used to estimate reliably the temperature of objects, then quite stringent tests could be made to enhance recognition rates. Unfortunately, the analytic interpretation of FLIR data at long range is complicated by many effects such as sun-angle, wind, smoke, surface composition, etc. Furthermore, the sensor hardware itself is subject to

unpredictable electronic noise, disturbances and failures. Only
some of these effects can be alleviated and then (due in part to
the classified nature of the sensor) only statistically.

Among the conventional gray level modifications considered
useful for producing more manageable imagery are the rather simple
histogram mapping techniques. Figure 2.1a illustrates the gray
level histogram of an unmodified image. The gray level range is
defined by eight bits--256 gray levels--and can be seen to exhibit
significant non-uniformities of response. Moreover, from a processing point of view, 256 gray levels do not effectively reflect
the true gray level range and contrast. A simple 2-bit shift
operation, converting 8-bit pixels to 6 bits, has the effect seen
in Figure 2.1b of smoothing the histogram while reducing the gray
level range to 64 gray levels. This technique if continued for
further shifts would ultimately combine significant peaks corresponding to object/background contrast. However, the conversion
from 8-bit to 6-bit was found to be justified, as it alleviated
non-uniform sensor response without destroying target discriminability.

If one assumes that a scene consists of the juxtaposition of
objects of uniform temperature taken from a small number of such
temperatures, then it is possible to convert the image into one
with only a few different gray levels present. An attempt at
adaptive requantization is described in [13]. Briefly, an iterative process constructs a new histogram from the previous version
by identifying gray level peaks and having them gain strength
(i.e., points) from neighboring non-peaks while the non-peak
areas are thereby depleted. The result is a mapping from the original gray level domain to a new sparse set of gray levels. The
resulting quantized images (Figure 2.2) seem not to have lost
object/background discriminability.

2.3 Image smoothing

In the previous section, preprocessing steps were described
which contributed to the interpretation of a scene as a mosaic of
uniform sensor responses. The techniques considered the gray level
population only. Proximity was not involved. In this section,
we discuss attempts to smooth the image spatially so that nearby
points from the same region will have more nearly identical gray

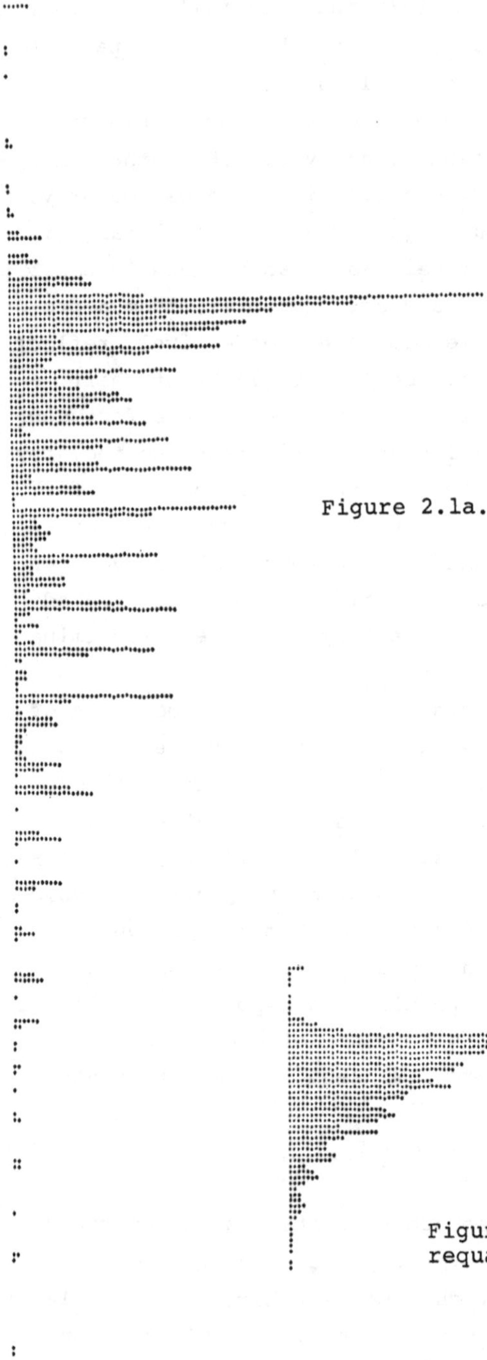

Figure 2.1a.   256-level histogram.

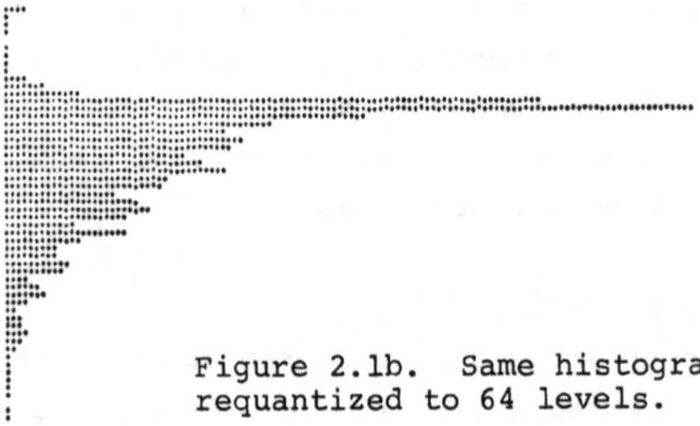

Figure 2.1b.   Same histogram
requantized to 64 levels.

a.

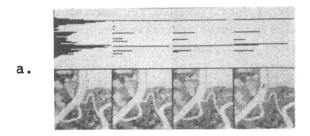

b.

c.

Figure 2.2.   Result of four iterations of the
peak sharpening process using
neighborhood sizes of 2, 3, and
4 for (a-b), sizes 2, 4, and 5
for (c).

levels. There are a number of justifications for spatial image
smoothing. First, by making the image spatially more uniform,
one increases the probability that points belonging to the same
region will be treated identically. Thus, the point sets extracted by thresholding will appear better defined with fewer pinholes
and fewer isolated points. This is reasonable since the chosen
image resolution is intended to cover any object with numbers of
pixels. The second reason for smoothing is to eliminate insigni-
ficant local changes of contrast. Otherwise the output of edge
detection operations based on differencing would contain many tiny
spurious edges which tend to obscure the proper edge signals.
Third, the statistical properties of a smoothed image are more
representative of the true situation. Thus, many decisions based
on the statistics of the smoothed image are more reliable.

Two methods of image smoothing were investigated. In a first
attempt, the mean value of a fixed neighborhood about each point
replaced the point's value. Figure 2.3a shows the effect of
replacing each point of a step edge by its mean value (blurring).
As is evident, blurring smears edges. Figure 2.4a-d illustrates
blurring for several target windows, and also shows the histograms
of these windows before and after blurring. Note that blurring
tends to blend peaks in histograms, thus making thresholding more
difficult. Also, small faint objects tend to become less distinct.

A second approach to image smoothing has the property of pre-
serving edges. At each point of an image, the median value of the
gray levels over a kxk neighborhood is computed. The value of k
depends on the amount of local noise variation. For the original
images, a 5x5 neighborhood size was chosen. Figure 2.3b illustrates the effects of median filtering on a step edge. Note that
the median does not increase the ramp width. Thus edges do not
smear. This is demonstrated in the two-dimensional case in
Figures 2.5-2.7 for a tank image. Median filtering does, however,
round off sharp corners. This was not a serious problem in this
data base. Figure 2.4e-f illustrates a number of median filtered
windows and their histograms. The general algorithm for median
computation over k^2 points is of order k^2. However, better
results may be obtained when evaluating a running median, by
making use of the high autocorrelation of gray level in most
images. The cumulative histogram of the k^2 data points is

a. Mean filtering   b. Median filtering

Figure 2.3.   Effect of filtering on
                step edges using a five
                point neighborhood.

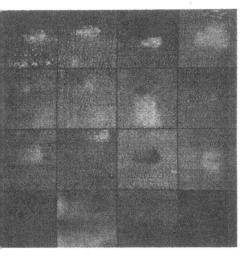
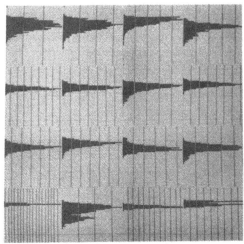

a. Originals.   b. Histograms of (a).

Image Reference: 3R   4T   6T   24T
                   34R   35R   41R   52R
                   21A   22A   23A   37A
                   14N   20N   26N   38N

Figure 2.4.   Comparison of mean and median
                filtering.

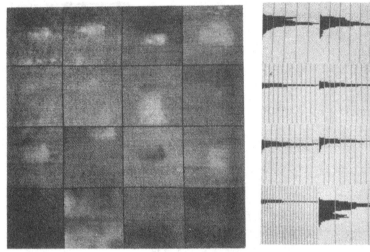

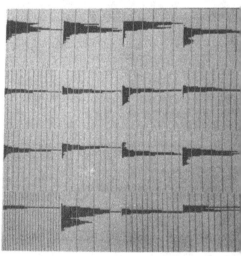

c. 3x3 mean filtered
windows.

d. Histograms of (c).

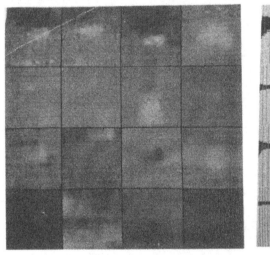

e. 3x3 median filtered
windows.

f. Histograms of (e).

Figure 2.4. (continued)

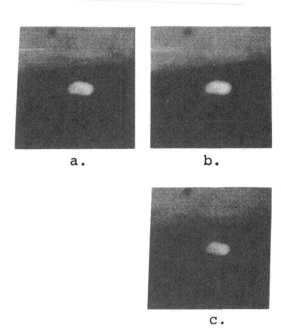

a.   b.

c.

Figure 2.5.   Gray level images.

a.   Original FLIR image of a tank.
     Note the noise content and the
     presence of a thin noise line at
     the upper left.

b.   Mean filtered image using a 5x5
     square neighborhood at each
     point. The tank appears blurred,
     as does the border between the
     road (dark) and the grass (light).
     The thin noise line is smeared
     into the background.

c.   Median filtered image using a 5x5
     square neighborhood. The tank
     contours appear sharper, while
     overall the image has been
     smoothed.

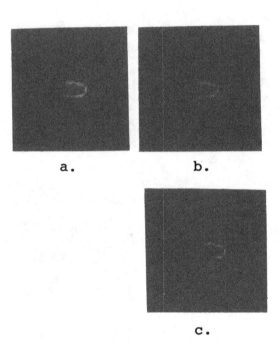

a.   b.

c.

Figure 2.6.   Results of Edge Detection

Each of the windows was subjected
to an edge detection operation which
detects the most significant edge
at each point over four orientations.
Note that edges surround the various
regions in the image but that the
edges in the median filtered image
(c) are sharper and have more contrast than those in the mean filtered
image (b).

a.   Edge detection response for the
     original image.

b.   Same as above for the mean filtered
     image.

c.   Same as above for the median filtere
     image.

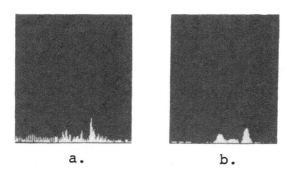

a.   b.

c.

Figure 2.7.   Edge Cross Sections

A single line of the edge detection
image passing through the tank is
displayed with height corresponding
to edge value. Notice that the
median filtered response exhibits a
thinner, higher peak corresponding to
a sharper, more contrasting edge
than the mean filtered response.

a. A single line of edge response from
    Figure 2.6a.

b. Same as above for Figure 2.6b.

c. Same as above for Figure 2.6c.

maintained in a vector of length d (e.g., d=64). The k deletions and k insertions are interleaved in pairs. Each (deletion, insertion) pair isolates a region of the vector which must be modified. The smaller this region on the average, the less work to be done. If the deletion and insertion in a given pair affect the same bin, no change is necessary. The length of the region of change in the cumulative histogram is the expected gray level difference of points at distance k. This corresponds to a variogram value, v(k). After updating, the vector is binary-searched for the median. Thus the number of vector operations is k·v(k), followed by log d operations to binary-search the updated vector. The sum k·v(k) + log d should be quite small for relatively smooth images.

3. Edge detection

The extraction of edge features has proved useful in a number of project areas. Section 4 will describe threshold selection methods which utilize edge information. Edges are also used in the critical step of the Superslice algorithm (Section 6). In this section, we discuss the variety of edge operations investigated and a method of thinning edge response so as to locate the apparent edge.

3.1 Comparison of methods

Methods for edge detection abound in the literature (for a survey, see [14]). Some of the simplest methods involve convolutions of templates with an image. A number of these were considered in the current work. These include:

Laplacian: $|e - (a+b+c+d+f+g+h+i)/8|$, where the neighborhood of e is

```
a b c
d e f t
g h i u
v w
```

Roberts Gradient: $\max\{|a-e|, |b-d|\}$.

Three-by-three: $\max\{|a+b+c-g-h-i| , |a+d+g-c-f-i|\}$

2x2 Difference:

$1/4*\max\{|d+e+g+h-f-t-i-u| , |b+c+e+f-h-i-v-w|\}$.

(In other words, the value corresponds to the maximum of the differences between 2x2 averages over adjacent pairs of

horizontal and vertical neighborhoods. This scheme extends
to diagonals also.

4x4 Difference: This is the same as the 2x2 difference except
that averages are taken over 4x4 neighborhoods.

8x8 Difference: The same as the previous except that averages
are taken over 8x8 neighborhoods.

Experiments with these operators indicated that the Laplacian
(which is a second difference), the Roberts Gradient and the 3x3
Gradient were too sensitive to minute changes in gray level. The
differences of averages operators produced better output by virtue
of the increased amount of smoothing on each side of the edge.
Knowledge that typical edge width in the windows was three pixels
suggested that the 4x4 operator could span the edge ramp (to give
the maximum gradient value) while remaining sensitive enough to
detect the edges of small faint regions.

3.2 Edge thinning

In the world of man-made objects, edges correspond to the
juxtaposition of surfaces and shadows. In a well focused image,
edges should appear sharp and should extend in some direction for
some length. (In the natural world, the boundaries of regions are
not necessarily as sharply defined, e.g., for trees, fields, etc.)
The output of the operators described in the previous section,
however, is generally smeared at or near the true edge location.
Nonetheless, for certain types of image understanding it is necessary to localize the edge so that it lies along the object boundaries. Given a knowledge of the edge detector, it is possible to
design a process which accepts the output of the operator and
which produces a thinned representation of the edge at the location of maximum edge response.

It is not sufficient to consider simply those points of maximum response, since this would force adjacent points in the direction of the edge to compete. This problem can be alleviated by
taking into account the computed local direction of the edge and
by placing into competition only those points which are normal to
the direction of the edge. In practice, a directional mask is
associated with each edge point oriented normal to the direction
of the maximum edge response at that point. The center point is
then deleted (assigned zero response) if any point within the

mask has a greater response. There are four masks:

```
            x x x          x                      x
   x     x     x        x x                    x x
   x x 0 x x ,  0   ,        0        ,    0        ,
   x     x     x              x x      x x
            x x x            x          x
```

one associated with each principal edge direction. The process,
called "non-maximum suppression," operates simultaneously on all
edge values to produce a "thinned" edge map. Figure 3.1
illustrates the process.

4. Threshold selection

The properties of a pixel in a single sensor image are its
position and its gray level. Our knowledge of the imaging environment allows us to predict an object's gray level more accurately than its position. In fact, the whole point of cueing is to
locate a target. Thus one has little a priori information about
target position; however, inasmuch as gray level is related to
thermal emission in FLIR data, there are some fairly powerful
heuristics available to aid in target recognition. For example,
we may choose to assume that operating vehicles are warmer than
the immediate background and that they radiate uniformly over
their surfaces. Naturally, such assumptions are not always possible. In cold weather, metal loses heat faster than the ground;
at close range, fine thermal detail is visible and the uniformity
assumption fails. Nor are these assumptions meant to be exclusive, e.g., we do not claim that every object region warmer than
its surround is a target. The power of these heuristics is to
suggest approaches which capture essential problem domain knowledge.

In this project, the force of the heuristics of the previous
paragraph is to emphasize methods which isolate distinct gray
level regions from their surrounds. The simplest of such methods
is thresholding -- the assignment of all points whose gray levels
are greater than a predetermined level (the threshold) into a
single class of potential object points. The filtering, aggrega-
tion and ultimate classification of these points are the subjects
of subsequent sections. In this section, we discuss our investigations of numerous methods for single and multiple threshold
selection.

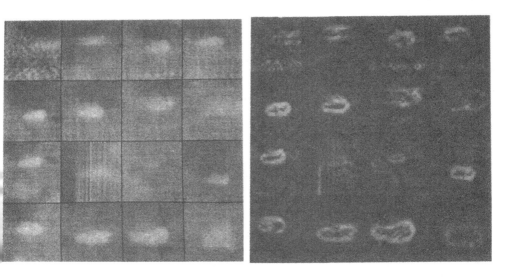

Originals.   Edge detector output.

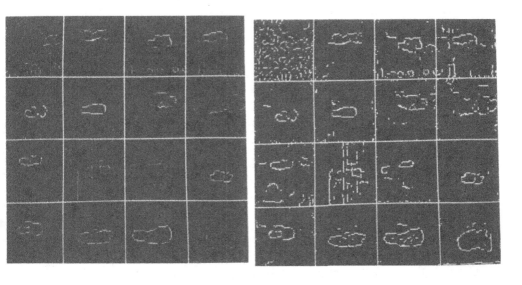

Thinned edge map.   Thinned edge map thresholded
                         to display only edge values
                         > 2.

Figure 3.1.   Results of edge detection and non-maximum
                suppression on 43 tank windows.

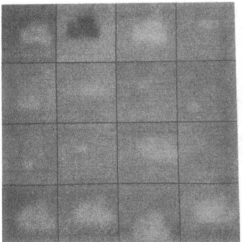

Originals.

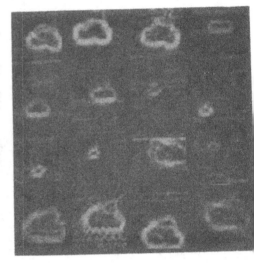

Edge detector output.

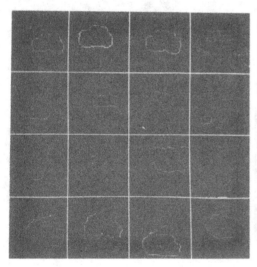

Thinned edge map.

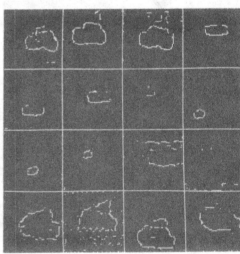

Thinned edge map threshold
to display only edge value
> 2.

Figure 3.1.   (continued)

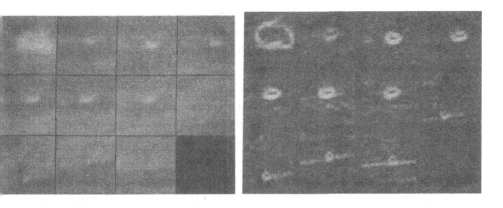

Originals.   Edge detector output.

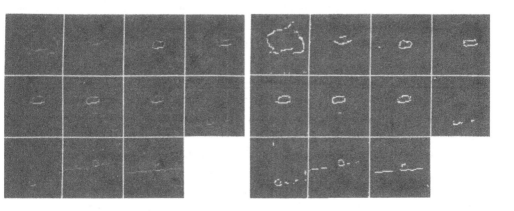

Thinned edge map.   Thinned edge map thresholded
                         to display only edge values
                         > 2.

Figure 3.1. (continued)

There is a progression in these methods which corresponds on the one hand to the need for increased sensitivity in choosing the "right" threshold and, on the other hand, to the deemphasis of the commitment to that particular threshold. However, we still retain the notion that for each object region in the image there is a "best" threshold. In the worst case, every possible threshold yields a target region which is invisible (unextractable) at every other threshold. One must therefore be prepared to threshold at any gray level and within that thresholded image to discern the target regions and to ignore the noise regions. These last comments appear to call for the selection of every gray level as a value at which to threshold. Indeed, given sufficient parallel hardware and powerful target/noise discrimination criteria, this brute force approach could lead to a reliable and sensitive target cuer. A further discussion of this option is in Section 6 and some relevant experiments are to be found in Section 8. The remainder of this section describes techniques for finding appropriate thresholds when hardware and throughput considerations allow only a few thresholds to be utilized per frame.

4.1 Threshold selection based on edge values

In Section 1.1 a model was proposed for images consisting of objects and background, each with characteristic gray level distributions. If the gray level histogram of the image is markedly bimodal, one may choose the threshold at the valley between the two peaks (possibly shifted towards the smaller peak when using a maximum likelihood estimate). However, the smaller the object, the less likely the histogram is to exhibit strong bimodality. The background distribution engulfs the object's gray level range and tests for bimodality are inconclusive.

One approach [15] to solving this problem has been to select from the original image a set of points that are as likely to fall within the object as within the background. If one examines the output of operators which respond to edges, then high values should correspond to points falling at or near object edges. The mathematical model has shown the gray level distribution to be unimodal with a peak at the mean. Thus, these points are as likely to lie on the object as on the background and their mean value should correspond to the desired threshold.

A brief description of the threshold selection method is as follows: Let $e(i,j)$ be the edge value computed at (i,j) and let $g(i,j)$ be its gray value. Then the chosen threshold is $\bar{g} = \text{AVG}\{g(i,j) \mid e(i,j) \geq t\}$, where t is lowest edge value considered significant. Computationally, two arrays are needed. One array, $\text{TOTAL}_0, \ldots, \text{TOTAL}_{63}$, accumulates the gray level g for each edge value e between 0 and 63; i.e., $\text{TOTAL}_e = \text{TOTAL}_e + g$. The second array, $N_0, \ldots, N_{63}$, tallies the number of points at each edge value. The desired average gray level $\bar{g} = (\sum_{i \geq t} \text{TOTAL}_i) / (\sum_{i \geq T} N_i)$.

Two parameters were treated in the experimental work: the choice of edge operator and the edge significance level t. Previous work with edge operators indicated that the 4x4 difference of averages operator was superior to the others as an edge detector in FLIR scenes. Experiments in threshold selection showed that thresholds chosen based on this operator were better overall [1].

The proper selection of a value for t is important because this parameter controls the size and quality of the sample points of high edge value used to compute the gray level threshold. Setting t too high decreases the statistical reliability of the sample; while a small t may admit too many noise values. The choice of t depends on the expected amount of object edge. Obviously, many assumptions are built into this notion, e.g., that the window contains only a single object of known size, shape, contrast, resolution, etc. In a tactical situation, one could make estimates of these parameters based on situation data. Based on estimates of target size, t was chosen as the edge value corresponding to the 95th percentile. This estimate was shown by experiment to provide good thresholds for the windowed data set. This is illustrated in Figure 4.1.

The sensitivity of the chosen gray level threshold to different choices of t was tested and a graph of the threshold was plotted as a function of the gradient cutoff t; see Figure 4.2. There is a tendency for this graph to drift toward the mean gray value as t is decreased. The chosen threshold is stable for large objects. For small objects, the choice is quite sensitive to the bin size.

The approach above and several variations [5] can be viewed as methods of decision surface selection in (gray level, edge value)

Originals.

1T	2T	3T	4T
6T	8T	9T	10T
11T	12T	13T	14T
15T	16T	17T	21T

Image reference numbers.

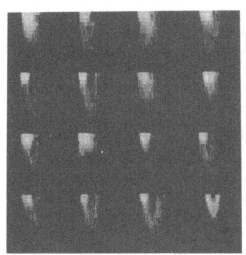

2-D Histograms.

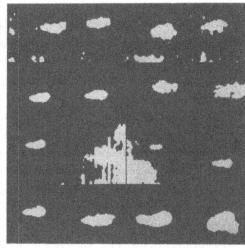

Thresholded windows after shrink/expand (see Section 5.1).

Figure 4.1. Results of thresholding and post-processing 43 tank windows.

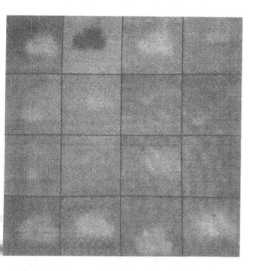

22T	23T	24T	26T
28T	31T	32T	33T
34T	35T	38T	40T
42T	43T	45T	46T

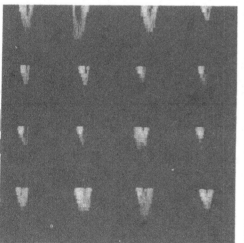
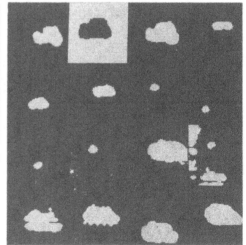

Figure 4.1. (continued)

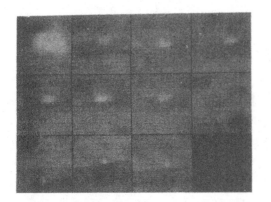

48T	50T	51T	52T
53T	54T	55T	56T
57T	58T	59T	

 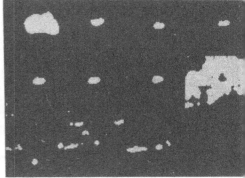

Figure 4.1.   (continued)

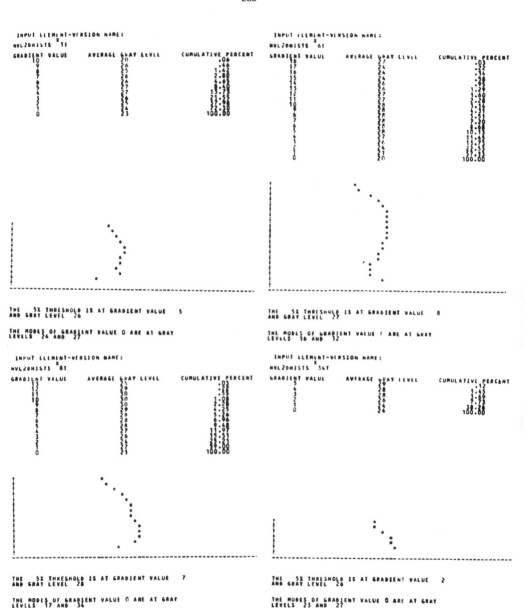

Figure 4.2. Graph of selected threshold as a
function of percentage edge value
cutoff. Abscissa: gray value
increases to the right; ordinate:
gradient decreases up the axis.

256

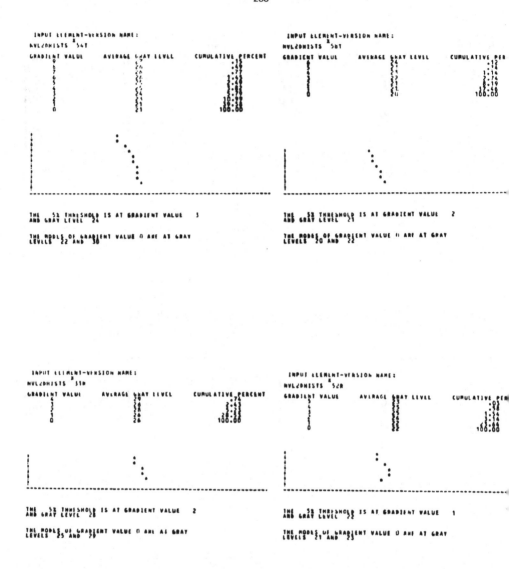

Figure 4.2.   (continued)

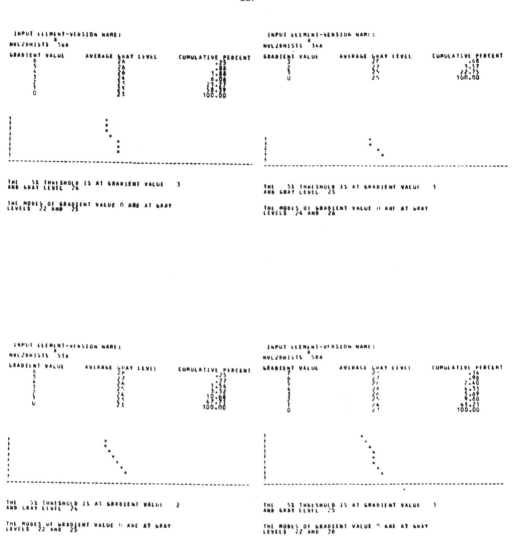

Figure 4.2. (continued)

258

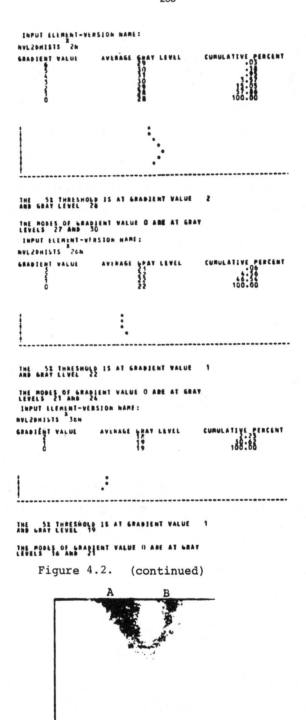

Figure 4.2.   (continued)

Figure   4.3.   Ideal 2-D histogram of a scene
containing an object and back-
ground with noise.

space. This space is visualized as a two dimensional histogram with gray level along one axis and edge value along the other. Figure 4.3 displays such a 2-D histogram for a hypothetical object on a background. Points at A represent background while object points (perhaps with some noise) cluster at B. The bottom part of the U-shaped region contains high-edge value points. As we have pointed out, the average gray level of these points is a good threshold. Figure 4.1 illustrated 2-D histograms for several target windows.

One may consider a threshold as a vertical decision surface separating object from background. Non-vertical partitions of the space have also been investigated [2] and were found to be capable of adding more points to the boundaries of object regions without substantially increasing the amount of noise. Several other partitioning schemes which were considered are discussed in [5].

4.2 Slice range selection

The methods discussed above predict a single threshold to be applied to an image. For images known to contain a single object class or for small windows, the use of a single threshold is appropriate. However, in general, no single threshold will separate all objects of interest from the background. It is therefore necessary to extend our threshold selection concept to allow the choice of multiple thresholds.

Our approach is to produce clusters of points corresponding to region borders and to associate the average gray level of each cluster with a threshold for the corresponding region. Edge detectors select at each point the maximum difference of averages of adjacent neighborhoods over several directions. By suppressing non-maximum responses normal to the selected direction (i.e., across the edge), thin contours result which appear to surround object regions (see Section 6.2). A by-product of this process are points with very low edge value, including values which truncate to zero. Such points correspond to the interiors of homogeneous regions. Figure 4.4 illustrates thinned detector responses with region interior maxima included. After thinning, each remaining point is plotted using edge value and average gray level in a two-dimensional histogram. Figure 4.5 shows examples of images together with their 2-D histograms based on thinned edges.

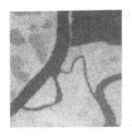

a.   b.

Figure   4.4a.   LANDSAT window of Monterey, CA.
              b.   Thinned edge detector response
                    (thresholded).

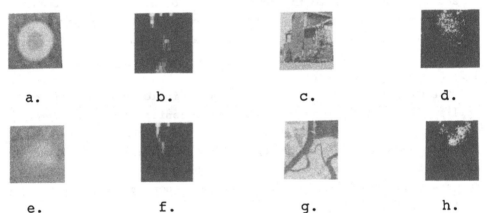

a.   b.   c.   d.

e.   f.   g.   h.

Figure   4.5a.   Disk (gray level 30) within ring (gray
                    level 40) within background (gray
                    level 20).
              b.   2-D histogram of (a) with gray level as
                    x-axis (increasing left to right) and
                    edge value as y-axis (stretched -- in-
                    creasing from top to bottom). Interior
                    of background is leftmost, topmost
                    cluster.
              c.   Window containing house.
              d.   2-D histogram of (c).
              e.   Window containing tank.
              f.   2-D (stretched) histogram of (e).
              g.   LANDSAT window of Monterey.
              h.   2-D histogram (thinned edge vs. average
                    gray level).

Two types of clusters are produced: <u>interior clusters</u> represent the interiors of regions, <u>edge clusters</u> represent boundaries
between regions. The size of a cluster (i.e., the number of
points in it) is closely related to properties of the region it
describes. Thus interior clusters relate both to the area of the
region and to the size of the neighborhood over which the local
operations (edge detection, non-maximum suppression) are defined.
For small object regions, there may be <u>no</u> points sufficiently far
from the object boundary to resist suppression. Thus, interior
clusters may be indistinguishable from noise, or may be nonexis-
tent.

Clusters of points at higher edge values are more likely to be
significant (based on our homogeneity assumptions). The size of
an edge cluster is therefore related to the perimeter of the
surrounded region in the image. Since perimeter increases
(roughly, for digital images) as the square root of area, the edge
clusters for objects of moderately different areas should, nonetheless, be of comparable size. A priori estimates of size are
of use in discriminating true edge clusters from random noise.

Each edge cluster corresponds (ideally) to these interior
clusters whose locations can be determined from the location of
the edge cluster. Thus a threshold derived from the edge cluster
will separate the interior clusters. However, care must be taken
not to split an interior cluster at a threshold since this introduces random noise regions. Figure 4.6 illustrates a compound
decision surface in the 2-D histogram of a multi-object image.
For further discussion see [16].

4.3 Variable thresholding

Previous approaches to thresholding apply the same threshold
to all points of the image. In [17], Nakagawa adapts the work of
Chow and Kaneko [18] to interpolate a best threshold for each
point of the image. Briefly, the image is divided into small
windows (say 32x32) and a test of gray level histogram bimodality
is made for each window. A best threshold is chosen for each
bimodal window and thresholds are interpolated to all image points.
A binary image results when each threshold is applied to its corresponding pixel value. Figure 4.7 compares fixed thresholding
and variable thresholding for several FLIR frames. Nakagawa

a.

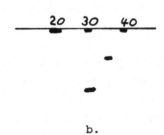

b.

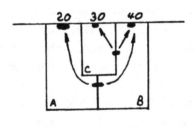

c.

Figure   4.6a.   Adjacent object regions on
background (same as Figure
4.5a).
b.   2-D histogram.
c.   2-D histogram partitioned into
classification regions.

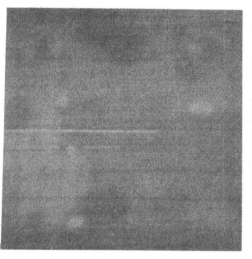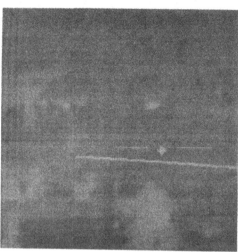

a.

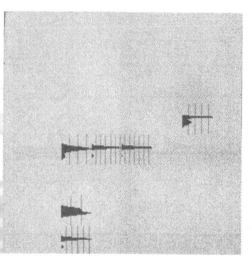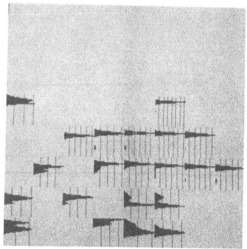

b.

Figure   4.7.   Comparison of fixed and variable
                 thresholding.

         a.   Two FLIR frames.
         b.   Two-Gaussian approximations to those
               32x32 window histograms that were
               judged to be bimodal.

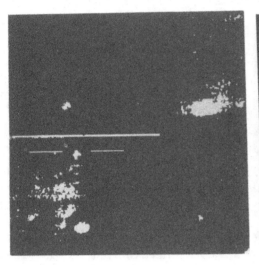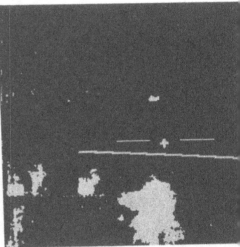

c.

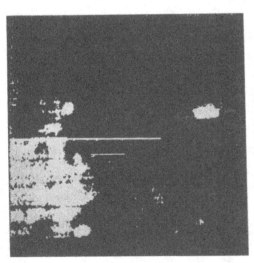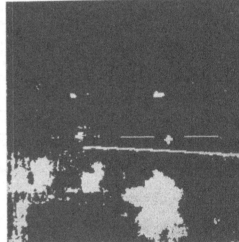

d.

Figure   4.7 (continued)

    c. Results of applying the interpolated
       point thresholds to (a).
    d. Results of applying a fixed threshold
       to (a).

extended this method to allow multiple thresholds (for multi-object adjacencies). Figure 4.8 illustrates the results.

5. Noise cleaning and component labeling

5.1 Shrink/expand and min/max

The result of thresholding is a binary valued image. It often contains isolated points and small noise regions which are artifacts of the thresholding and may not be readily visible in the original image. Smoothed images tend to have fewer (but larger) noise regions. One may delete noise regions by postprocessing the thresholded image.

The method consists of multiple applications of two processes: "shrink" and "expand." The purpose of the sequence of shrinks is to shrink objects in a uniform manner so that small or insubstantial objects disappear entirely. The sequence of expands is meant to regrow the remaining shrunken objects to their original size. The result of the shrinks/expands is the elimination of tiny regions (presumed to be noise regions).

Each shrink or expand requires the simultaneous or "parallel" application of a local replacement rule at every point of the thresholded image. The form of the shrink rule is as follows: Eliminate all 1's adjacent to 0's. Zero values are unchanged. Such a rule decreases the number of 1's in the thresholded image; thus, the image "shrinks." Only 1's surrounded by 1's will survive a shrink. The number of successive shrinks determines the mimimum diameter of a surviving region.

The expand rule is similar to the shrink rule: rewrite a 0 as a 1 if any of its neighbors are 1's, but leave 1's unchanged. Thus points adjacent to 1's become 1's, thereby increasing the number of 1's. If we wish to restore objects (that were not eliminated) to about their original sizes, t shrinks should be followed by t expands. Such a shrink/expand sequence produces an image whose 1's correspond to (a subset of the) 1's in the untransformed binary image. Thus, for example, isolated 1's are eliminated, and objects joined by narrow necks of 1's may become disconnected. Also, thin protusions from a region of 1's will disappear. Figure 5.1 illustrates the shrink/expand algorithm for both the 4 and 8 neighbor cases and $t = 1,2,3$ (the numbers of

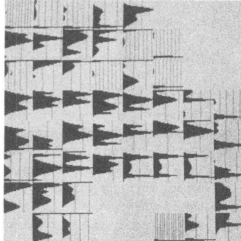

a.   b.

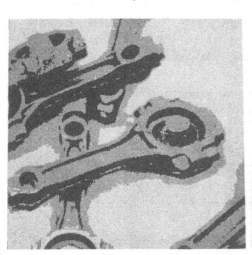

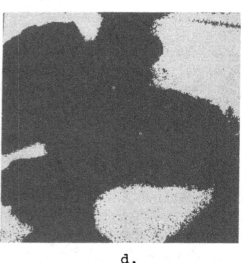

c.   d.

Figure   4.8.   Comparison of fixed and variable
                       thresholding.

                    a.   Machine parts image.
                    b.   Two- and three-Gaussian approximations
                         to those window histograms that were
                         judged to be bi- and tri-modal.
                    c.   Three level pictures obtained after
                         interpolating the multiple thresholds
                         determined from (b) and applied to (a).
                    d.   Results of applying a fixed threshold
                         to (a).

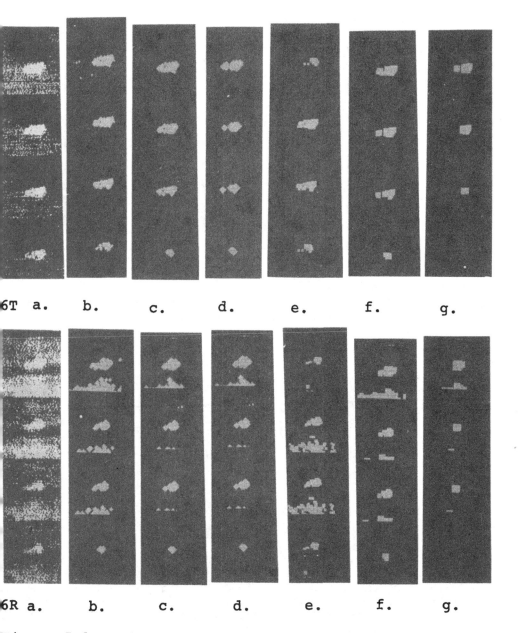

Figure 5.1. Effects of iterating SHRINK/EXPANDS (S/E's).
    a. Original images - each column is a single image
       thresholded at four different values.
    b. 4-neighbor rule - one S/E
    c. 4-neighbor rule - two S/E's
    d. 4-neighbor rule - three S/E's
    e. 8-neighbor rule - one S/E
    f. 8-neighbor rule - two S/E's
    g. 8-neighbor rule - three S/E's

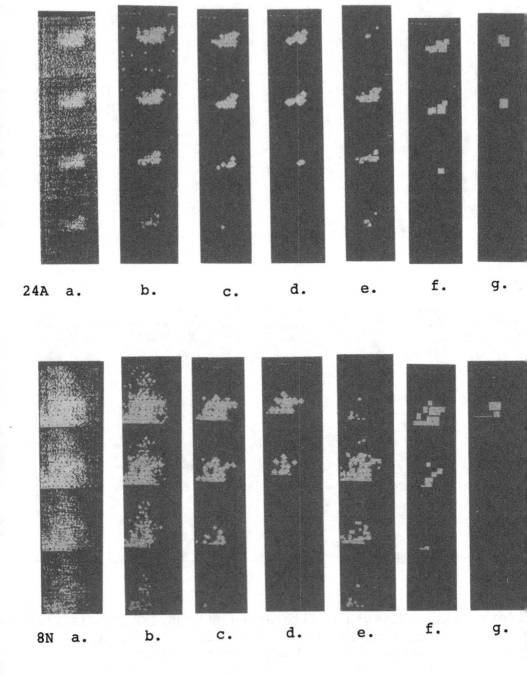

24A a.   b.   c.   d.   e.   f.   g.

8N a.   b.   c.   d.   e.   f.   g.

Figure 5.1. (continued)

shrinks and expands used).

A generalization of the shrink rule was formulated to fill pinholes and conserve small region shape as follows: delete a 1 if at least k of its neighbors are 0's (0's remain unchanged). The original shrink rule corresponds to k = 1. If k > 1, it takes more zero evidence to convert a 1 to 0. The generalized expand is analogously defined: Rewrite a 0 as 1 if it has at least k 1's as neighbors (1's remain unchanged).

However, the generalized expand rule is not quite as generous in providing new 1 values, although it does fill pinholes in sufficently large regions. Figure 5.2 provides a comparison for t = 1, 2 and k = 1, 2, 3. The shrink/expand rule with t = 2 and k = 3 applied to each image point and its 8-neighbors provides efficient noise cleaning with most noise regions eliminated, pinholes filled, and only a modest amount of target shape distortion.

One may further generalize this process for application prior to thresholding. This technique, called "precleaning", involves a sequence of local MIN/MAX operations applied to the gray level image (analogous to shrink/expand applied to a binary image). The resulting precleaned image may now be thresholded as desired. The above threshold regions are as they would have appeared after shrink/expand processing. Figure 5.3 illustrates the process. This work is described in [19].

5.2 Connected component extraction

The result of thresholding is a binary image. After noise cleaning operations filter this image (as needed), it still remains to aggregate points into identified (labeled) regions. A process which labels the individual disjoint regions in the binary image, in a single raster scan, is well known in the literature [20]. It is described briefly here.

A set of 1's in a binary image is connected if any two points in it can be joined by a path (sequence) of pairwise adjacent points lying in the set. A maximal connected set is called a connected component. The algorithm to be described produces the (unique) decomposition into connected components, labels the individual components, and constructs for each connected component a descriptive feature vector. Although we do not specify the features, it is assumed that they are all extractable from a raster

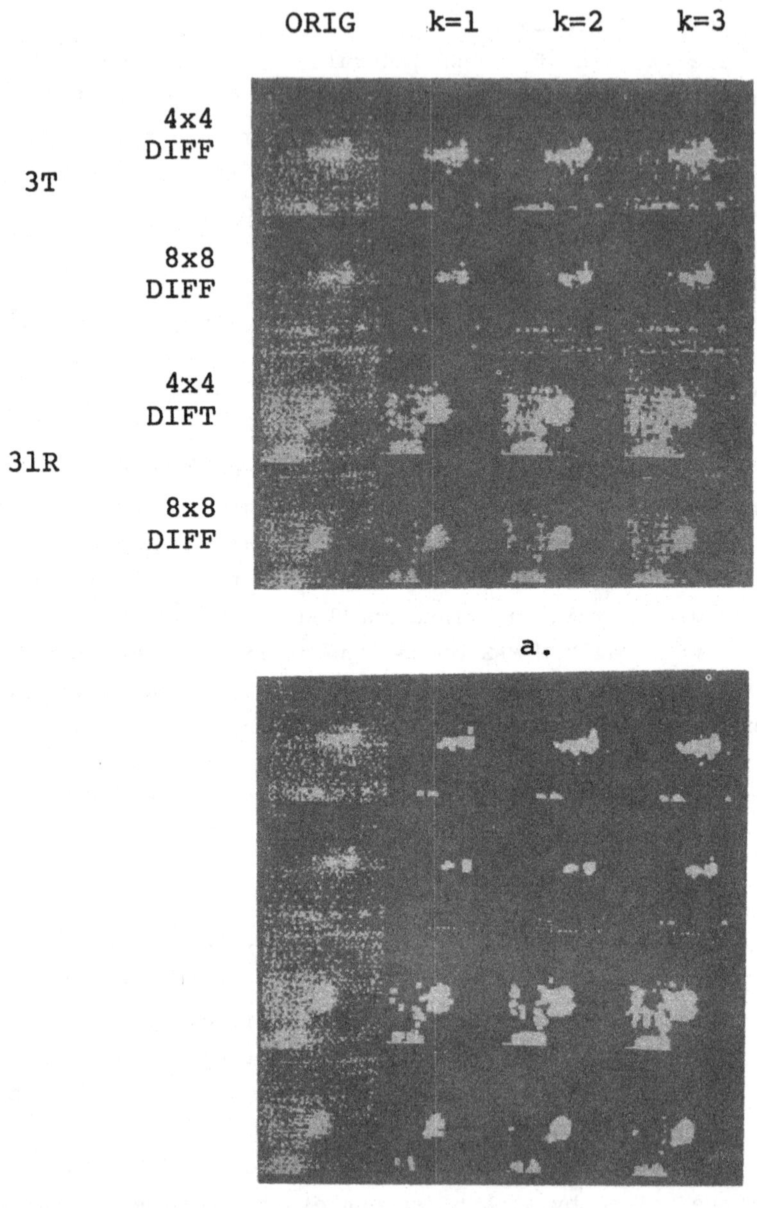

a.

b.

Figure 5.2. Leniency in SHRINK/EXPAND definitions for
             windows thresholded by two methods.
         a. 4-neighbor rule, one S/E, k=1,2,3
         b. 8-neighbor rule, one S/E, k=1,2,3
         c. 4-neighbor rule, two S/E's, k=1,2,3
         d. 8-neighbor rule, two S/E's, k=1,2,3

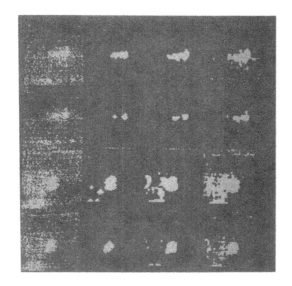

c.

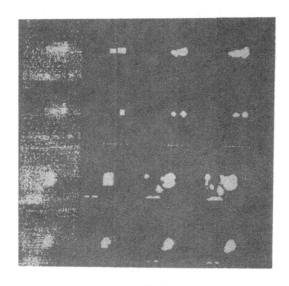

d.

Figure 5.2. (continued)

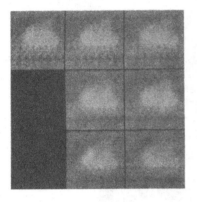

Key:

	4-nbr.	8-nbr.
Original	MIN·MAX	MIN·MAX
	$MIN^2 \cdot MAX^2$	$MIN^2 \cdot MAX^2$
	$MIN^3 \cdot MAX^3$	$MIN^3 \cdot MAX^3$

(a)

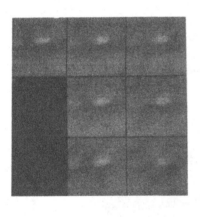

(b)

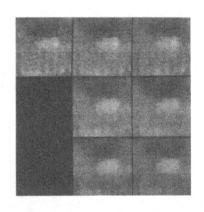

(c)

Figure 5.3.

Results of applying repeated local MIN and repeated local MAX to three FLIR images. In each
part, the upper-left picture is the original; the
second column uses 4-neighbor local MINs followed
by 4-neighbor local MAXes (1, 2, and 3 repetitions,
in the first, second, and third rows); and the
third column is analogous, using 8-neighbor operations (i.e., including the diagonal neighbors).

scan using a 3x3 processing window. Additional storage is available to hold the feature values for the components. Section 7.2
describes the features.

When a new region is encountered during a raster scan, it is
assigned a vector of registers to store its feature values. As
the region is being tracked on the same row or continued on the
next row, values continue to be accumulated into its feature
vector. In order to specify the correspondence between a region
and its register vector, a label is created and assigned to each
point of the region which has already been visited. The label
will identify the appropriate register vector, usually by some
indexing scheme. Region points found to be adjacent to already
labeled region points inherit that label and contribute their
feature values to its register vector.

Often a region encountered for what is thought to be the
first time may on a later row prove to be connected to a previously encountered region. Such regions are called subcomponents.
Inasmuch as feature values were being maintained separately for
each subcomponent, it becomes necessary to combine the feature
values (eventually) and to create a flag that signifies that the
two subcomponents belong to the same component. These flags reside in the label equivalence table. This table can be stored
either as a bit matrix or as a list.

Since region labels propagate from point to point, we must
also keep the labels of those points in the preceding row that
are neighbors of unexamined points in the current row, with the
labels of those examined points in the current row. The amount of
storage necessary for labels of points is thus only a single row.

The label assigned to a component should designate whether the
component is above or below threshold. If the background is not
partitioned into regions (i.e., is ignored) by the algorithm then
the data structure becomes simply a list of above-threshold regions. This is suitable for many applications, e.g., infrared
target cueing. In general, though, the containment relation
defines a tree structure. It is evident that if two components
of a binary image are adjacent then one encloses the other. However, if more than one object-background transition has been detected, one cannot know which encloses which from strictly local
information at the time of the initial label assignment. The

determining condition is "which region terminates first?" The region terminating first is enclosed by the adjacent region. Thus whenever a region terminates, the data structure is updated to reflect the containment relation. When a region is initiated it is entered onto an "active" list -- the list of unterminated regions. At the end of each row, the active list is compared with the list of component labels of the current label row. Any active component whose label does not appear in the current row is known to have terminated. Additionally, when overlapping regions are combined, the discarded label is deleted from the active list.

It is possible to modify the above to create a description of each connected component's boundaries. Such a description is called a "chain encoding" and is discussed in [20].

5.3 Fuzzy thinning

Objects which are everywhere elongated are often thinned down to a "medial line" for the purpose of extracting thickness-invariant topological features of the objects. The basic strategy for thinning is to iteratively delete border points (but not end points) of an object which do not locally disconnect it. For binary images, various parallel algorithms exist. The recent extension of the topological concept of connectedness to fuzzy subsets allows us to generalize thinning to gray level images [21]. Given thin dark objects on a light background, we define gray level thinning to be the successive replacement of points by the minimum gray level of their neighbors if those changes do not affect the local fuzzy connectedness for any pair of neighbors. The result of applying such an algorithm is a set of high gray level "curves" lying on the ridges and peaks of high gray level in the original picture. If the original picture is noisy there will be many local peaks; so while thinning is defined for unsegmented pictures, a local threshold is necessary to overlook these small noise peaks. Unlike binary thinning, however, we no longer need to distinguish between border and interior points since thinning a homogeneous region will not significantly change the gray level of any point; only a slight smoothing results. The results of experiments with this technique are described in a technical report [22]. See Figure 5.4 for examples of this process.

a.

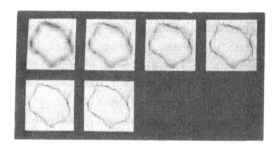

b.

Figure   5.4a.   Iterations 0-3 of fuzzy thinning
                  on LANDSAT window of Monterey.
          b.   Iterations 0-5 of fuzzy thinning
                  on the output of an edge detect-
                  or.

6. Superslice

The object extraction task is somewhat simpler for FLIR imagery than for visible-light imagery since the objects of interest (military vehicales) are generally compact regions of (more or less) uniform thermal intensity. For this reason, thresholding has been chosen as an appropriate method of segmenting the scene. However, one can criticize threshold selection schemes on a number of grounds. First of all, if a window contains no object then thresholding it is dangerous, since above-threshold noise regions may often produce probable looking "objects." Secondly, if more than one object is present in the window then a single threshold will not suffice. Thirdly, if an object overlaps several windows then there may be no consistent representation of an object (i.e., no representation using a single threshold). Attempts to divide the scene up into overlapping windows, so that objects of maximal size are guaranteed to lie completely within a single window, answer this last objection at the cost of greatly increased overhead. In any case, the size of the smallest thresholdable region -- as well as the particular threshold chosen -- depends on the window size, the coarseness of the grid, and the type of statistical test used to determine if a region is thresholdable. One would prefer, however, to be able to extract a small region regardless of the clutter and noise beyond its borders.

Another objection to pure thresholding is the presence of noise regions in addition to object regions. Noise regions may be difficult to distinguish when based on size, shape, or gray level features. The broader and higher the valleys of the gray level histogram, the more likely that the noise regions will be extensive and numerous.

A final objection concerns the design of optimal thresholding techniques in which the optimality is based on a statistical model of the gray level population. In situations where an object contrasts strongly with the background, there may be a number of thresholds at which the object appears well defined. As the threshold decreases through this acceptable range, each object exemplar is contained within a slightly larger one. Thus although the exemplars may each look reasonable, the optimality criterion for the thresholding does not necessarily choose a "best" exemplar. This is because the optimality condition was based on the whole window rather than on the component corresponding to the object.

For these reasons, a segmentation method which does not require a commitment to a single threshold in arbitrarily chosen regions of an image is preferable. Our method uses thresholding as a means of discovering candidate object regions. Candidates are then accepted or rejected based on the coincidence of an edge map with the region boundary. The surviving object regions are compared with the survivors of other thresholds, and those that best match the edge map are used to describe the actual objects in the image. Thus, while a number of thresholds are used, only the one defining the greatest coincidence of thresholded region border and (thinned) edge is deemed valid for a particular region. This method can be considered as defining a best exemplar for each object region.

6.1 Algorithm

The algorithm consists of several steps as follows: median filtering; extraction of an edge mask by edge detection and thinning; thresholding; forming connected components; and object validity checking. For a given picture, smoothing and edge map extraction need to be done only once; whereas thresholding and the subsequent steps are to be performed over a range of thresholds sufficient to extract any objects in the picture.

Figure 6.1 illustrates the basic concepts involved. Figure 6.1a shows several object windows along with a number of possible thresholds for each. Note that it is not at all obvious which threshold is best. However, when the edge map (Figure 6.1b) is overlaid on the thresholded picture (Figure 6.1c), we have much better guidance. Figure 6.1d shows the object region extracted from each window using the method to be described.

A number of steps of the Superslice algorithm have been discussed in previous sections: smoothing (Section 2.3), edge detection and thinning (Section 3.2), threshold selection (Section 4.1) and connected component extraction (Section 5.2). However, several problems associated with threshold selection deserve mention:

a) The omission of a threshold from consideration increases

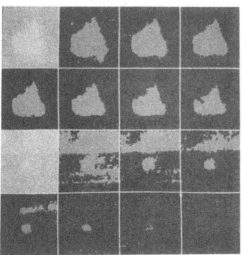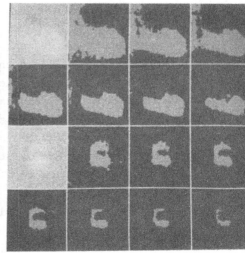

a.

b.

Figure   6.1a.   Four target windows (large tank,
                 small tank, truck, APC) thresholded
                 at seven different gray levels.
         b.   Edge maps (thresholded for visibility).

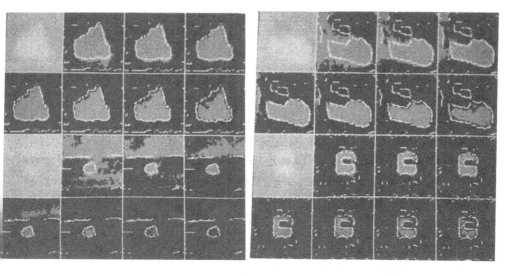

c.

d.

Figure   6.1c.   Edge maps from (b) overlaid on
                 (a).
          d.   Object regions extracted by the
                 Superslice algorithm.

the probability of missing extractable regions.

b) The greater the number of thresholds considered, the greater the false alarm rate.

c) The speed of the algorithm is approximately linear in the number of thresholds used.

The probability of missing an object region due to the omission of a single threshold is the product of the probability that the scene contains an object region and the probability that the object region is discernible (by the algorithm) at exactly the omitted threshold. Although knowledge of the a priori probability is dependent on a model for the scene (which does not at present exist), experiments have demonstrated that an object region which is discernible at all by the algorithm can be extracted over a range of thresholds -- dependent, of course, on the steepness and homogeneity of the edge region bordering the object. Noise regions, on the other hand, do not tend to persist over a range of gray level thresholds. This tradeoff may therefore be posed as follows: By sampling at every kth gray level, we reduce the workload to a fraction (1/k) without appreciably increasing the false dismissal rate; however, we lose some redundancy in the extracted data which would help us discriminate object regions from false alarms.

The false alarm rate is a function of input window size, as well as a function of the number of thresholds and the positions of the thresholds in the overall gray level histogram. Certain thresholds are worse than others in producing false alarms -- specifically, those at or adjacent to peaks in the histogram.

After thresholding and connected component extraction, each component must be validated as to whether the extracted region really corresponds to an object in the scene. If one considers validity checking to be a classification process, then one can compute a large number of potential features and, using standard techniques, determine a discriminant function. We have established three heuristics to be of value. One is that objects should be "well-defined," i.e., have discernible borders. Note that not all real-world regions satisfy this constraint. For example, in LANDSAT scenes, forest, urban areas and clouds can blend into their surrounds with no discernible edge. The second

heuristic is that an object's interior should "contrast" with its
surround. In this study, contrast is based on gray level difference. However, other local features including texture measures
are worth considering as defining object interior. The third is
that the region size lie within an acceptable range. The size
test is applied first, eliminating any region with fewer than 20
or more than 1,000 points.

"Well definedness" of a region is measured by the percentage
of border points which correspond spatially to (match) actual edge
points in the edge map. "Contrast" is measured by the absolute
difference of average gray level between the border region of the
component and its interior. Figure 6.2 shows a scatter plot of
these two features for the regions extracted from a set of windows.
A reasonable discriminant based on these two features appears to
be: match > .5 and contrast > .6 -- i.e., at least 50% of the
border matches the edge map, and the contrast is at least .6 gray
levels (out of 64). Note that neither feature is by itself reliable enough to discriminate noise regions from object regions.
Optimal discriminants may be computed based on several models.
Regardless of the particular model chosen, the discriminant value
can be interpreted as a "score" for the component. Components
with very low scores are discarded as pure noise. In practice, we
have used the match measure as a score for objects which were
above the pure noise threshold.

The score is important in comparing (nested) object regions
corresponding to the same object. When an object is thresholdable
at gray levels $t_1 > t_2 > ... > t_k$, this gives rise to k connected
components, $C_{t_1} \subseteq C_{t_2} \subseteq ... \subseteq C_{t_k}$. Since each C_{t_i} represents the
same object, we call each an "exemplar." In general, we wish to
select a single exemplar as the best representative of an object.
The score provides a criterion for selecting among exemplars.
Thus, one could choose the exemplar C_{t_j} with the highest score.
It is not always easy, however, to determine the nested sequence
$\{C_{t_i}\}$. In particular, if one object thresholdable at gray level t
is contained within another thresholdable at gray level t' < t,
then regardless of the comparative difference between the two
scores, we would want to retain C_t and $C_{t'}$. This situation can be
handled by assuming that nested components whose areas are

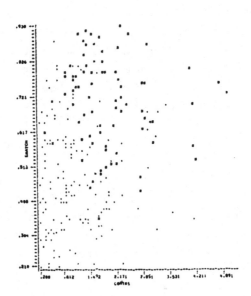

Figure 6.2. Scatter diagram plotting
well-definedness against
contrast for a set of noise
regions (plotted as periods)
and object regions (plotted
as hash marks).

sufficiently different (say, 50% change in size) correspond to different (although nested) objects. In thermal images, this might correspond to a warm vehicle with a hot engine compartment, or to a vehicle on an asphalt road. The results of applying the algorithm to a set of 16 APC windows are illustrated in Figure 6.3. Note that in almost all cases (the negative image was not processed), the resulting labelled images contain the target regions (as well as other regions).

In summary, the algorithm for region extraction consists of the following steps:

1. Smooth the image, if necessary (to promote clean thresholding).

2. Extract a thinned edge picture.

3. Determine a gray level range for thresholding.

4. For each gray level in the range:

    a. Threshold the smoothed image.

    b. Label all connected regions of above-threshold points.

    c. For each connected region:

        i. Compute the percentage of border points which coincide with significant thinned edge points.

        ii. Compute the contrast of the region with the background.

        iii. Classify the region as object/non-object based on the size, edge match and contrast.

5. Construct the canonical tree for the set of object regions based on containment.

6. Prune the containment tree by eliminating adjacent nodes which are too similar.

6.2 Conformity - a measure of region definedness

The Superslice algorithm relies on the heuristic that thresholded object regions are distinct from background because they contrast with their surround at a well-defined border. The coincidence of high contrast and high edge value at the border of a thresholded region is an example of the use of convergent evidence supporting the assertion of the object region. The definedness of the border may be evaluated as the percentage of the border points which coincided with the location of thinned edge (locally maximum edge response). Thus a match score of 50% means

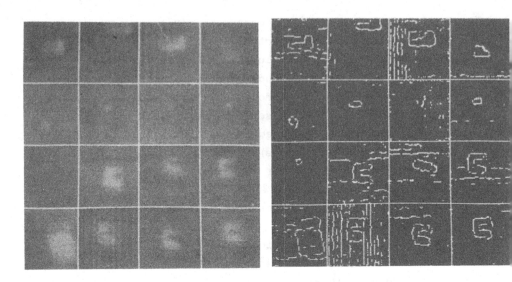

a   b

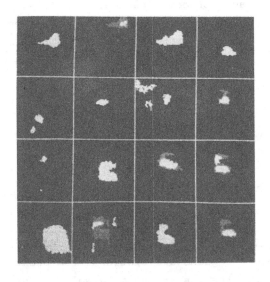

c

Figure   6.3a.   Sixteen APC windows.
                  b.   Edge maps (thresholded for visibility).
                  c.   Object regions extracted by the
                       Superslice algorithm.

that half the border points are accounted for as being on the edge. However, it does not mean that the matched points adequately represent the object. Figure 6.4 illustrates two cases of 50% match. (Matched points are indicated by thick strokes.) Clearly, the second case is a better representation than the first.

The traversal of the border of a thresholded region induces an ordering on the matched points. Let $r_1, \ldots, r_n$ be the runs of matched points encountered during a border traversal. By connecting the proximal ends of runs along the traversal, one creates a polygonal approximation to the thresholded region. We define "conformity" as the measure of match of the polygonal approximation to the thresholded region. High conformity means that the region is well-represented by its approximation regardless of the actual percentage of matched border points. Figure 6.4a illustrates low conformity, while Figure 6.4b shows good conformity.

Conformity is evaluated as the ratio of the absolute difference in area (between the two polygonal representations) to the area of the threshold region. Experiments have indicated its utility as a feature for discriminating noise from objects. A quantitative study of its discrimination value is described in Section 8.4.2.

6.3 Hyperslice - An algorithm for recursive region extraction

The algorithm (Hyperslice) described here is an amalgam embodying the recursive control structure of Ohlander [23] and the object extraction techniques of Superslice. Hyperslice consists of the following steps [24]:

1. Preprocessing - image smoothing, thinned edge map extraction.
2. Initialize the extracted region mask (ERM) to the empty mask. Initialize the available points mask (APM) to the entire mask.
3. Compute histograms for all feature images based on the APM.
4. Determine a "best" slice range over all current histograms and slice the corresponding image.
5. Generate submasks for regions satsifying the Superslice criteria. Add them to the ERM; delete them from the APM.
6. Apply algorithm steps 3-5 recursively to the background

a.   b.

Figure   6.4a.   Contour whose matched edge points
                            (thickened strokes) exhibit poor
                            conformity.

           b.   Contour showing good conformity.

 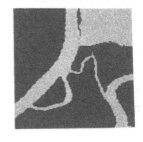

a.   b.

c.   d.   e.

Figure   6.5.   Recursivě region extraction on
                          Monterey image.

           a.   LANDSAT window.
           b.   Edge map.
           c.   Histogram of (a), with selected slice
               range indicated.
           d.   Mask of slice range. Within range
               points are white.
           e.   Extracted regions mask.

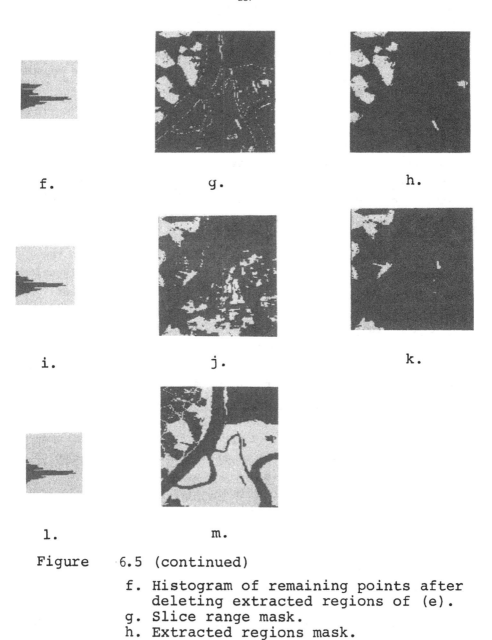

f.

g.

h.

i.

j.

k.

l.

m.

Figure 6.5 (continued)

    f. Histogram of remaining points after
       deleting extracted regions of (e).
    g. Slice range mask.
    h. Extracted regions mask.
    i. Histogram of remaining points.
    j. Slice range mask.
    k. Extracted regions mask.
    l. Histogram of remaining points.
    m. Mask of remaining points.

set (APM). The algorithm should also be applied recursively to each submask added to the ERM, since the extracted region may be a union of regions discriminable by some other feature.

Several comments are in order. First, the slice ranges chosen for Hyperslice should be rather liberal (i.e., extending beyond valley bottoms in the histogram), since points not corresponding to well-defined regions will be returned to the APM. The resulting histograms appear more natural (not "carved-out") for this reason. Secondly, the resulting decomposition is order-dependent, i.e., different results may be obtained if the order of selection of slice ranges is changed. If two adjacent regions in the image contribute adjacent peaks in the histogram, then points in the intersection of the overlapping slice ranges will generally belong to the shared edge region. Whichever region is sliced first will tend to accrete more of these points. Since these points lie at or near the true edge, they tend to increase the edge match criterion for that region. Once they are removed from the APM, they are not available to the adjacent region. Consequently, the edge match criterion of the adjacent region may suffer. This is most likely to occur for adjacent regions which lack a strong common border. The 2-dimensional histogram approach in [16] can detect adjacency along weak borders. In practice, the edge match criterion is relaxed somewhat from demanding actual coincidence to allowing proximity (e.g., a region border point adjacent to a thinned edge point is counted as a match).

The algorithm has been implemented as an interactive system of programs. Several examples illustrate its ability to segment images based on gray level alone (i.e., no other features were used to aid the segmentation). Figure 6.5 depicts a window of an ERTS frame of the Monterey area in California. The water area contrasts sharply with the land and very little noise is extracted and subsequently returned to the APM. The subsequent slices extract light and dark fields which contrast with the undifferentiated background region.

The second example is derived from Ohlander's house scene. The average of the three color bands provides the gray-scale. The resulting image has been smoothed by 3x3 median filtering. The first slice range extracts the sky regions and the bright crown of a bush. Next the shadow regions appear along with the bushes. The somewhat darker grass is extracted in the third slice range. Finally, the brick is extracted. Figure 6.6 illustrates this sequence.

Images such as the Monterey and house images are difficult to analyze since regions need not be well defined due to the complexity of light reflections and shadows. Nonetheless, this algorithm provides a mechanism for retrieving those regions which are well-defined.

7. Feature extraction

7.1 Feature design

In this section, as in most work dealing with pattern classification, a "feature" is taken to be some numerical quantity which can be calculated for each object to be classified. ("Shape" is not a feature, since many features, such as height/width, measure characteristics of the shape.) To be consistent with a high processing rate throughout, all features used in this study are based on accumulatable quantities. That is, a number of crude features have been chosen (listed in Table 7.1a) which are defined at each pixel. The value of any of these features for a region is just the sum of the values over all the pixels of the region. These crude features can be accumulated as the image is being segmented, and are therefore immediately available for any region as soon as it has been completely extracted. The descriptive features actually used are simple functions of these accumulatable quantities, so that once any region has been extracted, brief calculations produce all the information required for classification of that region, with no further reference to the original image. One additional feature, "conformity," has been obtained for many of the images. This feature requires rather more postprocessing after region extraction, and is included as a nearly optimum measure of one region characteristic which should be of importance in target detection: cooccurrence of the region perimeter and points of high brightness gradient. This gives a useful standard for measuring the adequacy of the rapidly calculated feature (E&P, in Table 7.1c) which is used as a measure of the same property.

A decision rule is effectively a mapping from the feature space

a.

b.

c.

d.

e.

f.

g.

h.

Figure 6.6. Recursive region extraction on house
image.

a. House window.
b. Edge map.

c,f,i,l,o. Histograms after successive deletion
of extracted regions. New slice range
are indicated.
d,g,j,m. Slice range masks.
e,h,k,n. Extracted region masks.
p. Mask of remaining points.

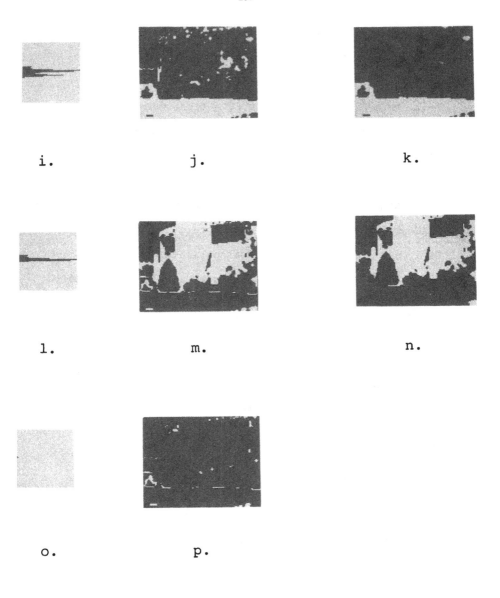

i.   j.   k.

l.   m.   n.

o.   p.

Figure   6.6 (continued)

a. Accumulatable features per connected component

	Symbol	Meaning
1.	N	Area
2-3.	SX,SY	$\Sigma X, \Sigma Y$ - first moments
4-6.	SX^2, SY^2, SXY	$\Sigma X^2, \Sigma Y^2, \Sigma XY$ - second moments
7.	P	Perimeter point count
8.	E	High edge point count
9.	SPE	Total edge value on the perimeter
10.	SIG	Total interior gray value
11.	SPG	Total perimeter gray value
12-13.	SG, SG^2	Total gray level, total squared gray level

b. Intermediate quantities

1.	X_{AVE}	$4 * \sqrt{SX^2}$
2.	Y_{AVE}	$4 * \sqrt{SY^2}$
3.	R^2	$SX^2 + SY^2$
4.	V	$SG^2/N - (SG)^2/N^2$

Table   7.1.   Features.

c. Recognition features

1. h/w $\qquad$ Y_{AVE}/X_{AVE}

2. (h/w)' $\qquad$ $|X_{AVE}-.8*Y_{AVE}|/\sqrt{X_{AVE}*Y_{AVE}}$

3. (h*w)/A $\qquad$ $X_{AVE}*Y_{AVE}/N$

4. (h+w)/P $\qquad$ $(X_{AVE}+Y_{AVE}-4)/P$ } shape

5. diff $\qquad$ $(SX^2-SY^2)/R^2$

6. skewness $\qquad$ $|SXY|/R^2$

7. asymmetry $\qquad$ $((SXY)^2-SX^2SY^2)/R^4$

8. SDEV $\qquad$ $\sqrt{V}$

9. Gray level difference $\qquad$ $SIG/(N-P) - SPG/P$ } brightness

10. E & P $\qquad$ (Number of perimeter points at high edge local maxima)/P

11. E_p $\qquad$ SPE/P

d. Special features

1. conformity $\qquad$ (See Section 6.2)

Table 7.1, continued

294

to a lower-dimensional space (the decision space) in which each
point is associated with a fixed class. While this structure is
very general, commonly used decision rules are very severe speci-
alizations of this general scheme. Usually the initial mapping
is produced by a set of polynomial functions on the features, one
function for each dimension of the decision space. Within this
space, the class regions are usually separated by planar boundaries. Thus, the Fisher method utilizes a single linear mapping
onto the line, which is bisected by a point (at the Fisher
"threshold") to establish the two class domains. Specialization
of decision rules places sharp restrictions on what constitutes an
appropriate feature.

To discriminate tanks from trucks, a naive observer might
point out that one need only examine the shapes. One more familiar with computational measures would recognize that the shape
of an object involves a great many features, but might suggest
that the height-to-width ratio would be one useful feature. However, height-to-width, width-to-height, log(height-to-width), etc.
are all quite distinct features, one of which may be highly effective in the desired decision while others may be totally useless.
Useful features must thus satisfy a number of conditions, some of
which are general, the others being imposed when particular simple
decision rules are to be applied. The present classification
study has considered linear and quadratic classifiers, a decision
space with no more dimensions than the number of classes, and
simple boundaries for each class within the decision space.
Several levels of restriction on the features to be used with such
a classifier can be stated:
1. Each feature must exhibit a different distribution for
   each of at least two classes.
2. The classes should tend to fall in different value ranges
   for each feature, since class assignments in the decision
   space will be to connected regions.
3. When the classifier utilizes sample means and variances to
   estimate parameters for the mapping (as those used here
   do), the true feature distributions of each class should
   be unimodal, approximately symmetric about the mode, and
   with a minority of points contained in the wings of the
   distribution.

4. For use with <u>linear</u> classifiers, each feature should have
   a distinctly different mean for at least two classes. For
   use with <u>quadratic</u> classifiers, it is only necessary that
   some range of values tend to characterize one class, while
   the other class predominates on the complement.

Despite these "rules" for good features, it should be noted
that for a multi-feature decision scheme, none of these rules is
essential. However, only when some of the features are very
strongly correlated can the above principles be violated without
destroying the classification, and while this situation is not
necessarily to be avoided, it makes interpretation of decision
rules much more difficult. Moreover, as a practical matter,
features which fail to have the above properties normally turn out
to be ineffective (or worse, countereffective) when employed in
automatic classification. Since one is not really restricted in
the particular form of the features to be used (but only in the
underlying characteristic being represented) one may as well assure that the features being considered are, as far as possible,
<u>individually</u> effective means of class discrimination.

Finally, one more restriction should be stated.

5. The features should <u>not</u> reflect characteristics which
   effectively delineate the sample classes, rather than the
   true classes.

This, of course, is the familiar failing of "small" samples,
but may appear even in apparently large enough samples. In our
data base (Section 8.1), several such "extraneous differentiations"
did arise. In cases where a large number of features are employed
in a classifier, there must always be doubt about whether condition 5 will hold. It is this condition, more than any other,
which restrains the number of features which can usefully be included in a classifier. If an arbitrarily large number of features are measured for a particular set of classified samples, it
is virtually certain that spurious characteristics will allow
them to be well separated by a decision function based on those
features, but there is no reason to expect anything other than
random classification of new samples. The problem is sufficiently
pervasive that a simple means of dealing with it could almost be
elevated to a principle:

5'. Features should be included in a classifier only if they

identify true differences between the classes more than
they do spurious differences between the samples.

While the above rule may seem obvious, it is important to rea-
lize that including additional features that do not discriminate
between classes makes the classifier _worse_, as the features may
very well distinguish the class samples, even though they do not
distinguish the classes. (Self-classification of the training set
improves, while classification of independent test sets degrades.)
Class differences must be _effectively_ reflected in the feature
to make it safe to use. "Height-to-wdith" ratio is a dangerous
feature to include in a linear classifier for target vs. non-
target since its mean values for target and non-target classes may
not be greatly different (though the distributions may differ
greatly), so that small spurious differences in sample means may
produce most of the "strength" of the feature. In a quadratic
classifier, however, the problem would be much less severe, since
the discrimination provided by the feature more nearly matches
the requirements of the decision function employed.

7.2 Computation

The principal attributes of image regions which can be used
to identify them are shape and relative brightness. Corresponding
locally accumulatable properties are pixel coordinates, and
functions of them, and gray level, and functions of it. Additional information can be obtained from the contrast between the
region and its surround at the region boundary. One can know as
one examines each image point whether it is in the interior of a
region, on the region boundary, or in the background. Statistics
of interest can therefore be accumulated separately for these
classes. Finally, the pre-computed edge value (gray-level
gradient) is associated with each point, and these values may be
accumulated or may be used to index subsets of points (e.g., "high
edge" points) for which other quantities may be accumulated separately. The accumulated features actually used are all of one or
the other of the above types, and were listed in Table 7.1a.

The features calculated for use in classification studies are
given in Table 7.1c-d. They are further divided into two
groups -- those that are purely shape measures, and those that
depend in some way on the brightness of the region (or some part

of it). Many of the functions appear to be straightforward measures of significant characteristics, but others seem less
straightforward. The criteria for choosing the specific functional forms used are discussed in Section 8.4. A discussion of
the relative utility of the features appears in that same section.

8. Region Classification and Experimental Results

8.1 Data base description

For a description of the complete "NVL" data base and its
ground truth see [1]. From it a set of 174 128x128 windows were
selected, extracted, requantized, median filtered and sampled 2
to 1. The set consists of 164 target windows (75 tanks, 34 trucks,
55 APC's) and 10 non-target (noise) windows. Figure 8.1 displays
this set of windows and their identifiers.

8.2 Overview of classification

There are two general approaches to classification of objects
into a preassigned set of mutually exclusive categories. The
first might be called "semantic" classification. Each category
is examined for particular characteristics which distinguish its
members from those of every other category being considered. These
characteristics are used to identify each object submitted for
classification. (Difficulties, of course, occur if an object has
none of the "key" characteristics, or has "key" characteristics
suggesting more than one classification. Such an occurrence indicates that the classes suggested simply do not include everything within the domain of interest, or are not truly mutually
exclusive -- at least as defined by the set of "key" features.)
This is a form of classification which is ubiquitous in human
experience. Unfortunately, in many cases of practical importance,
the objects to be classified cannot be characterized by properties
which will always be observed within one class, and never in any
other class. If the classes really are well-defined, this difficulty may arise because of the need to classify using noisy or
poorly resolved data. It may also occur because characteristics
quite plain to human observers may defy expression as calculatable
quantities (one vehicle may be "sleek and speedy looking", another
"squat and out-of-date"). For whatever reason, when such incom-

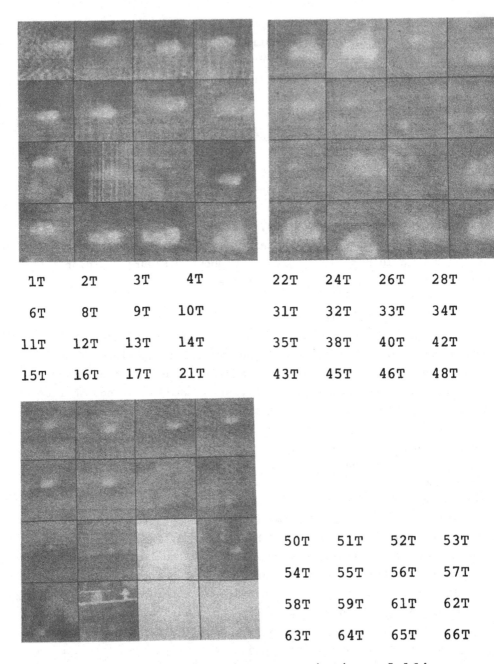

1T	2T	3T	4T		22T	24T	26T	28T
6T	8T	9T	10T		31T	32T	33T	34T
11T	12T	13T	14T		35T	38T	40T	42T
15T	16T	17T	21T		43T	45T	46T	48T

50T	51T	52T	53T
54T	55T	56T	57T
58T	59T	61T	62T
63T	64T	65T	66T

Figure   8 .1.   NVL data base consisting of 164
             target windows and 10 non-target
             windows.

         a.   75 tanks.

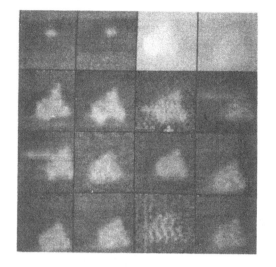

68T	69T	73T	74T
75T	76T	78T	79T
80T	89T	92T	95T
99T	105T	109T	110T

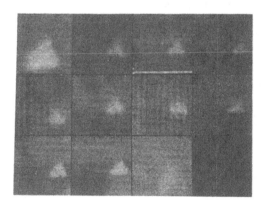

114T	122T	123T	124T
125T	126T	127T	128T
129T	130T	131T	

Figure   8.1 (continued)

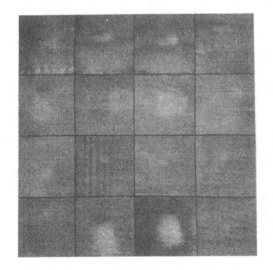

3R	4R	6R	9R
18R	22R	24R	26R
31R	32R	33R	34R
35R	41R	47R	51R

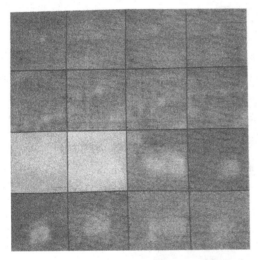

52R	53R	54R	55R
56R	57R	58R	59R
71R	72R	77R	100R
104R	109R	132R	133R

134R 135R

Figure   8.1 (continued)
b. 34 trucks.

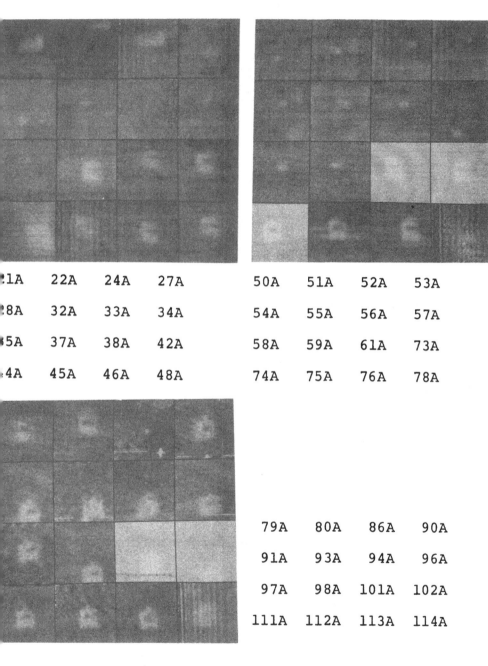

21A	22A	24A	27A
28A	32A	33A	34A
35A	37A	38A	42A
44A	45A	46A	48A

50A	51A	52A	53A
54A	55A	56A	57A
58A	59A	61A	73A
74A	75A	76A	78A

79A	80A	86A	90A
91A	93A	94A	96A
97A	98A	101A	102A
111A	112A	113A	114A

Figure   8.1 (continued)

c. 55 APC's.

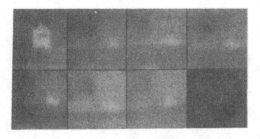

115A   122A   123A   125A

127A   129A   130A

c.   APC's (continued).

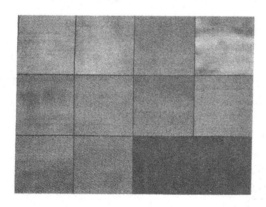

2N   8N   14N   20N

26N   32N   38N   44N

50N   56N

d.   10 non-target windows.

Figure   8.1 (continued)

pletely characterized problems arise, a method is required which
provides a computable "best guess" classification. All such
methods accept a number of (usually numerical) features which are
assumed to be relevant to the classification intended. The distribution of these features for a large number of objects whose
identity is already known is then used to provide a rule which
assigns a class to an object given the n-tuple of features measured for that object. Typical rules of this sort are simple
polynomials over the features, whose values are used to determine
the class assignments.

"Statistical" classification finds the best rules for a fixed
class under some (usually very restrictive) assumptions about the
way the features ought to be distributed. Since the data available in this study appear not to provide enough resolution to produce a semantic classification, we have utilized a procedure which
includes a statistical classification component. A completely
statistical classifier was not used, however. The full procedure
consists of a semantic pre-classification of regions which could
not represent targets, followed by a statistical classification of
the "reasonable" regions. This approach was chosen primarily to
ensure greater robustness in the resulting classification scheme,
as will be discussed more fully below.

Finally, it is important to analyze the types of errors made
by a classifier. For example, a well-behaved classifier should be
wrong more often on distorted images than on undistorted ones.
This type of performance may be tested by training a classifier of
the same type on a "training set" of half the samples, distributed
evenly through the classes. The resultant classifier can then be
used to reclassify the whole data set. If the "training" and
"test" results are similar, then the classifier is judged fairly
stable. If the results are good, then the classifier can be considered fairly powerful.

It is important to distinguish between human interaction in
classifier design and human interaction in the operation of the
classifier. The former is permissible since the classifier is
fixed once it has been effectively designed and trained. No
further human assistance is allowed and the classifier is applied
in an automatic fashion to the test set.

8.3 Detailed classification description

The objects to be classified in this study are connected
regions of an input picture, extracted by thresholding the image.
More than one threshold may have been used on any given picture,
so the regions need not be disjoint; rather, one may be entirely
contained in another. For each region, a feature vector containing information about shape and brightness (as described in
Section 7) is used as the sole source of information about the
region for classification. The extraction procedure has somewhat
preselected these regions, so that every region examined has at
least minimal (20%) correspondence between its perimeter and the
high-edge points, has at least minimal contrast (.2 gray level)
and is of roughly appropriate size (between 20 and 1000 pixels).

8.3.1 Stage 1: pre-classification

If the classification is thought of as a two-stage process
(shown schematically as Figure 8.2), the first stage is a crude
"semantic" classifier which identifies some regions as having
properties which indicate that they are not targets. Thus, all
targets have similar height and width, seen at any aspect angle.
Any region with h/w greater than 3 or less than 1/3, then, may be
confidently rejected from further consideration. Similarly,
targets "should" show some minimal contrast at their perimeters,
a good edge-perimeter overlap, and small targets should be of
nearly uniform brightness. All these criteria are set by esta-
blishing numerical thresholds such that at least 95% of the sample
targets satisfy the criteria.

This is called "semantic" classification, rather than a very
crude statistical classification, because the particular criteria
used have been chosen to distinguish the targest on the basis of
physical characteristics of true target images. A statistical
classifier, even if it arrived at the same scheme, would be asses-
sing discriminatory ability on the sample of classified regions
provided for training, and could reflect any peculiarities which
happened to distinguish the categories in that sample. (In the
NVL data, APC's often exhibit an asymmetry which is due to the
fact that most of those in the sample appear in only a single
aspect. An apparently good statistical classifier could be formed
which would unhesitatingly identify any APC in some other aspect

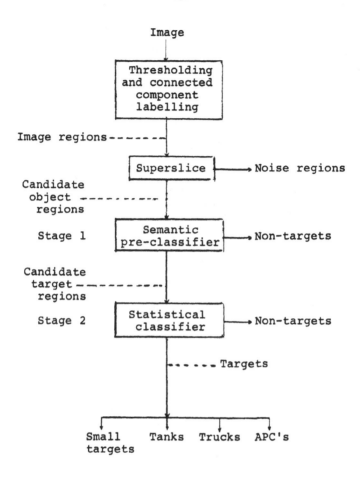

Figure 8.2a. The classification process.

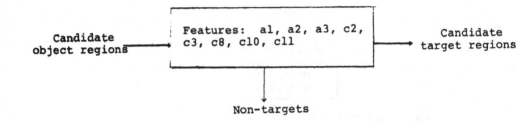

Figure 8.2b. Stage 1 - the pre-classifier
(for feature list, see
Table 7.1).

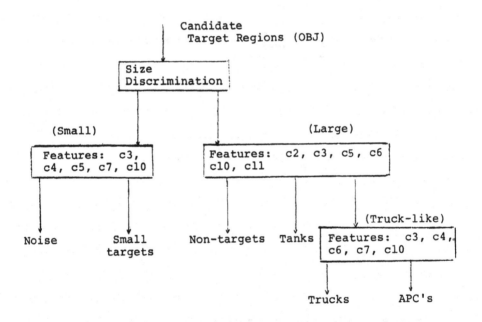

Figure 8.2c. Stage 2 - the classifier
(for feature list, see
Table 7.1).

as a tank.)

This pre-classification examines individual features to determine whether they could be reasonably associated with true targets, and discards "ridiculous" cases. A side-effect of this sorting is to assure that feature values seen by the subsequent statistical classifier are never very far from their characteristic values. This makes the classifier much better-behaved than one which accepts non-normally distributed features (as most do) that have not been "critiqued."

8.3.2 Stage 2: statistical classification

Once the set of extracted regions has been reduced to a set of bright, compact, reasonably uniform regions, statistical classification is used to assign a class to each particular combination of features (or rather, to its associated region). A great many kinds of statistical decision rules exist. Access to the MIPACS [25] interactive system allowed us to design a decision tree (each node of which is a standard classifier) for efficient classification. The system allows individual decision functions to be either linear (e.g., Fisher), quadratic, or maximum likelihood, and provided a convenient mechanism for selecting which decisions to make, and just which features to use at each decision point.

The basic structure selected was shown in Figure 8.2c. The first node actually represents a non-statistical selection. Because of the wide range of apparent sizes of the target images (from 25 to 1000 pixels) and the consequent wide range in visible complexity of detail, it was quickly determined that statistical classifiers would not provide good discrimination over the entire size range. (Almost every feature measured showed substantial correlation with apparent size, and since the various sample classes happened to have rather different image size distributions, our earliest classifiers used that factor as a main classification indicator.) Therefore, the first step in the classification is a simple split on image area -- with all regions of less than 95 pixels going to the "small" subtree, and the remainder passing into the "large" subtrees. For several reasons, principally a presumed lesser urgency for detailed identification of small or distant objects and the fact that in the smallest images no significant differences between the various target classes are apparent, the small regions are simply sent to a node which classifies them as (small) "target" or "non-target" -- the specific type of target is left unspecified. For the large regions, a two-stage process followed. As neither APC's nor trucks are particularly well characterized by the features used and their distributions are very similar, they were merged into a composite "truck-like" class. Any region found to be in this class is then assigned as APC or truck by a Fisher discriminant. (A major reason for this breakdown is that it permits fairly large samples to be used at an important decision point and relegates use of the sparsely sampled truck class to a relatively inconsequential discrimination.) The principal decision was therefore between the "tank" and "truck-like" classes and the "non-target" class. Two different approaches were tried for making this decision, both based on a quadratic maximum-likelihood discriminant. These are described more fully in Section 8.4. One approach ("fixed classes") applied the maximum likelihood criteria directly to the tank, truck-like, and non-target classes. The second approach included two "reject" possibilities as well -- non-target, and unclassified target. (Notice that the non-target label is applied either if a region looks sufficiently like a "typical" non-target or if the best label implies too unlikely a value for the features measured.) The latter approach was included to further minimize reliance on characterizing non-targets in detail.

Given the tree structure for the classification, the kind of classifier and the set of features at each node were determined. The number of features which can reliably be used depends on the size of the sample set used for training. Assuming that the features are chosen so as to avoid apparent vagaries in the set of exemplars, one can confidently use an additional feature for each ten samples in the smallest group, and sometimes may use up to one-third the sample number (for a linear classifier). As quadratic classifiers utilize more detail of the presumed distribution one is restricted to the conservative end of that range. These rules of thumb, while not universally valid, are nonetheless useful guides.

By merging the truck and APC classes, we allow comfortable use of a quadratic classifier on five or six features at the main decision node, while the smaller samples make a linear classifier or a three or four feature quadratic classifier more reasonable at the lower node. The "small" node could utilize five or six features -- but one is hard-pressed to find even that many which provide any discriminatory power at all. (However, one feature, E&P, is very powerful indeed.)

8.4 Experimental results

8.4.1 Feature selection

As in any classification problem, much of the initial feature selection for the vehicle recognition task was carried out informally. This phase is largely introspective, determining characteristics of the images that seem helpful for human judgement, then identifying some features that suitably reflect these characteristics. This initial feature set (conveying "shape" and "relative brightness") is listed in Table 7.1, Section 7. All of these features seem appropriate for use with linear or quadratic classifiers.

The features were examined in several ways. First, histograms for each feature were produced for every sample class. These histograms were examined to see whether the sample distributions satisfied the criteria noted in the last section. The differentiation that appeared was interpreted as to whether it was a true difference between classes, or simply a sampling anomaly. (At this stage too, particular features might be replaced by similar features of slightly different functional form, to better satisfy the requirements of automatic classification.) Second, those features that seemed to have some merit were ranked for classification power at each node of the decision tree. The "Automask" method, available within MIPACS, was used ([25]). Briefly, Automask finds, for each feature, its "share" of the total dispersion both between and within sets, and finds the single feature which produced the greatest comparative variance between sets. This feature is then deleted from consideration, and the other features reexamined to find the next best feature, and so on. The relative merits of the features for each node are shown below.

Node	Good features	Usable features
Small	E&P	(h/w)', (h*w)/A, (h+w)/P, diff, skewness, asymmetry
Large	E&P, diff	(h/w)', (h*w)/A, skewness, asymmetry, E_p
Trucklike	E_p, asymmetry	(h/w)', (h+w)/P, skewness, E&P

Shape features:

In the first stage, the (h/w)' height-to-width feature was useful in identifying small bright streaks as non-targets. In the statistical classifier for small targets, shape features were individually very weak in distinguishing targets from non-targets. For large targets, diff was the best shape feature at node LARGE; all the others but asymmetry were also of some use. At node TRUCK-LIKE, on the other hand, asymmetry was the best shape feature, with the remainder of no value.

Brightness-related features:

Edge-border coincidence (E&P) was by far the strongest single feature for both nodes involving target/non-target discrimination (OBJ and LARGE). For small targets, it provides nearly all the discrimination in the second stage. For large targets, it provides evidence which is well complemented by shape information—both must be included for adequate performance. Also very useful, particularly at stage 1, is E_p, which provides substantially different information from E&P. Gray level variance is used to some effect in the first classifier stage, but is not effective in the second stage. Perimeter contrast information appears to be much more effectively conveyed through E_p than dgl.

These rankings, while not dependable when taken alone, have been very helpful in suggesting which features could usefully be included in decisions at each node and which should be omitted. This was especially helpful in the case of the shape features, for which estimates of relative merit were not obtainable.

The final stage of feature testing was experimental. Features suggested either by Automask or by the problem definition were included in decision functions, and self-classification attempted. In many cases, the results were not satisfactory and one or more features were added or deleted until "good" results were obtained. If too many features were present in this classifier, features were removed until the best classification obtained with an acceptable number of features was found.

8.4.2 Classification

The NVL data base as windowed for classification purposes consists of:

> 75 Tanks
> 34 Trucks
> _55_ APC's
> 164 Target windows
> _10_ Non-target windows
> 174 Total windows

Associated with each window was a liberal threshold range extending from the shoulder of the background peak gray level to the
highest gray level at which there was significant sensor response.
Although these ranges were manually selected, this is not a significant intereference with the automatic nature of the algorithm
since the gray level ranges can be chosen by a simple scheme which
identifies the background peak and proposes every threshold above
the peak. (If a coarse temperature calibration is available, this
task is even simpler.) See Section 8.4.3 for further discussion.

The Superslice algorithm was run on these windows using the
selected gray level ranges. Connected components whose contrast,
edge-perimeter match score and size were within tolerance were
retained. The resulting sets of regions are described by the
containment forests in Table 8.1. Within each containment tree,
Superslice selects the best exemplar(s) for the candidate object
region based on edge match. Thus, every tree has one or more
best exemplars associated with it. All other (non-exemplar)
regions are suppressed since the algorithm has proposed better
representatives for classification.

Each containment tree is manually labelled as either "target-
related" (containing regions associated with the target) or noise
(spatially apart from a target region) so that false dismissals
can be determined.

Of the 164 target windows, two windows (64T, 86A) had containment forests with no target-related regions present. At this
stage, the false dismissal rate is 2/164 ~ 1% for Superslice.
Determination of a false alarm rate is inappropriate since the
discrimination performed by Superslice is "object vs. non-object,"

Window Reference Number	Lowest Threshold	Containment Forests
1T	23	X(N,TTT(PPPPP,PP),NNN,N(N,NN),NN);NN
2T	23	TTTTTTT
3T	25	TTTTTTT(PP,P);NN;NN
4T	30	TTTTTT
6T	25	TTTTTT
8T	26	TTTTT
9T	24	TTTTTT(P,P)
10T	25	TTTTTT
11T	25	TTTTTTTT;NN
12T	22	X(PPPPP(P,P(P,P)),N)
13T	20	XX(N,TTTT);N
14T	22	TTTTTTTT
15T	30	TTTTT
16T	24	TTTTTTT
17T	26	TTTTT
21T	26	TTTTT
22T	25	TTTTTT
24T	29	TTTTT
26T	26	TTTTT
28T	27	TTT
31T	27	TTT
32T	21	X(TTTT,N,N)
33T	23	VTTTT;N
34T	26	TTT
35T	24	TTTT;N
38T	24	TTTTTTT
40T	23	TT;NN;N
42T	24	TTTTT(P,P(PP,PP))

Table 8.1. Containment forests of regions extracted by Superslice(Tanks). "AB" means that region A contains region B. "A(B,C)" means that region A contains the disjoint regions B and C. "A;B" means that A and B are disjoint regions in the window. Underlined letters denote "best" exemplars of the target region. Target trees begin at lowest threshold.

Legend:
- T target
- P partial target
- X target with additional noise
- O target invisible in noise
- N noise region
- F fiducial mark
- V target region not present at this threshold

43T	26	TTTTT
45T	25	TTTT̄TT
46T	26	TTTT̄TT
48T	24	TTT̄TTTTT
50T	22	OTTTT̄
51T	24	TT̄T̄TT
52T	23	TTTT̄T
53T	23	TTT̄TT
54T	23	TTT̄TT
55T	23	TT̄TTT
56T	22	T̲;N̄;N
57T	22	TTT;NN;N
58T	20	X(̄NN,NN,TT)
59T	21	X(TT,NN);N̄;N
61T	43	TTT̄TTT
62T	24	TTTT̄;N
63T	24	TTT;N
64T	28	FFF̄FF;N;N (no target region found)
65T	46	T
66T	47	T̄T
68T	26	T̄TTT;N
69T	26	TTT̄T;NN
73T	43	TTT̄TTTT
74T	45	TTTT̄T
75T	22	TT̄TTTT(P(P,P),P)
76T	23	TTTT̄TTTTTTT
78T	27	TTTTTTT(̄P,P)
79T	24	T̄TT(PPPP,PPP)
80T	22	TTT̄T(P,PPPPP(P(P,P),PP))
89T	23	TTTT̄TTTTTT
92T	22	TTTTT̄TTTTTTT
95T	24	TTTTTTT̄TTT
99T	21	TTTT̄TTTTTTTT
105T	24	TTTTTTTT̄TT(P,P,P)
109T	28	TT(̄PPPP,PPPPP,P(PPPP,PP))
110T	24	T̄TTTTTT
114T	25	TTTTT̄TTTTT
122T	20	T̄TTTTT
123T	22	TTTT̄TTT
124T	21	TTT̄TTTT
125T	24	TTTTTT̄
126T	23	TT̄TT
127T	24	T̄TTTTTTT
128T	23	TTT̄TTTT
129T	24	TTTT̄TTTT
130T	25	TTTT̄TT
131T	26	TT̲T̄TT

Table 8.1. Continued.

Window Reference Number	Lowest Threshold	Containment Forests
3R	23	X(TTT,NNN(NNNN,NNNNN));N
4R	22	TTTTTT;N;N;NNN
6R	23	OTTTTTT;NN
9R	23	X(TTTT,N(NN,N),NN,N,N)
18R	26	VTTT;N
22R	24	TTTTTT
24R	28	X(X(TTT(PP,P),N))
26R	27	TTT;N
31R	26	OTTTT
32R	21	X(PP,N,N,N);NN
33R	23	X(X(TTT,N),N
34R	24	VVTTT;N;N;N
35R	23	TTT;N;N;N
41R	25	TTTTTTTTTTT
47R	25	TTTTTTTTTTTT
51R	25	TTT;N;N
52R	23	TTT
53R	24	TT
54R	23	TT;N
55R	23	VTTT;N;N
56R	24	TTTTTT;NNN
57R	24	TTTT;NNN;N;NN
58R	24	TTTT;NN
59R	23	TTTT;NN;N;N
71R	44	TTTTT
72R	46	TTT;NN;N
77R	27	TTTTTT(P,P)
100R	23	TTTTTTT
104R	27	TTTTTTT
109R	27	TTT(P,PPP)
123R	27	X(TT(P,P),N)
133R	27	TTTT
134R	27	XTTT(P,P)
135R	26	TTTT

Table   8.1.   Continued.   (Truck windows)

Window Reference Number	Lowest Threshold	Containment Forests
21A	26	TTTTTT
22A	22	TTTTTT
24A	28	TTTTT
27A	27	VTTT;N
32A	25	TT
33A	25	T;N;N
34A	26	TTT
35A	25	TT
37A	27	TTTTTTT
38A	23	TTTTT
42A	24	TTTT(PP,PP)
44A	28	TTTTTTTT
45A	26	TTTT;N;N
46A	26	TTTTTT
48A	26	TTTTTTT
50A	24	TT
51A	25	TTTT;N;N
52A	25	TT;N;N
53A	24	TTT;N;N;NN
54A	25	TTT
55A	26	T
56A	25	TTTT
57A	24	TTTT
58A	25	TTTTT
59A	24	TTTTTTT
61A	41	TTTTTTT
73A	43	TTTTTT
74A	43	TTTTTTT
75A	25	TTTTTTT;N
76A	26	TTTTTTTTT
78A	31	P(PP,P)
79A	25	TTT(PPPP,PPP)
80A	24	TTTTTTT
86A	24	FFFFF;NN;N;N (no target related region found)
90A	25	TTTTTTTTTT
91A	26	TTTTTTTTT
93A	26	TTTTTTTT(P,P)
94A	26	TTTTTTTT
96A	27	TTTTTT
97A	24	TTTTTTTT;N
98A	24	TTTTT
101A	44	TTTTT
102A	44	TTTTT;N
111A	24	TTTTTTTTT
112A	24	TTTTTTTTT
113A	23	TTTTTTTT
114A	29	X(TT(P,P),NN)
115A	24	TTTTTTTTTT(P,P)
122A	23	TTT
123A	24	TTTTTT
125A	24	TTTT
127A	24	TTTT
129A	26	TTTT
130A	23	TTTTTT

Table   8.1.   Continued.   (APC windows)

not "target vs. non-target," and there is no ground truth for the number of objects (including targets, hot rocks, trees, etc.) in the frames.

The next stage - preclassification - performs possible-target vs. non-target screening. [For the purpose of building the screening criteria and subsequent classifier, a single exemplar per target was hand-chosen. No other target-related regions were considered; all noise regions, however, were retained.] Of the 162 target windows, the preclassifier retained 161 for a false dismissal rate of 1%. In addition, 44 noise exemplars also survived as possible targets. The false dismissal was 66T (small, very faint).

After preclassification, 150 selected target exemplars and all 44 noise exemplars were split into a training set (74 targets and 22 noise regions) and a test set (76 targets and 22 noise regions). The training set was used to design the optimum decision rule. It was felt that similar results in classifying both sets would then indicate that the classifier had utilized robust characteristics of the target class and thus could be expected to give similar results on further data of the same type.

A linear discriminant was used at the trucklike node while a maximum liklihood discriminant was used at the small target/non-target node. Five features were used at both nodes, of which four were the same: (h*w)/A, (h+w)/P, asymmetry, E&P. The fifth feature was diff for the small target discriminant and skewness for the truck/APC discriminant. The large targets are divided into three classes (tank, truck/APC, other) by a quadratic maximum likelihood discriminant using six features: (h/w)', (h*w)/A, diff, skewness, E&P and E_p. Two different procedures for classifying large regions (> 94 pixels) were tested. One procedure attempted to discriminate between four fixed classes (tank, APC, truck, other); the other procedure used three classes (tank, APC, truck) and two "reject" categories (non-target, unidentified target). Both used identical polynomial maps into decision space. In the latter classifier, however, the maximum likelihood class assignment of a region had to be significantly better than for random noise regions (otherwise, the non-target class was assigned) and significantly better than the next best target class assignment (otherwise, it was called an unidentified target).

The detection results using the fixed class classifier on the

150 selected target exemplars are summarized by:

	Train	Test	Total
Large	53/53	53/55	106/108
Small	20/21	20/21	40/42
Total	73/74	73/76	146/150

where "M/N" means "M successes out of N tries." This classifier thus appeared to be robust.

Table 8.2 displays the results of this classifier for all extracted regions, including all target and noise exemplars. A false dismissal for a window containing a target occurs when no target exemplar (at any of the thresholds) is classified as a target (i.e., classified as tank, truck, or APC). Similarly, a false alarm is any noise exemplar (i.e., not associated spatially with a target region) classified as a target. However, multiple exemplars for the same noise region are counted only once. In effect, we are counting the image regions (as opposed to exemplars) which are classified as target regions by at least one exemplar. If a region is, in fact, a target region and some exemplar of it is called a target, that is a success. If no exemplar is so called, then a false dismissal has occurred. Finally, if the so-called target region does not, in fact, contain a target, then a false alarm has occurred.

The classifier results consist of 6 false alarms and 3 false dismissals from the 162 target windows and 2 more false alarms from 10 non-target windows. No window contained more than one false alarm cue. Details are as follows:

False Dismissals	False Alarms
32R	3T
35R	11T
33A	3R
	56R
	59R
	86A
	2N
	8N

Thresholds

Frame	20	21	22	23	24	25	26	27	28	29	30	31	32	33	34	35	36	37	38	39	40	41	42	43	44	45	46	47	48
1T				[0	0	+	+	+	+	+	+	+	0	0	0]														
2T				[+	+	+	+	+	+	+	+]																		
3T						[0	0	0	0	+	+	+]																	
4T										+	+	[+	+	+	0	0]													
6T						[+	+	+	+	+	+]																		
8T								[+	+	+	+]																		
9T							[0	0	0	+	0]																		
10T					[0	0	0	0	+	+]																			
11T						[+	+	+	+	+	+]																		
12T		[0	+	0	0	0	0]																						
13T	[0	0	+	+	+	+	0]																						
14T				[+	+	+	+	+	+	+]																			
15T											[+	+	+	+	+]														
16T						[+	+	+	+	+	+]																		
17T						[+	+	+	+	+]																			
21T						[+	+	+	+	+]																			
22T						[+	+	+	0	+]																			

Table   8.2   Region classification (tank windows).

Each entry represents the outcome of the classifier for the purpose of target detection. Brackets indicate the range of thresholds considered for each window. "+" means that the target was detected at that threshold. "0" means that the target was dismissed. "_" indicates a false alarm for that threshold. No window had two or more distinct false alarm regions.

Thresholds

Frame	20	21	22	23	24	25	26	27	28	29	30	31	32	33	34	35	36	37	38	39	40	41	42	43	44	45	46	47	48
24T										[+	+	+	+	+]															
26T							[0	+	+	+	0]																		
28T							[	+	+	+	]																		
31T								[	+	+	]																		
32T	[				0	0	+	0	]																				
33T				[				0	]																				
34T				[				+	+]																				
35T				[0	0		+	+]																					
38T				[0	0	0	0	+	0	0	]																		
40T			[	+	+		+	]																					
42T				[+		+	0	0	+	0	0	]																	
43T					[+		0	0	+	+	+]																		
45T					[+	0	0	+	+	+	+]																		
46T					[0	0	0	0	+	+	+]																		
48T				[+	+	+	+	0	+	0	+	0	]																
50T			[+	+	+	+	0]																						
51T			[+	+	+	+	+	+	+]																				
52T			[+	+	+	+	+	0]																					
53T			[+	+	+	+	+	+]																					
54T			[+	+	+	+	+	+]																					
55T			[+	+	+	+	+	+]																					
56T			[+		]																								
57T		[+	+	+			]																						

Table 8.2. Continued.

Thresholds

Frame	20	21	22	23	24	25	26	27	28	29	30	31	32	33	34	35	36	37	38	39	40	41	42	43	44	45	46	47	48
58T	[0	+	+		]																								
59T	[0	+	+		]																								
61T																							[+	+	+	+	+]		
62T					[+	0	+	+]																					
63T					[+	+	+]																						
64T								[		0	0	+	0	+	+]														
65T																										[+]			
66T																											[0		0]
68T						[+	+	+]																					
69T						[+	+	0]																					
73T																								[+	+	+	+	+	+]
74T																										[+	+	+	+]
75T				[+	+	+	+	+	+]																				
76T				[0	+	+	+	+	+	+	+	+	+	+	0]														
78T								[+	+	+	+	+	+	+	0]														
79T					[+	+	+	+	0	+]																			
80T				[+	+	+	+	+	+	+]																			
89T				[+	+	+	+	+	+	+]																			
92T				[+	+	+	+	+	+	+	0]																		
95T				[+	+	+	+	+	+	+]																			
99T	[0	0	+	+	+	+	+	+	+	0]																			
105T					[+	+	+	0	0	0]																			
109T								[+	+	0	0	0	0]																

Table 8.2. Continued.

Thresholds

Frame	20	21	22	23	24	25	26	27	28	29	30	31	32	33	34	35	36	37	38	39	40	41	42	43	44	45	46	47	48
110T					[0	+	+	+	+	+	+]																		
114T						[+	+	+	+	+	+	+	+	+	0]														
122T	[+	0	+	+	0]																								
123T				[+	+	+	+	+	0]																				
124T			[0	+	+	+	+	0	0]																				
125T					[+	+	+	+	0]																				
126T				[0	+	+	+	+]																					
127T						[+	+	+	+	+	+	0]																	
128T				[	+	+	+	+	+	0	0]																		
129T				[	+	+	+	+	+	+	+	0]																	
130T						[+	+	+	+	+	0]																		
131T							[0	+	+	+	0]																		

Table 8.2. Continued.

Thresholds

Frame	20	21	22	23	24	25	26	27	28	29	30	31	32	33	34	35	36	37	38	39	40	41	42	43	44	45	46	47	48
3R				[+	+	+	0								]														
4R			[+	+	+	+̲	0	0	]		–	–																	
6R				[+	+	+	0	+	+]																				
9R				[0	+	+	0	+	]																				
18R							[	+	+	0	]																		
22R				[0	0	+	0	+	0]																				
24R									[+	+	+	0	+	0	0]														
26R							[	0	+	0	]																		
31R							[	+	+	+	0]																		
32R	[0	0	0	]																									
33R				[	0	0	+	+]																					
34R				[	0	+	+]																						
35R				[0	0	0]																							
41R						[0	+	0	+	+	0	0	0	0	0	]													
47R						[+	+	+	+	+	+	0	+	0	0	]													
51R						[0	+	0	]																				
52R				[0	0	+	]																						
53R				[0	+	]																							
54R				[0	+	;																							
55R				[	0	+	0]																						
56R				[+	+	0̲	0̲	0̲	0	+]																			

Table 8.2 (continued): Truck windows.

Thresholds

Frame	20	21	22	23	24	25	26	27	28	29	30	31	32	33	34	35	36	37	38	39	40	41	42	43	44	45	46	47	48
57R					[+	0	+	+		]																			
58R					[+	+	+	+		]																			
59R				[0	+	+	0		]																				
71R																									[+	+		+	0]
72R																										[+	+	+	0]
77R							[+	+		+	+		+	0]															
100R				[0		+	+		+	+]																			
104R							[+	+		+	+		+	+]															
109R							[0	+	+		+	+	0]																
132R							[+	+	+	+	0]																		
133R							[+	+	+	+	0]																		
134R							[+	+	+	+	0]																		
135R						[+	+	+	+	+]																			

Table 8.2. Continued.

Thresholds

Frame	20	21	22	23	24	25	26	27	28	29	30	31	32	33	34	35	36	37	38	39	40	41	42	43	44	45	46	47	48
21A							[+	+	+	+	0	0]																	
22A			[+	+	+	+																							
24A									[+	+	+	+			]														
27A							[0	+	+	+	]																		
28A								[	+	+	0]																		
32A						[+	+		]																				
33A						[0			]																				
34A						[0	+		+		]																		
35A						[0		+		]																			
37A				[+	+	+	+		+		+	+		+		]													
38A				[+	+		+		0]																				
42A					[+	+	+		+	0]																			
44A									[+	0	+	+	0	+	0		]												
45A							[+	+	+	0	]																		
46A							[0	+	+	0	]																		
48A							[+	+	+	+	0]																		
50A					[+	0	]																						
51A						[0	+	+	0	]																			
52A						[0	+		]																				
53A					[+	+	+]																						
54A						[+	0	0	]																				
55A						[+			]																				
56A					[+	0	+	0	]																				

Table 8.2 (continued): APC windows.

Frame	20	21	22	23	24	25	26	27	28	29	30	31	32	33	34	35	36	37	38	39	40	41	42	43	44	45	46	47	48
57A					[+	0	0	0]																					
58A						[+	0	+	+]																				
59A					[0	+	+	+	0]																				
61A																						[+	+	+	+	+	+	+]	
73A																								[+	+	+	+	+	+]
74A																								[+	+	+	+	+	+]
75A					[+	+	+	0	0	0]																			
76A							[+	+	+	+	+]																		
78A											[+	0	0]																
79A						[0	+	+	0	+]																			
80A					[+	+	+	+	+	+	+]																		
86A					[_	_]																							
90A							[+	+	+	+	+	+	0	0]															
91A							[+	+	+	+	+	0	+]																
93A							[+	+	+	+	+	+	0]																
94A							[0	+	+	+	+	+]																	
96A								[+	+	+	+	+]																	
97A					[+	+	+	+	+	+	+]																		
98A					[+	+	+	+	+	+	+]																		
101A																								[+	+	+	+	+]	
102A																								[0	+	+	+	+]	
111A				[+	+	+	+	+	+	0]																			
112A					[+	+	+	+	+	0	0]																		
113A					[+	+	+	+	+	0]																			
114A								[+	+	+	+	+	+]																
115A						[+	+	+	+	+	+	+	0]																

Table 8.2.   Continued.

Thresholds

Frame	20	21	22	23	24	25	26	27	28	29	30	31	32	33	34	35	36	37	38	39	40	41	42	43	44	45	46	47	48
122A				[+	+	0]																							
123A					[+	+	+	0	+	,0]																			
125A					[+	+	+	+]																					
127A					[+	+	+	+	]																				
129A								[+	+	+	0]																		
130A				[+	+	+]																							

Table 8.2. Continued.

Thresholds

Frame	20	21	22	23	24	25	26	27	28	29	30	31	32	33	34	35	36	37	38	39	40	41	42	43	44	45	46	47	48
2N								[	—					]															
8N								[				—	—		]														
14N	[			]								—	—																
20N					[		]								]														
26N		[				]																							
32N			[		]																								
38N	[			]																									
44N			[				]																						
50N			[			]																							
56N	[				]																								

Table   8.2   (continued):   Noise windows.

Figure 8.3a displays the 6 (total) false dismissals. Masks of
the 8 false alarms along with their gray level windows are shown
in Figure 8.3b.

The question of how target identifications can be made in this
environment of multiple exemplars, while secondary to the task of
detection, is an interesting one. Since each exemplar in a containment tree can be classified independently, there are many ways
of arriving at a final region label. Section 8.5 discusses the
use of context and considers the identification of object regions
from the classifications in their containment trees as an example
of context. We discuss the issue here simply from the point of
view of critiquing the classifier performance. For each containment tree containing at least one exemplar as a target, we chose
the target type of the exemplar with the best edge-match (E&P)
score in the tree and used that target type to designate the
region. In the event that the "best" exemplar was not described
as a target, we labelled the object region "unknown target". Only
large targets were considered, since small targets while detectable
were not considered identifiable.

In a test which classified all best exemplars of large targets
(55 tanks, 21 trucks, 36 APC's) the between-types confusion matrix
was:

classified as

		T	Tr	A	UT
	T	40	5	6	4
A priori	Tr	6	8	7	0
	A	9	5	20	2

where "UT" is the "unknown-target" type. The 8 false alarms were
classified as 1 truck, 2 APC's, and 5 small targets. Between-
class confusion is high, with tanks being the most successful
class. Trucks and APC's were often confused with tanks. A number
of reasons can be advanced for this performance. First, tanks
were the most numerous target and therefore could be identified
most confidently. Second, large APC's appeared with the wooden
wave deflection board in view, producing a characteristic "c"
shape. No attempt was made to utilize this special knowledge.

64T   66T   32R   35R

36A   86A

a.

3T	11T
3R	56R
59R	86A
2N	8N

b.

Figure   8.3.   Classification results for NVL
data base.

      a.   Six false dismissals.
      b.   Eight false alarm region masks
          with their gray level windows.

Third, the large targets appeared in only a single aspect and no generalized shape descriptors separating the different types could be extracted reliably. It seems most sensible to model the target types as three-dimensional objects and to derive discriminators from their inherent shape and size differences from all aspects.

The second classifier (which applied a threshold to reduce the false-alarm rate) did not improve classification as might have been expected. Any threshold which would have reduced the number of false alarms also caused a number of false dismissals. Thus while the method might be of use, its utility could not be judged on the limited data set available especially since there is no model relating the false alarm rate to the false dismissal rate.

We may summarize the principal classification results as follows: the false dismissal rate of the system is less than 4%, giving a system detection rate of 96%. The false alarm rate, based on the number of false alarm regions per unit area, is 8 false alarms in 174 (128x128) windows. Assuming there are 500x800 pixels per frame and that a target occupies about 1/10 of a window, we conclude that the total processed area corresponds to about 6 frames. Thus the false alarm rate is 8/6 or 1.3 per frame. A separate test of the false alarm rate was made using a set of four 512x512 pixel frames (Figure 8.4). All available targets were detected. In addition, 4 large false alarms and 8 small false alarms were detected (see Figure 8.5). However, 5 of the 8 small false alarms corresponded to fiducial marks. Moreover, one large false alarm (in F1) appears to be a target. In any case, 7 false alarms in 4 frames agrees well with the previous estimate of the false alarm rate.

8.4.3 Threshold selection evaluation

Our method of threshold range selection was described previously. However, it bears repetition in this section. Using the histogram of gray levels (perhaps of the previous image), choose as a range the sequence of gray levels from the mode to the highest gray level with appreciable response (e.g., more than 5 points). The previous subsection demonstrated that this brute force approach gave excellent system detection efficiency. Naturally, the liberal range of thresholds has important effects on system architecture.

Figure   8.4.   Four 256x256 frames (after median
                  filtering and sampling).

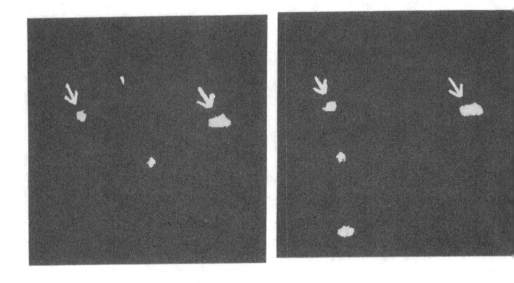

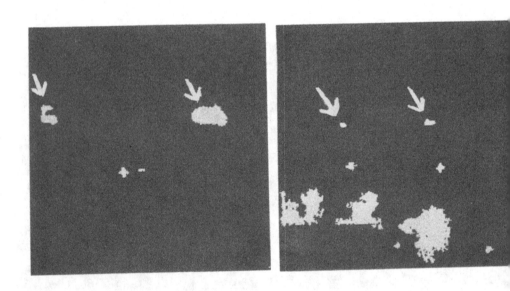

Figure   8.5.   Cued regions in the four frames
of Figure   8.4.   All targets
were detected (masks indicated
with arrows), along with 12 false
alarms (5 corresponding to
fiducial marks).

Since the number of thresholds used determines the time cost (in a sequential implementation) or the hardware replication cost (in a parallel implementation), it is appropriate to consider methods which can accommodate a limited number of thresholds. "Intelligent" methods of threshold selection are discussed in Sections 4 and 9. We wish to consider "brute force" methods which select thresholds at every gray level, at every third gray level, etc.

As may be seen from Table 8.2, correct target detections for single windows tend to occur in extended runs. Table 8.3 provides a histogram of run lengths. In general, large targets had better constrast and their detections were stable over long runs. Small targets were fainter and were detectable over only a few thresholds at most. Table 8.3 shows what percentage of the targets were detected within runs of I or longer for I = 1,2,... . Thus the false dismissal rate would be 11% if every other threshold in the range were omitted. Since there were so few false alarms, it is not possible to give comparable statistics of any reliability, but any scheme which considers fewer exemplars is bound to detect fewer false alarms.

From a slightly different point of view, we might consider how to allocate a fixed number of thresholds within a given gray level range. Suppose that five thresholds are implemented in parallel hardware. Thus, for a gray level range of 10, thresholds would occur at every other gray level; for a range of 20, thresholds would occur at every fourth gray level. If we use the gray level ranges indicated by brackets in Table 8.2 and distribute N (=1,2,3,...) thresholds equally spaced (where feasible) throughout the range, we compute the following results:

N	# False Dismissals	# False Alarms
1	25	1
2	14	3
3	7	7
4 and above	5	8

Thus, for four or more thresholds equally spaced throughout the available gray level range of each window, no additional false dismissals occurred beyond those already dismissed using the whole

Run length	# of windows	Cumulative count	% of 164 windows
0	5	164	100
1	17	159	97
2	25	142	87
3	29	117	71
4	27	88	54
5	19	61	37
6	12	42	26
7	10	30	18
8	8	20	12
9	7	12	7
10	3	5	3
11	2	2	1

Table   8.3.   Statistics of longest runs of correct target detections in 164 target windows.

range. Interestingly, for small N the increase in false dismissals
is just about compensated by the decrease in false alarms. One is
doubled as the other is halved.

Naturally, the threshold ranges depend both on window size and
on window content. It is therefore not likely that three
thresholds will be sufficient in practice. The best choice of N,
the number of thresholds, will result from estimating the probabi-
lity/cost tradeoff for faint targets. Given a range of x gray
levels for target regions, N should be about x/2 or x/3, which
for the current data base suggests that N should lie between 5 and
10. For an extension to image sequences, see Section 9.1.

8.4.4 Classifier extension

An attempt was made to apply the classifier derived from the
NVL data base to a different set of thermal images. The Alabama
data base is a set of imagery taken with a thermoscope. The
actual sensor data are classified; radiometric noise was added to
mask the source. Figure 8.6 exemplifies the type of imagery involved. The gray level histograms are not smooth and in some
cases runs of gray level bins contain no points. Median filtering (using odd sizes) cannot be used to smooth such images since
it preserves false contours. Median filtering using even sizes
provides a small degree of smoothing. We elected to smooth by
locally averaging over a 2x2 neighborhood just to introduce sufficient gray level variation so that 5x5 median filtering would be
effective.

The resultant images were windowed and threshold ranges were
selected. The Superslice algorithm was then applied in order to
extract candidate object regions. It was necessary to increase
the contrast threshold since the inherent contrast (including
false contours was higher than in the NVL data base. With this
adjustment, the Superslice algorithm extracted regions corresponding to 64 out of 65 targets. After classification, 60 out of
65 were detected. In addition, there were 3 false alarms in the
48 64x64 windows considered (although one of the false alarms
appears to be a target missing from the ground truth).

8.5 Classification and context

Our approach to the target cueing problem has been to extract

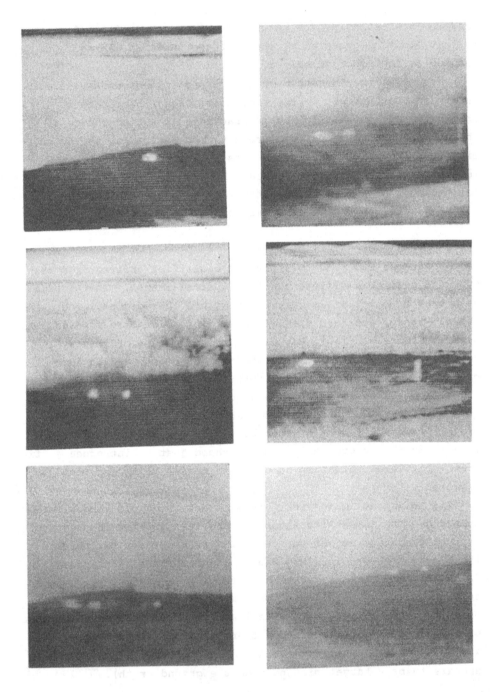

Figure   8.6.   Alabama data base (selected frames).

337

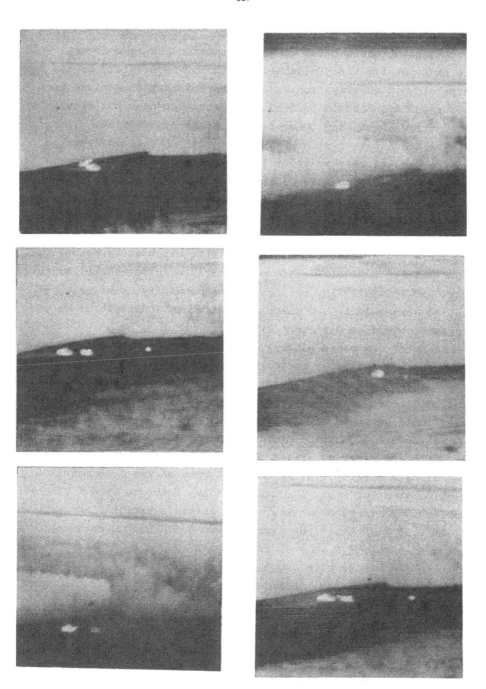

Figure   8.6   (continued)

and classify object regions independently of one another. That
is, segmentation is based on the assumption that the object regions
are individually thresholdable, though not necessarily by the same
threshold. Classification is based on information derived from
measurements on the individual components but does not take into
account the intra- and inter-frame context of a region.

The Gestalt laws of grouping (see [26]) are of interest in
this respect since they refer to factors that cause some parts to
be seen as belonging more closely together than others. These
rules are applications of the basic principles of similarity which
assert that region association is partly defined by region resemblance.

There are several types of similarity which could be used with
FLIR imagery, e.g. similarity of appearance (size, shape, brightness, etc.), similarity of location or proximity, similarity of
spatial arrangement, and temporal similarity (multiple views of
the same object in different frames).

Whenever one can confidently group a set of N objects as
being similar (based on one or more of the types of context discussed above), it may be advantageous to classify them collective-
ly (The Compound Decision problem) rather than independently
(The Simple Decision problem).

The compound decision problem can be stated briefly as follows:
There are a set of states of nature $\Omega = \{1,2,...\gamma\}$ and a set
of actions $A = \{1,2,...s\}$, associated with an rxs loss matrix L_{ij}
being defined for every $i \in \Omega$ and $j \in A$. When the same decision
problem is confronted N times, there exists a vector $\vec{\theta}_N =
\{\theta_1, \theta_2, ...\theta_N\}$ of states of nature where $\theta \in \Omega^N$ and a corresponding
vector $X_N = \{x_1, x_2, ...x_N\}$ of random variables. θ_k denotes the
state in the kth problem and the distribution of x_k is $P(x_k|\theta_k)$.
For a given θ_k, x_k is independent of other x's and θ's. In other
words

$$P(\vec{x}_N|\vec{\theta}_N) = \prod_{j=1}^{N} P(x_j|\theta_j)$$

We do not assume that the θ's are necessarily independent.

The loss in the compound decision problem is taken to be the
average of the losses incurred at each of the N decisions and the
compound risk is defined correspondingly.

If all the observations $\vec{X}_N$ are at hand before the individual decisions must be made, one can use a compound decision rule $\vec{t}_N = \{t_1, t_2, \ldots t_N\}$ where $t_k = t_k(j|\vec{X}_N)$ for each $\vec{X}_N$ is a distribution over A, according to which the kth action is chosen. Also one can define a sequential compound decision rule if only the observations $\vec{x}_k$ are at hand before the kth decision is made.

It is possible to work out a decision procedure which is compound Bayes against the distribution $G(\vec{\theta}_N)$ where $\vec{\theta}_N \in \Omega^N$ (for the details see Abend [27]).

It would be desirable, in principle, to make effective use of context in general and of the compound decision rule in particular as a way of combining related observations. Naturally, this would require a data base which is sufficiently structured to provide the necessary context. However, a recasting of the problem makes another type of context available.

Consider a set of nested regions (exemplars) produced by the Superslice algorithm. We wish to investigate how these regions can be treated in ensemble as defining (perhaps) a target region. This suggests the following experiment: Given a set of object regions generated by Superslice, classify them independently. Choose a nested region of significance: namely, a subtree in the containment forest (corresponding to a given window or frame) all of whose paths from the root to the terminal nodes are of length $\geq$ nt where $0 \leq t \leq 1$ and n is the number of thresholds used by Superslice. This insures that for a proper choice of t we only consider nested regions which keep appearing for a large fraction of the total number of thresholds.

For each such nested region (subtree), suppose that there is a class, say, w (tank, APC, truck, or noise) such that M of the N objects in the subtree have been assigned to w and M $\geq$ tℓ where ℓ is the length of the longest path in the subtree. (This rule insures that for a proper choice of t the chosen class w really dominates the subtree.) We then assign class w to all N objects in the subtree. Otherwise, we leave the classifications unaltered.

In an experiment using the NVL data base, 315 objects generated by Superslice from 52 windows were considered. The objects were hand picked to belong to the a priori classes tank, APC, truck and noise, and were then classified into five classes, viz. Tank, APC, Truck, Small target, and Noise. The corresponding confusion matrix is shown in Table 8.4a.

We then applied the majority logic context rule on all the
containment forests (52 of them) for t = .5; the resulting confusion matrix is shown in Table 8.4b.

A comparison between the two matrices shows an improvement in
the false dismissal rate. The false alarm rate is left unchanged,
since no significant nested regions (for t = .5) could be found
where the noise class dominated the target class. Within the target classes we find a marked improvement in the self-classification of tanks and APC's. However, more trucks in the second case
have been misclassified into APC's. This is presumably not due to
an error in the majority logic rule, but rather due to the inabi-
lity of the classifier to discriminate trucks from APC's.

The majority logic context rule is not necessarily a superior
classification procedure, since Superslice considers only the best
exemplars and may therefore produce a better classification. However, the present study does support the relevance of low-level
context for classification validation.

9. The Dynamic Environment

The work described heretofore has considered the analysis of
single frames. However, inasmuch as the sensor is capable of
generating 30 frames per second and the hardware is capable of
analyzing about 3 frames per second, it is worthwhile to investigate how information culled from sequences of frames can improve
the performance of the system. There are two ways in which sequence data can be helpful. First, a high scanning rate allows a
succession of views of the same scene with only a small amount of
change (dependent on platform motion). Thus, image statistics
should be relatively stable and multiple measurements may allow a
reduction of the standard deviation of feature values. Second,
the use of motion information can provide a better description of
the object regions in a scene. For this project only a small data
base of ten sequential frames was available (Figure 9.1). The image
content and quality are similar to those of the NVL data base.
The sequence corresponds to every other frame from the FLIR sensor
over a span of 2/3 of a second. The images show a tank against a
background of trees, and fade away more with each frame. While
this data base was not large enough to permit meaningful tests, it

		Classified as			
	Tank	APC	Truck	Small Target	Noise
Tank	28	1	2	4	19
APC	10	26	15	35	22
Truck	6	10	10	27	23
Noise	6	1	1	7	62

A Priori (row label, vertical)

Table 8.4a. Independent classification confusion matrix

		Classified as			
	Tank	APC	Truck	Small Target	Noise
Tank	40	1	0	0	13
APC	13	38	11	30	16
Truck	6	15	6	27	22
Noise	6	1	1	7	62

A Priori (row label, vertical)

Table 8.4b. Majority logic classification confusion matrix

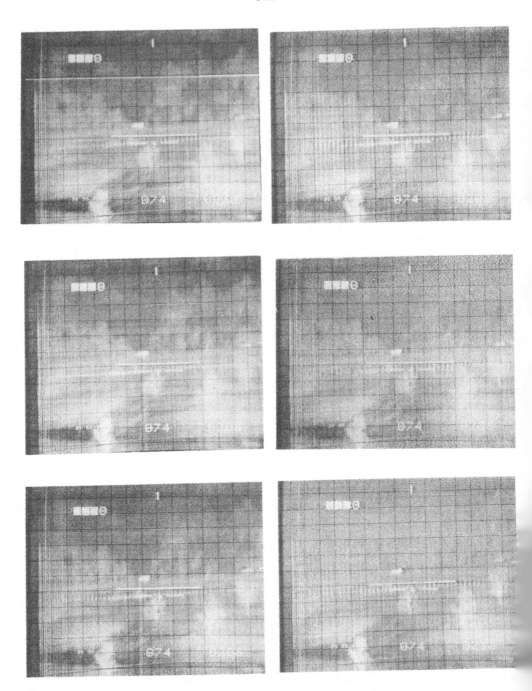

Figure   9.1.   Ten sequential frames.

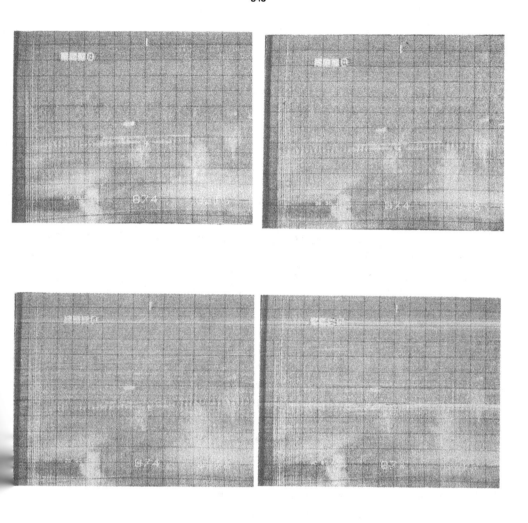

Figure   9.1.(continued)

did allow some exploratory work.

9.1 Threshold selection

One does not expect (time-) adjacent frames to differ radically and therefore it should be possible to use good thresholds from the previous frame to segment the current frame or at least to guide the selection of thresholds in the current frame. A sequence of 10 windows was extracted and smoothed (Figure 9.2) and a best threshold was chosen for each. Figure 9.3 shows the effect of choosing a lower threshold or a higher threshold. As may be noted, the adjacent thresholds have a fairly negligible effect on the target region although there is a sizable change in the amount of noise (which can be eliminated by shrink/expand noise cleaning.) However, if one considers the sequence of best thresholds as determined by the border/edge match score (Table 9.1), there is a large shift (from gray level 27 to 17) even in this short sequence of frames. Thus no single threshold is appropriate for the whole sequence. Nonetheless, the previous threshold when used on the current frame is a fairly good choice. This suggests the following approach: In a single pass over the frame, segment the current frame using the best threshold(s) from the previous frame and simultaneously compute the best threshold(s) for this frame (to be applied to the next frame in sequence). The advantage of this scheme is that the frame is not stored, thereby realizing a considerable saving in chip size and complexity.

A somewhat different approach attempts to distribute N thresholds across the threshold range dynamically. Suppose the threshold range is X gray levels. It would take X/N frames to investigate each threshold in the range. However, as mentioned earlier, X/N is likely to be ≤ 3. Thus the entire gray level range capable of harboring targets can be sampled every 3 frames. At a projected processing rate of 3 frames per second, the range would be sampled once per second. A hybrid approach is also appropriate, devoting K of N thresholds to the most likely gray levels and letting $N-K$ thresholds "rove" over the rest of the applicable gray scale.

9.2 Region tracking

The Superslice algorithm builds a forest-like structure of

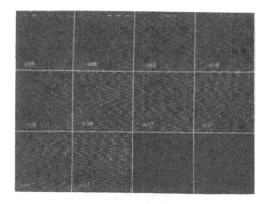

a.

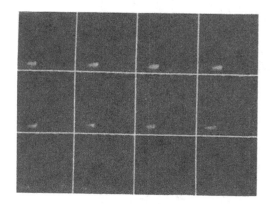

b.

Figure   9.2a.   Ten 64x64 windows from the sequential
                   data base.

          b.   5x5 median filtered windows of 128x128
                originals, then sampled 2 to 1.

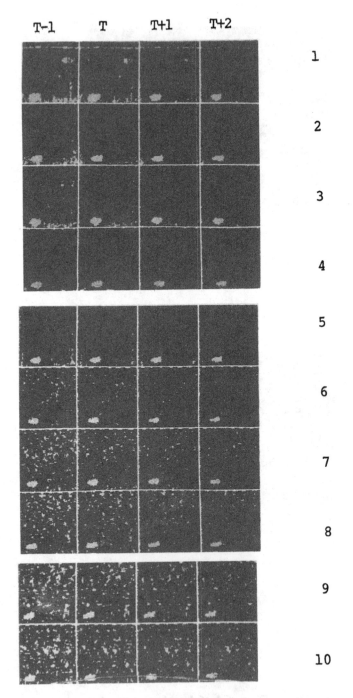

Figure   9.3.   Effect of choosing lower or higher thresholds. The column labeled T shows the result of applying the chosen threshold to each window in the sequence. Columns T-1, T+1, T+2 show the results of using thresholds 1 lower, 1 higher, and 2 higher, respectively.

| Threshold | Sequential Window # | | | | | | | | | |
	#1	#2	#3	#4	#5	#6	#7	#8	#9	#10
14	26	29	34	47	35	49	54	74	68	69
15	34	29	42	35	43	48	54	88	82	79
16	52	35	48	49	43	64	72	88	83	72
17	60	43	52	51	57	74	81	84	82	81*
18	53	51	72	58	72	72	90	90*	84*	69
19	54	53	76	67	70	76*	93*	87	71	65
20	59	60	85	75	72	59	89	66	75	65
21	67	67	87*	85	72	59	88	66		62
22	67	66	87*	100*	75*	50	80	63		50
23	67	70	87*	100*	68	42	80	63		
24	67	72	87*	97	68	38	80	63		
25	71	70	79	97	73	33	83	61		
26	76	76	81	85	69					
27	79*	79*	62	58	68					
28	76	77	64	54	68					
29	75	75	62	43	52					

Table   9.1. Percentage border/edge match as a function of threshold for the sequence data (maxima indicated with "*").

regions from each frame. Within each structure, a sequence of
nested regions which are roughly similar in size (but arising from
different thresholds) constitutes a set of exemplars of a possible
object. In addition, a certain number of accidents tend to be
present. Regions of either type are called "candidate object
regions". The frame to frame tracking process attempts to dis-
cover consistent temporal sequences of candidate object regions
by selecting one exemplar per candidate object per frame, according to a dynamic programming model (see [28]).

Two evaluation functions, S and D, are used. The static evaluation function $S(c)$ defines a figure of merit for each candidate
object region c. The Superslice algorithm provides such a figure
of merit based on contrast and well-definedness. The assumption
is that the best exemplar for an object region is identified by
having the greatest figure of merit. The dynamic evaluation function $D(c,c')$ defines the similarity of one candidate object region
(c) to another (c'). This is evaluated by considering the scaled
differences between the feature vector of c and that of c'. If c
is a perfect exemplar then $S(c) = 0$ and $D(c,c) = 0$.

Let $\{c_{ij}; j = 1,...,N_i\}$ be the set of candidate regions in
the ith frame, $i = 1,...,M$. We define the dynamic programming
problem as: find $\{c_{i\pi_i}; i = 1,M\}$ such that $T(C_{M\pi_M})$ is minimum over
all selection functions, π. The solution is achieved by the
following:

Basis step: $T(c_{1j}) = S(c_{1j}); j = 1,...,N_i$

Iterative step: $T(c_{i+1,j}) =$

$$S(c_{i+1,j}) + \min_{K=1}^{N_i} \{T(c_{ik}) + D(c_{ik},c_{i+1,j})\}$$

$$\text{for } j = 1,...,N_{i+1}$$

The above procedure finds the minimum cost sequence of candidate
object regions. Candidate regions which are accidental are
unlikely to persist from frame to frame; thus their D terms are
likely to be large, thereby increasing the total cost of any
sequence which includes them. Note that there will be many sequences which are only slightly more costly than the minimum.
These suboptimal sequences will be based on other exemplars for
the same object. The optimal sequence is thus optimal for the

particular formulations of S and D. Giving more weight to S and
less to D will tend to select best exemplars; while the reverse
weighting will tend to favor frame to frame consistency. A semantic model can provide guidance.

In general, the image sequence may contain more than one object. The scheme described above identifies the "best" object
region sequence. In order to extract region sequences corresponding to other objects in the image sequence, we must delete all
candidate object regions accounted for by the optimal sequence.
The inherent data structure specifies which regions are exemplars
for each object. By deleting all candidate object regions in each
frame which are similar to the selected region of the optimal
sequence (i.e., contain it or are contained in it), we can set the
stage for another application of dynamic programming. This process is repeated until only very poor (high cost) sequences are
obtained. Presumably at this point all objects have been accounted for.

Occasionally, a deletion step may leave a particular frame
empty of candidate object regions. This may occur for two reasons:
All objects were accounted for by the last dynamic programming
step, or the candidate region proposer failed to elicit an exemplar for an actual object. In the former case, the process will
have terminated. The latter case can be handled by associating
a fixed "empty frame" cost which is the price paid for skipping a
frame. Of course, one can't know which case applied. The conservative approach is always to assume the second case and apply the
empty frame cost. The termination criterion will then be based
on a threshold for the total cost.

The problem of an object leaving the field of view can be
handled in a different manner by flagging candidate object regions
which lie on the border of the image. A partial sequence whose
last element is flagged but which overall has low cost can be accepted as depicting an object which has moved off the image.

The dynamic programming algorithm described above has been
implemented and tested on a sequence of ten windows of FLIR data
containing a tank (Figure 9.4). These windows were already
smoothed by a 3x3 median filter to provide better response to
thresholding. The Superslice algorithm extracted a modest number
of candidate object regions. Figure 9.5 displays these regions

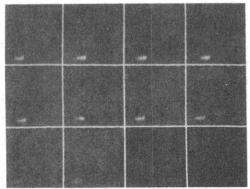

Figure   9.4.   A sequence of 10 median filtered
windows of a tank.

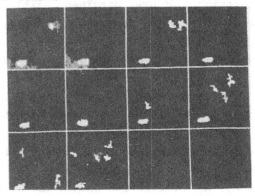

Figure   9.5.   Output of the Superslice algorithm.

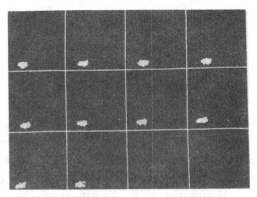

Figure   9.6.   Optimal sequenced regions using
dynamic programming.

(although for nested sequences only the best static exemplar is displayed). The solution to the dynamic programming problem was computed and the exemplars which correspond to the solution are shown in Figure 9.6. There are of course many suboptimal solutions which are quite similar to this one. Their cost is not significantly greater than the minimal cost. When the indicated regions were deleted along with all other similar candidates, the only remaining regions corresponded to noise and any minimal cost path attempting to span several frames was substantially more costly than the optimal path or any of its similar suboptimal paths. It seems reasonable therefore to establish thresholds for static and dynamic cost in order to prune the search space.

10. Concluding remarks

The work described in this paper resulted from the consideration of a specific problem environment, that of object detection in FLIR imagery. Nonetheless, our intent was not to produce a "special purpose" solution having limited generality. Rather, it has been our goal to develop concepts and approaches which would be of use in a wide variety of applications and would contribute to more successful image understanding.

References

1. Algorithms and Hardware Technology for Image Recognition, First Quarterly Report, Computer Science Center, Univ. of Maryland, College Park, MD, July 1976.

2. Algorithms and Hardware Technology for Image Recognition, First Semiannual Report, Computer Science Center, Univ. of Maryland, College Park, MD, October 1976.

3. Algorithms and Hardware Technology for Image Recognition, Second Semiannual Report, Computer Science Center, Univ. of Maryland, College Park, MD, April 1977.

4. Algorithms and Hardware Technology for Image Recognition, Third Semiannual Report, Computer Science Center, Univ. of Maryland, College Park, MD, October 1977.

5. Panda, D. P., "Segmentation of FLIR Images by Pixel Classification", University of Maryland, Computer Science TR-508, Feb. 1977.

6. Panda, D. P., "Statistical Properties of Thresholded images", University of Maryland, Computer Science TR-559, July 1977.

7. Panda, D. P., "Statistical Analysis of Some Edge Operators", University of Maryland, Computer Science TR-558, July 1977.

8. Hueckel, M., "A Local Visual Operator Which Recognizes Edges and Lines", JACM, Vol. 20, 1973, pp. 634-647. [Erratum: JACM, Vol. 21, 1974, p. 350.]

9. Hueckel, M., "An Operator Which Locates Edges in Digitized Pictures", JACM, Vol. 18, 1971, pp. 113-125.

10. Hummel, R. A., "Edge Detection Using Basis Functions", University of Maryland, Computer Science TR-569, August 1977.

11. Mero, L., Vassy, Z., "A Simplified and Fast Version of the Hueckel Operator for Finding Optimal Edges in Pictures", Proc. 4th Intl. Conf. on Artif. Intelligence, Tbilisi, USSR, Sept. 1975, pp. 650-655.

12. Shaw, G. B., "Local and Regional Edge Detectors: Some Comparisons", University of Maryland, Computer Science TR-614, December 1977.

13. Peleg, S., "Iterative Histogram Modification, 2", University of Maryland, Computer Science TR-606, November 1977.

14. Davis, L. S., "A Survey of Edge Detection Techniques", Computer Graphics and Image Processing, Vol. 4, 1975, pp. 248-270.

15. Weszka, J. S., Rosenfeld, A., "Threshold Selection Using Weighted Histograms", University of Maryland, Computer Science TR-567, August 1977.

16. Milgram, D. L., Herman, M., "Clustering Edge Values for Threshold Selection", University of Maryland, Computer Science TR-617, December 1977.

17. Nakagawa, Y., Rosenfeld, A., "Some Experiments in Variable Thresholding", University of Maryland, Computer Science TR-626, January 1978.

18. Chow, C. K., Kaneko, T., "Automatic Boundary Detection of the Left Ventricle From Cineangiograms", Comput. Biomed. Res. 5, 1972, pp. 388-410.

19. Nakagawa, Y., Rosenfeld, A., "A Note on the Use of Local MIN and MAX Operations in Digital Picture Processing", University of Maryland, Computer Science TR-590, October 1977.

20. Milgram, D. L., "Constructing Trees for Region Description", University of Maryland, Computer Science TR-541, May 1977.

21. Rosenfeld, A., "Fuzzy Digital Topology", University of Maryland, Computer Science TR-573, September 1977.

22. Dyer, C. R., Rosenfeld, A., "Thinning Algorithms for Grayscale Pictures", University of Maryland, Computer Science TR-610, November 1977.

23. Ohlander, R., "Analysis of Natural Scenes", Ph.D. Thesis, Carnegie-Mellon University, Pittsburgh, PA, December 1976.

24. Milgram, D. L., Kahl, D. J., "Recursive Region Extraction", University of Maryland, Computer Science TR-620, December 1977.

25. Stockman, G. C., "Maryland Interactive Pattern Analysis and Classification System, Part I: Concepts", Dept. of Computer Science, University of Maryland TR-408, College Park, MD, September 1975.

26. Wertheimer, M., "Principles of Perceptual Organization", in Readings in Perception, D. C. Beardlee and M. Wertheimer (eds.), p. 122, Van Nostrand-Reinhold, Princeton, NJ, 1958.

27. Abend, K., "Compound Decision Procedures for Unknown Distributions and for Dependent States of Nature", Pattern Recognition, L. Kanal, Ed., Washington, DC, 1968, pp. 207-249.

28. Milgram, D. L., "Region Tracking Using Dynamic Programming", University of Maryland, Computer Science TR-539, May 1977.